Decoding Afro-Cuban Jazz:
The Music of
Chucho Valdés & Irakere

By
Chucho Valdés
&
Rebeca Mauleón

Graphic Design : Attila Nagy
Cover Design : Linda McLaughlin
Illustrations of Cuban instruments : Lissa Herschleb

©2018 Comanche Publishing LLC and Rebeca Mauleon-Santana.
English version published by Sher Music Co., www.shermusic.com
P.O. Box 445, Petaluma, CA 94953
All Rights Reserved. International Copyright Secured. Made in the USA
No part of this book may be reproduced, posted online or duplicated in any way
without written permission from the publisher.
ISBN 978-0-9976617-2-9

Chucho Valdés at the SFJAZZ Center, November, 2016. PHOTO CREDIT: RICK SWIG

TABLE OF CONTENTS

Table Of Contents i
About This Book ii
About The Authors vi
Chapter I   •   The Music Of Cuba: An Overview 1
Chapter II   •   Demystifying The Cuban Clave 21
Chapter III •   Chucho Valdés: A Biography 37
Chapter IV   •   A Brief History Of Irakere 53
Chapter V   •   Afro-Cuban Folk Genres 65
Chapter VI   •   The Songs 87
                 Mambo Influenciado 106
                 Misa Negra 108
                 Neurosis 116
                 Bacalao Con Pan 120
                 Aguanile Bonkó 124
                 Claudia 129
                 Calzada Del Cerro 133
                 El Tata Cimarrón 137
                 Lo Que Va A Pasar 149
                 Anabis 155
                 San Francisco 162
Chapter VII •   Questions For The Maestro 165
Discography 170
Bibliography 173
Glossary 180
Appendix A: Afro-Cuban Rhythm Glossary 190
Appendix B: Annotated List Of Works 201
Appendix C: Referenced Audio Recordings 208
Index 210

ABOUT THIS BOOK

"Music is a more potent instrument than any other for education, because rhythm and harmony find their way into the inward places of the soul." – Plato

"I'm hoping that the true creative spirit and artistry of Cuban musicians will be recognized globally."
– Herbie Hancock

• • •

• **WHAT** IS THIS BOOK, **WHO** IS IT FOR, AND **HOW** DO I USE IT?

In the summer of 2014, Chucho Valdés and the newly-minted rendition of his Afro-Cuban Messengers performed an unforgettable four-night run of concerts in San Francisco, including a remarkable afternoon master class on the history and evolution of Cuban music. The long-awaited appearance was a clear example of the Bay Area's continuing advocacy for Cuba's top musicians, and was particularly memorable given the fact that Chucho's sidemen were all nearly half his age, having learned and benefitted from the Maestro's place in the Afro-Cuban musical canon. We were witnessing the torch not just being passed, but being carried together by two generations: the elder, one of the music's chief architects, and the younger, a band of extraordinarily talented and capable ambassadors, all of whom were "nurtured" and raised on the music of Irakere, one of Cuba's most influential ensembles in the post-revolutionary era. Each night was the epitome of musical joy for those of us diehard fans, enthusiasts, aficionados and practitioners, with a level of artistry and technical brilliance that seldom achieves such heights.

During one of those summer days in San Francisco, Chucho and I proceeded to gather the members of his band in the dressing room on the morning before the master class, and agreed that somehow we would trace several hundred years of Cuba's musical evolution in a fluid way, combining demonstration and conversation, and open things up to audience Q&A at the end. The first time we attempted anything like this together was in 1993 in Havana at the National Art School (La Escuela Nacional de Arte, or "ENA"). Fast-forwarding to 2012, we invited Maestro Valdés to present a similar master class for an advanced group of high school jazz musicians, this time focusing on the repertoire of Irakere and the band's use of traditional Cuban musical forms, culminating in a jam session between Chucho and some very lucky young players.[1]

More recently, 2015 would mark a turning point in Chucho's trajectory as he set out to honor the legacy of the band he launched forty years before, Irakere. It was, in fact, a request from his Afro-Cuban Messengers band members, who suggested creating a tribute to the band whose repertoire had shaped and inspired them during their years of study at Cuba's art schools and conservatories. What began as a tribute concert would eventually lead to a successful international tour (including another marvelous stint at the SFJAZZ Center in October), and yet another GRAMMY-winning recording for Maestro Valdés.[2] It was this momentum that led to the idea for this book. In Chucho's mind, it was clear that the body of work he had developed decades before was not only relevant to the younger aspiring

---

[1] The students in question were members of the SFJAZZ High School All-Stars, which is a high-level training program for advanced jazz musicians from the San Francisco Bay Area.
[2] Valdés won a GRAMMY Award for his 2015 recording *Tribute to Irakere: Live in Marciac* (Comanche Music). To date Chucho has received 6 GRAMMYs and 3 Latin GRAMMYs.

ABOUT THIS BOOK

artists of today, but could also be shared with professional musicians as well as educators and music historians around the world as a guide for advanced Afro-Cuban jazz study.[3]

So at the most basic level, the question of "what" this book is can be understood as a type of "manual" on Cuban music performance practice *a la Chucho Valdés*. However, we also realized there would be a need to provide important **context** to these works, given the level of sophistication, depth and complexity of the music. There is great value in sharing not only the inner-workings of the music, but also the immensely broad history that has shaped its creation and evolution, not to mention the many individuals who contributed to it. The answer to the "who" part of the equation is not only for whom we are intending this book, but the many, many people who represent Afro-Cuban jazz as creators, innovators and architects, and this includes musicians both Cuban and non-Cuban. There is a lineage in every musical tradition, a seemingly endless and wonderfully entangled family tree of participants, known and unknown, and our fundamental hope is to shed some light on those who played a part in the story in order to frame Chucho's place in that lineage. Simply put: this book is for anyone who has a degree of curiosity about, admiration for, or obsession with Cuban music, from students to seasoned pros, and especially those seeking to interpret the music with any degree of integrity and authenticity.

And therein lies the challenge: what often proves to be a roadblock to genuine understanding of any musical genre is the level of inexplicable mystery or "magic" that simply cannot be written down, no matter how hard one may try. "How" to use a book like this will mean different things to different people, and if your entry point is limited by some lack of skill set, there will obviously be some "shedding" required to enable you to keep up or even begin to absorb what is being presented here. Our primary goal with this project is to **demystify** the elements that often prove frustrating to interpreters of Afro-Cuban music, and that sometimes tend to be glossed over or made to appear "off limits" to those "on the outside." Music doesn't always need to be so mysterious or untenable, and although no book can equate years or decades of musical immersion and dedication (nor those all-important "10,000 hours"), our hope is that this work will serve to **decode** some of the inherent elements that can seem daunting at first (or even second) glance. If you require some more fundamental knowledge before embarking on this journey with us, we suggest any of the method books, recordings and articles listed in the Bibliography and Discography to get you started. So the answer as to "how" to use this book seems fairly straightforward: **listen** to and **play** this music (including interpretations of Maestro Valdés' work by others), **analyze** the technical and musicological aspects of the works presented here, **dig deeper** into the historical origins of Afro-Cuban jazz music, **appreciate** the compositional process of a true virtuoso, **enjoy** the anecdotal references and very personal backstory behind this music, and **be inspired** to continue pushing this music forward.

• AUDIO REFERENCES

In the practical sense, the resources included at the end of this book should provide plenty of study material as well as access to important tools, including an index of links to the specific audio files referenced here (in Appendix C) available on the Sher Music website. For the eleven specific pieces presented in this book, we have provided **direct links to the audio tracks** of the original or definitive Irakere recordings (available for purchase via various digital download services) at

---

[3] In Cuba's music schools and conservatories, several of Chucho's compositions and arrangements had already been adopted as curriculum for jazz study.

ABOUT THIS BOOK

shermusic.com/decoding. To enhance your experience with this book, we recommend that you seek out these audio sources (as well as specific video links) as a way to deepen your understanding of the material. Given that this content is beyond our control or ownership, we suggest you visit the Sher Music website to access these tools.

CHARTS & MATERIALS

The song transcriptions contained in this book are presented as condensed mini-scores. Beyond the typical lead sheet, and similar in format to the presentation in the *Latin Real Book* (© Sher Music Co., 1999), these charts provide as thorough a blueprint of Chucho's arrangements without the complexity of an entire musical score. A bit more dense than the average lead sheet, these charts can certainly be used in a practical performance setting with a fair amount of preparation. In addition, the many fragments of folkloric percussion styles throughout the book should provide plenty of cues as to what rhythm section players are required to play during a given section, as well as content for further study and exploration. Again, combining this with an aural reference is key in properly interpreting the specific music being described. Furthermore, the rhythmical and stylistic content referenced throughout the book is summarized in Appendix A ("Afro-Cuban Rhythm Glossary"), providing as close to a "one-stop shop" guide for users on the multitude of Afro-Cuban styles and genres as possible. Some of this material was presented in the 1993 book *Salsa Guidebook* (also for Sher Music Co.); however, it is clear that the nature of this present work seeks to broaden the scope of how Afro-Cuban music performance practice can be laid out, so to speak. In addition, the term "salsa" does not accurately reflect the range and complexity, nor the historical authenticity, of this music, even though it certainly developed from the same source material.[4]

DEMYSTIFYING THE MUSIC

It goes without saying that Chucho's compositions, and in particular those he created for Irakere, require a level not only of technical proficiency but also a breadth of style and genre. Any musician seeking to experience the full effect of a given composer's work should, in fact, **play** these specific arrangements, and Irakere's music is certainly not for the faint of heart. The most critical asset for accurately or authentically interpreting Afro-Cuban jazz is the **rhythm section**, one with a thorough knowledge of the many traditional rhythms (both folkloric and popular), in addition to the vocabularies of jazz, classical music, and other genres. If you can check those boxes, the next hurdle becomes the **phrasing** within the horn section. The most seasoned jazz players often struggle with the difference between swing and a so-called "Latin" feel, finding it difficult to lock in comfortably with the rhythm section. But of course, not all jazz music is swung, and plenty of Afro-Cuban jazz tunes alternate between straight 8ths and swing 8ths, or go beyond those parameters to include more sophisticated concepts such as odd or mixed meter, metric modulation, and so on. The secret to being able to play Chucho's (and Irakere's) repertoire lies in the ability to master all of the varying styles and genres that have gone into the evolution of Afro-Cuban jazz, and that is one tall order! To understand the music is one thing; to actually play it at a level of mastery is quite another.

---

[4] Since the publication of the *Salsa Guidebook,* the author has attempted to set the record straight that while the roots of "salsa" music are admittedly diverse, the bulk of the source material comes from Cuban music. Salsa, unlike some of the music discussed here, became associated with a particular sound and era, with the benefit of marketing strategies that transformed a musical language into a product for commercial consumption. However, we can acknowledge the word "salsa" as a perfect metaphor for the extraordinary mixture that occurred as a result of many social, cultural, economic and even political events. The focus of this book highlights the evolution of a musical expression that in many ways mirrored that of salsa, but came out differently.

ABOUT THIS BOOK

- **THE ARRANGEMENTS**

To make this more accessible, we will be creating an unprecedented resource that will continue to grow as we include more and more content. For the first time, complete arrangements of the eleven songs contained in this book by Chucho Valdés himself will be available for additional purchase, as a first step in creating and sustaining an archive of Afro-Cuban jazz repertoire for students and professionals alike. Written for small to medium ensemble formats (mirroring Irakere's instrumentation over the years) and exploring the possibility of creating big band versions at a later date, these arrangements will provide musicians with access to one of Cuba's most important and prolific composers and arrangers. For over a half century, Chucho has created a body of work that has come to define Afro-Cuban music in myriad ways, and we encourage you to study and perform this repertoire so that it can live on beyond current generations. To learn more, please visit *cubanmusicacademy.com*.

• • •

ABOUT THE AUTHORS

Jesús "Chucho" Valdés is one of the world's greatest pianists and composers, an acknowledged architect of the postmodern era of Afro-Cuban jazz, and an exceptional musician exhibiting extraordinary fluency in and command of multiple languages. Part of an iconic lineage of pianists noted for shaping the evolution of contemporary Cuban music, Maestro Valdés has contributed to the musical lexicon as a prolific composer, arranger, and bandleader, ushering in an era of exploration in the decades following the Revolution in Cuba. From his early years under the tutelage of his father—the great Bebo Valdés—to his pioneering role as founder and musical director of one of the most groundbreaking bands anywhere, Irakere, Chucho has cemented his legacy as one of the most influential artists of our time. His extensive compositional output, along with his prolific recording and performing career, encompasses the gamut of musical traditions, with an ease and fluidity not often seen in one artist. In his capacity to convey a plethora of musical vocabularies in one breath, Chucho has created a singular approach that represents the culmination of extraordinarily rigorous classical training, a thorough knowledge of American jazz as well as Afro-Cuban folkloric and popular music genres, and an endlessly creative and inquisitive spirit. Known for his mentorship to and cultivation of generations of emerging young musicians, Maestro Valdés embraces his role as elder statesman much in the way Art Blakey did, by providing the ultimate "on-the-job-training" to young players in his workshop-like ensembles. At the three-quarter-century mark, Maestro Valdés shows no signs of slowing down, preferring to continue his quest for new sonorities, collaborations, and adventures.

Chucho wishes to thank:

"Olofin,[1] for giving me the best prize in the world: my parents, Bebo and Pilar.
My wife Lorena, for so much love.
Rebeca and Manolo, for their talents and dedication to this project.
Zenaida Romeu and Rosario Franco, for believing in me.
Susan Sillins, for her friendship.
Obatalá[2] and Mr. Julián, for strength and courage.
Lindsey Frank, for his invaluable help always.
May the music live on!"

○ ○ ○

Rebeca Mauleón is a pianist, author and educator who fell in love with Cuban music in her teen years and never let go. Her multifaceted career has encompassed a dedication to performance, research and pedagogy, with a deep respect and admiration for Cuba's music and musicians, among them Chucho Valdés. As a performer and recording artist, Mauleón has shared the stage and studio with many of the greats in Afro-Cuban and Latin jazz music, while simultaneously feeding her passions for ethnomusicology, production, composition and education. She has published several books and articles on Cuban music performance practice, including the *Salsa Guidebook* and *101 Montunos* (both for Sher Music), as well as serving as co-editor of the *Latin Real Book*, *Muy Caliente* and the *Latin Real Easy Book* (also for Sher Music) in addition to writing articles for *Keyboard* magazine, *Bass Player* magazine, *Modern Drummer*, *Mix* magazine and others. Rebeca's devotion to education

---

1 Olofi (or Olofin) is one of several manifestations of the supreme being in Yoruba mythology.
2 Obatalá is an orisha (deity) in the Yoruba pantheon.

ABOUT THE AUTHORS

includes her role as Director of Education at SFJAZZ (San Francisco Jazz Organization), as professor at the San Francisco Conservatory of Music, City College of San Francisco, and visiting professor at Mills College, in addition to serving as a clinician specializing in Afro-Caribbean and Latin jazz music. She is a fierce advocate for arts education equity and access, and continues to draw inspiration from those committed to making the world a better place through music.

Rebeca would like to thank the many artists, educators, researchers, scholars, colleagues and musicologists whose tireless efforts in documenting this all-important history have contributed to this book. To my teachers, including Lázaro Ros, Guillermo Barreto, Amelia Pedroso, Juan Formell, Librada Quesada, Emiliano Salvador, Gregorio "Goyo" Hernández, Enrique Plá, Merceditas Valdés, Tito Puente, Israel "Cachao" López, Bebo Valdés, Pauline Oliveros, Anthony Braxton, Jesús Blanco, Tomás Jimeno Diaz, Regino Jiménez, Zenaida Armenteros, Gonzalo Rubalcaba, Changuito, Carlos del Puerto, Miguel "Angá" Díaz, Teresa Polledo, Juan de Dios Ramos Morejón, David Bernstein, Maggie Payne, Chris Brown, Madeline Mueller, Mark Levine, Carlos Federico, Ellen Hoffman, Alvin Curran, and many, many others, for guidance and motivation along the way. To my family, for unconditional support, love and encouragement. To my proofreader Rusty Aceves, and colleague Michael Spiro, for literary and musical fact-checking. To the Lick-Wilmerding High School computing students, for indexing software. To Lindsey Frank, for legal and professional expertise. To Rick Swig, for his lovely photos. And finally, to Maestro Chucho Valdés, my deepest gratitude for countless years of inspiration, and for his trust in allowing me to collaborate in the publication of this book.

Dedication

We dedicate this book to all of those whose music has in some way shaped, transformed, inspired and contributed to the landscape of Afro-Cuban jazz. With gratitude to the ancestors, pioneers and innovators from continents near and far, and to those who continue this journey with us.

• • •

Rebeca Mauleón and Chucho Valdés at the SFJAZZ Center, October, 2015.
PHOTO CREDIT: RICK SWIG

The Music of Cuba: An Overview

CHAPTER 1

"La música es el alma de los pueblos. (Music is the soul of the people)." – José Martí

"What really swings is the music of the United States, Cuba, the Caribbean...and, of course, Brazil. The rest is all waltzes." – Antonio Carlos Jobim

• • •

There is something about the music of Cuba that seems to penetrate the soul. Certainly not every person, musician or not, has the same reaction, of course. An assumption can be made that you, the reader, are motivated by your admiration for our principal protagonist in this endeavor (Chucho Valdés), and that your interest in the subject matter is already informed by a deep respect for and awareness of Cuban music. Or, you may be a musician or educator seeking to broaden your knowledge of the musicological aspects pertaining to this music, or Afro-Cuban jazz in particular, and your motivation might have more to do with the application of this material to your own creative process. Whatever the reason may be, we welcome you into this exciting world, and hope you will find the information contained herein useful.

As with many projects of this nature, it is important to acknowledge that there is much more information available than could possibly be synthesized down to just one method book or musicological guide. Any attempt here to simplify or encapsulate the extraordinary history, evolution, and diversity of Cuba's music would be ludicrous; instead, we will offer a glimpse at some of its most poignant and essential aspects, with a goal to frame the contributions of such an influential artist as Valdés and his groundbreaking ensemble, Irakere. Of course, it is also significant to understand how Cuban music relates to that of other cultures, and how it has both shaped, and been shaped by, its neighbors near and far. What follows is a brief synopsis of Cuba's musical legacy, highlighting both cultural as well as historical events, and an endeavor to contextualize the music represented in this book so it can not only be understood, but widely disseminated.

• WHY "AFRO-CUBAN JAZZ"?

Cuba's music is largely a mixture of African and Spanish origins, with traces of indigenous elements, (namely percussion instruments). So why, then, is the term "Afro-Cuban" used to describe a music that is already inherently mixed? Simply put, the semantics have more to do with an anthropological "acknowledgement" of sorts, highlighting the inordinate amount of African influence that has clearly permeated virtually all music on the island. While vehemently rejected by some musicologists and historians even up through the early 20th century, afrocentricity in Cuban culture is undeniable, having penetrated all aspects of the arts, including music, dance, and vernacular theater.[1] The imprint of the Diaspora is manifested in all aspects of life in Cuba, no matter the outcome or outlet, and no matter the racial makeup of the Cuban person in question. As a multiethnic society, Cuba experienced a musical evolution resulting from the contributions of all races and classes of people, and over time, each genre or stylistic tradition eventually became accessible to all, regardless of their race or class, although that process has certainly been long and complicated. This said, it is clear that while the term "Latin jazz" may be more commonly used, it doesn't really describe the **lineage** that is represented in

---

[1] Ortiz, Fernando. *La Africanía de la Música Folklórica de Cuba,* and *La Música Afrocubana;* and The Gilder Lehrman Institute of American History, "Iberian Roots of the Transatlantic Slave Trade, 1440–1640."

CHAPTER 1
THE MUSIC OF CUBA: AN OVERVIEW

the music, although it certainly can be argued that Cuban rhythms are not the only ones utilized in Latin jazz music. For the purposes of this book, and in order to establish the cultural foundations for the eventual migration of Cuban music outward, as well as its immersion with American jazz, we will refer to the repertoire contained herein as "Afro-Cuban jazz." The term is credited to one of the genre's pioneers, Mario Bauzá, who along with his brother-in-law Frank Grillo "Machito," was at the forefront of some of the first experiments in the merging of jazz and Cuban music as early as the late 1930s in New York City. In his view, this "new" music was layered "like a lemon meringue pie: jazz on the top, and Afro-Cuban music on the bottom."[2] Another critical moment in this new musical marriage was the collaboration between bebop pioneer and trumpeter Dizzy Gillespie, and Cuban conguero and composer Luciano "Chano" Pozo, with the introduction of Cuban syncopated rhythms into the jazz band, and their now-classic composition, "Manteca."[3] It should be understood that the nomenclature is the least important aspect of this subject; it is simply a way to categorize and contextualize this particular body of work, no matter how widespread the influences are within it. To begin, let us briefly explore some of Cuba's cultural history.

• ROOTS & BRANCHES

fig. 1a

Before the arrival of the Spanish and other Europeans to the Antilles, there were three principal tribes or indigenous groups living in Cuba: the Ciboney (or Siboney), the Taíno, and the Guanahatabey. By the late 1500s, the majority of the native populations were wiped out through the brutality of the *encomienda* system to which they had been subjected, or by disease, genocide, or suicide in order to avoid capitulating to the demands of the Spanish.[4] The musicological evidence of their cultures can be observed in the few small percussion instruments that remained, such as the ***güiro*** and the ***maracas*** (fig. 1a), along with a number of indigenous words that have survived and endure today. Then, in the 16th century, slavery began on the island until it ended in 1867 (and was finally abolished in 1898), but not before **over one million Africans, mostly from West Central Africa**, endured the voyage through the Middle Passage, being forced to work on immense sugar and tobacco plantations. The profitability of slavery in Cuba increased after the neighboring country of Haiti successfully overthrew its French oppressors (between 1791 to 1804) and retreated from the manufacturing of sugar, resulting in Cuba's role as the leading sugar producer for the global market.[5]

Another important historical as well as cultural contribution in Cuba came by way of indentured Chinese workers, often regarded as a "forgotten diaspora," who toiled in both agricultural (mostly

---

[2] Bauzá, Mario. Interview from *Latin Music USA*, Episode 1, PBS.
[3] "Manteca," composed in 1947 by Dizzy Gillespie and Chano Pozo (with the arrangement by Gil Fuller), is considered one of the earliest compositions in the "Afro-Cuban jazz" genre, and acknowledged as the first jazz standard to incorporate the Cuban *clave*. Dizzy described the collaboration with Pozo during the creation of the piece, sharing its beginnings as a layering of percussive lines by the bass and horn section, which he transcribed as Chano dictated. Dizzy then wrote the bridge, and Gil Fuller "blew it up," creating the explosive arrangement that became an instant hit with jazz audiences. *Routes of Rhythm* (1984 PBS documentary film, originally titled *Roots of Rhythm*) interview with Dizzy Gillespie.
[4] The *encomienda* was a Spanish feudal system of indentured servitude organized by the Crown, entitling the conquerors to plots of land and a number of native servants.
[5] Gilder Lehrman Institute, Wikipedia, Ortiz and others.

The Music of Cuba: An Overview — Chapter 1

sugar) production as well as the construction of the island's railroads. Between 1847 and 1874, over 124,000 Chinese workers were brought to Cuba, almost all of them male.[6] In addition, many of these Chinese "coolies" joined in the fight for independence from Spain, becoming critical players in the insurrections during the late 1800s. In an article summarizing this little-known history, Lisa Yun captures the essence of their story: "As men with nothing to lose—most without families, completely severed from their birth-land, and trapped in a system of indenture that had become melded into slavery—the Chinese became *cimarrones* and *mambises* in a venture that offered no guarantee of survival."[7] Their musical contributions consisted of the introduction of instruments, and while seemingly modest, would remain embedded in Cuban folk and popular music. Two such instruments are the **suona** (double-reeded horn, referred to in Cuba as the *trompeta* or *corneta china*), which is still used today in the *conga santiaguera* (music for Carnaval) in Santiago de Cuba, and the **cajita china** (woodblock), which is often mounted to the set of *timbales* in popular dance bands, and a common element in the percussionist's arsenal (fig. 1b).[8]

fig. 1b

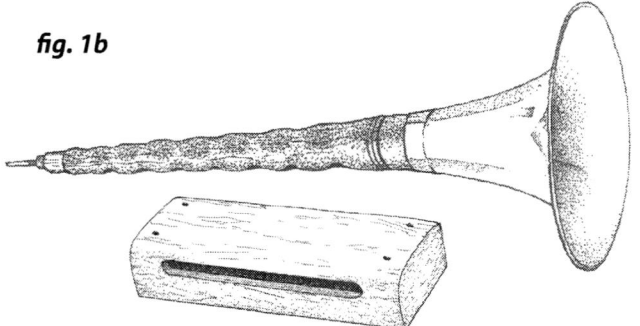

While Spanish music would provide the primary foundational elements in Cuba during the colonial era (as we will discuss further below), other European musics would also play important roles. Early on, the first newly created musical forms were directly imported from Europe (such as the Spanish *zarzuela*);[9] however, distinctly Cuban genres that developed by the 18th century were the descendants of other Western European root forms, as is the case with Cuba's national dance, the **danzón**. English and French popular dances would contribute to the *danzón's* stylistic evolution, beginning in the 1700s with the *contredanse*, which became "creolized" in Cuba as the **contradanza**. From the *contradanza*, the lineage would continue in the creation of the **danza**, followed by one of the island's first internationally-recognized 19th century forms, the **habanera**. Over time, many of these forms would experience a gradual "Africanization" or "creolization," as ethnographer Fernando Ortiz would observe, citing the process (over time) of mutual influence between folk and popular traditions.[10] Similarly, African traditions began to incorporate European (mostly Spanish) influences, as the slave populations were obligated to speak the language—and practice the religion—of their masters. Furthermore, as rural music migrated to the port cities of Santiago, Matanzas, Havana and others, the multiethnic face of Cuban music became a symbol of ongoing creativity and survival. By the mid to late 19th century, Cuban nationalism took hold, with many classically-trained musicians cultivating a repertoire that spoke to the blending of African and Spanish melodies, rhythms and instruments. However, African sacred as well as secular folkloric traditions were simultaneously able to retain many of their direct

---

[6] Hu Dehart, Evelyn. "Chinese Coolie Labor in Cuba in the Nineteenth Century: Free Labor of Neoslavery," *Contributions in Black Studies*, p. 4.
[7] Yun, Lisa. "Chinese Freedom Fighters in Cuba," *Afro Asia*, p. 32. The terms "cimarrones" and "mambises" (respectively) refer to "runaway slaves" and "Cuban guerilla independence soldiers" who fought against Spain during the Ten Years' War (1868-78) and the Cuban War of Independence (1895-98).
[8] Ortiz, Orovio, Mauleón and Triana.
[9] Chase, Gilbert. *The Music of Spain*, pp. 257-272.
[10] Ayala, Carpentier and Ortiz.

links to Africa, as demonstrated in the Yoruban-derived Santería religion (otherwise known as *regla de ocha* in Cuba). Through the establishment of mutual aid societies known as **cabildos**, members of the various African nations—and their descendants—were able to pass down their musical (and cultural) legacy through oral transmission.[11]

• SPANISH LINEAGE

From a cultural perspective, there is a deeply embedded consciousness in the Spanish-speaking world as to its European heritage, largely the result of the dominance of the Catholic Church (with its bounty of choral music), and the immense wealth of Spanish vernacular theater as well as popular music and dance traditions. Early music in Cuba during the beginnings of the 16th century drew a direct line from that which was popular in Spain dating back to medieval times, including genres such as the **villancico**, the **romance**, and the improvised vocal rhymes known as **coplas** (couplets).[12] These genres, combined with the music of the Church and the eventual arrival of Spaniards from various provinces, brought about a rich tapestry of regional music and dance traditions originating in Spain, and directly "imported" into Cuba. By the 17th century, the Spanish form of light opera known as the **zarzuela** came into vogue, eventually morphing into the *zarzuela cubana* (Cuban *zarzuela*) in the late 19th century and taken up by renowned composers such as Eliseo Grenet and, later on, Ernesto Lecuona.[13]

However, of the most influential genres of Spain, the two with the most wide-reaching impact are **música campesina** (regional country music from varying northern Spanish provinces), and **flamenco** (the centuries-old tradition of music, dance and song from the Southern province of Andalucía). The former originated in the tradition of the **trovadores** (Spanish troubadours), noted for their skill in the art of improvisational spoken and sung verses using one of the most commonly used poetic structures in all of Latin America, the **décima** (10-line octosyllabic poem). Primarily relegated to the Eastern provinces of Cuba and spreading outward, *música campesina* (now simply called **trova**) took root on the island during the 19th century and never let go, with generations of poets and improvisers developing a rich tradition of spontaneous as well as "composed" songs. (We will explore *trova* in a bit more detail shortly.)

Flamenco, on the other hand, has a much more complex and multicultural history dating back to the Byzantine Empire, encompassing dozens of subgenres, with a foundation in the music of nomadic gypsies, known as the Roma (or Romany). Consisting of a triumvirate of singing, music and dance (*cante, toque y baile*, respectively*)*, flamenco evolved from a diverse array of cultural influences, and provided much of the nuance in Cuban folk and popular music, especially *rumba*, as we will explore later. Flamenco music's most enduring influence—not only in Cuba but throughout the Americas— was the stylistic evolution of the **guitar**; at first glance, one might summarize the essence of the African-Spanish heritage in Cuban music as the drum meeting the guitar...and giving birth.

---

[11] The *cabildos* in Cuba were modeled after the Spanish *cofradías*, which were fraternities developed during the 14th century in Seville. In Cuba, beginning around the mid-16th century, the *cabildos* developed as a way for members of the same African tribe or nation to preserve elements of their cultural practices, including language, religion, music (predominantly through drumming), and dance. In effect, the *cabildo* was the principal way Africans resisted the cultural hegemony of their oppressors and preserved many aspects of their identity. These organizations still exist in Cuba today.
[12] Sublette, *Cuba and Its Music,* pp. 68-72.
[13] Ernesto Lecuona (1885-1963) was one of Cuba's most prolific composers, and a magnificent pianist. His repertoire has become standard in Cuban music education, and his compositions, including the classic "Malagueña," are performed around the globe. Sturman, Janet Lynn. "Zarzuela: Spanish Operetta,' *American Stage*, pp. 49-52.

The Music of Cuba: An Overview   Chapter 1

• AFRICAN LINEAGE

The primary African tribes brought to Cuba were the Yoruba, Congo and Dahomean peoples, and the results of their influence would shape the island's musical tapestry for centuries to come. Each nation found ways to preserve critical elements of its distinct musical expressions, both sacred and secular. As a result, members of these enslaved African nations, along with their descendents, became the conduits of the ensuing new music that would emerge. In Cuba, these principal tribes are referred to (respectively) as the **lucumí, bantú**, and **arará**, and each cultural group was able to develop—largely through the establishment of the aforementioned *cabildos*—an extraordinary wealth and variety of rhythms, songs, dances, religious practices, instruments, linguistic and idiomatic expressions, visual symbolism and social organization, all of which remain today as a testament to perseverance and cultural lineage.

Another fascinating example of the distinct ways in which African culture was preserved in colonial Cuba, was through the formation of a secret fraternal society known as the **Abakuá** (originating in the Calabar region of Southern Nigeria), which became a highly influential one in terms of the evolution of folk music, and its shaping of popular culture.[14] It should be noted that there are many additional cultural influences that invariably impacted the Cuban musical landscape during the colonial era, with varying degrees of cross-pollination between African nations over the centuries. Remember, while there certainly was preservation of these traditions (in the *cabildos*, for example), there was always the harsh reality of slavery and oppression.

Haitian influences also played a significant role in the development of Cuba's folk music, particularly in the area of Guantánamo, after migrants fleeing Haiti's Revolution settled in the region, bringing dance-drum traditions that represented their French-Creole heritage, including the practice of *vodun* (or *vodou*). Cuban **tumba francesa** is one such cultural tradition, combining African drumming, Creole singing, and French-influenced dance; its rhythmical elements, including the five-note *cinquillo* pattern, would go on to penetrate the European-derived *contradanza*, eventually leading to the evolution of Cuba's national dance, the **danzón**.[15]

Within African-derived music, there are several inherent characteristics that can be observed almost universally in all of the Diaspora, no matter the genre, country, instrumentation, era, etc. These primordial "Africanisms" include: **call-and-response singing** (antiphony), **polyrhythm** (or cross-rhythm), **improvisation, syncopation,** and **repetition**. Virtually all Cuban music contains some variation of these five attributes, regardless of the context (whether folkloric or popular, sacred or secular). Furthermore, the polyrhythmic element that is most prominent is the cross-rhythm of three against two, wherein a six or 12-beat count can be subdivided in halves or thirds (fig. 1.1). The tension is alleviated by the underlying pulse, which serves as an anchor: *(next page)*

---

[14] Miller, Ivor. "A Secret Society Goes Public," *African Studies Review*, p. 161.
[15] León, Orovio, Linares, Ortiz, etc. The *cinquillo* is a five-note pattern at the root of many Caribbean musical traditions, and is highlighted in Chapter II.

1.1 - Cross-Rhythms

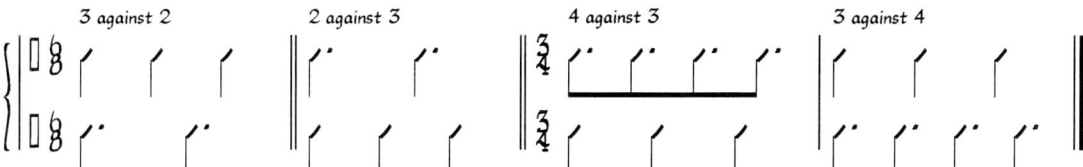

• AFRICAN SACRED AND SECULAR FOLK MUSIC

Taking into account the premise of this book to celebrate the repertoire of one of Cuba's most groundbreaking bands, let us acknowledge that among Irakere's most compelling attributes was its exploration of myriad African-derived folkloric genres. As with several Caribbean and South American countries, Cuba has experienced a high level of cultural preservation of both sacred and secular folkloric traditions, many of which have carried on despite being forgotten in Africa. In rural as well as urban communities, Yoruban, Congolese and Dahomean drumming traditions were largely maintained within the established *cabildos*, and while certainly undergoing transformation and variation, they have endured both in the context of sacred ritual as well as through popular expression, leading to the development of several genres that can be regarded as "mother musics."[16] Throughout the island, musicians from within spiritual drumming communities continue to pass on their sacred rhythms and chants through **oral transmission**; only recently has there been an attempt to document the hundreds if not thousands of rhythms, songs, dances, and ritual practices that have informed Cuban popular music and culture. For the most part, these rituals were preserved in secret during colonial times, and have carried forth the powerful legacy of the African Diaspora for centuries.

fig. 1c - Batá Drums

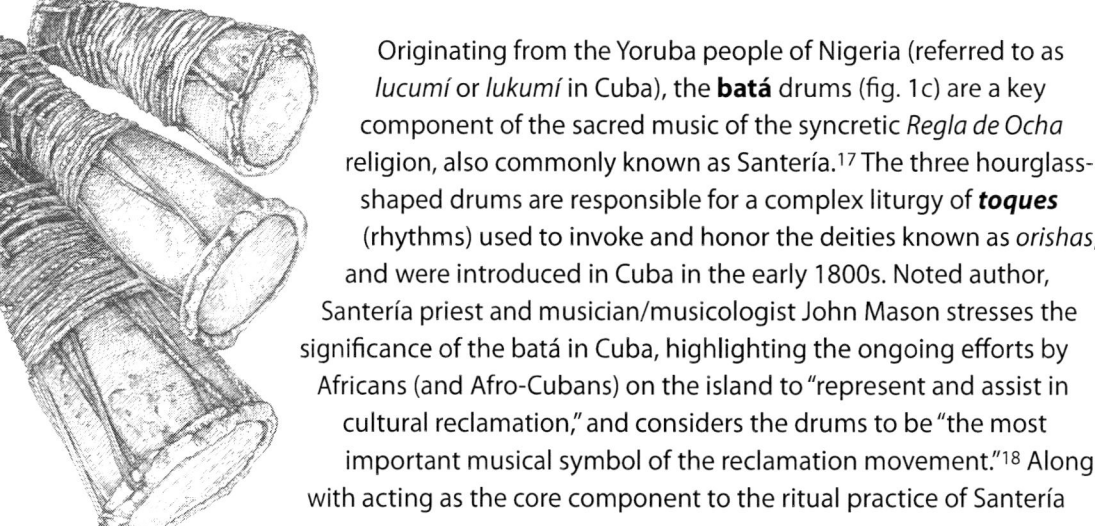

Originating from the Yoruba people of Nigeria (referred to as *lucumí* or *lukumí* in Cuba), the **batá** drums (fig. 1c) are a key component of the sacred music of the syncretic *Regla de Ocha* religion, also commonly known as Santería.[17] The three hourglass-shaped drums are responsible for a complex liturgy of **toques** (rhythms) used to invoke and honor the deities known as *orishas*, and were introduced in Cuba in the early 1800s. Noted author, Santería priest and musician/musicologist John Mason stresses the significance of the batá in Cuba, highlighting the ongoing efforts by Africans (and Afro-Cubans) on the island to "represent and assist in cultural reclamation," and considers the drums to be "the most important musical symbol of the reclamation movement."[18] Along with acting as the core component to the ritual practice of Santería

---

[16] In many countries in the Americas, one can witness a similar evolution of folkloric and popular traditions (stemming from both sacred and secular forms of African origin) that merged over time with varying European styles, resulting in new hybrids that serve as foundational genres. In Cuba, these "mother musics" include *son* and *rumba*, two of the most influential genres in all of Latin music.

[17] Religious syncretism in this case is a combination of Roman Catholicism and Yoruban polytheism and cosmology.

[18] Mason, John. Foreword to the book, *Carlos Aldama's Life in Batá: Cuba, Diaspora, and the Drum* by Umi Vaughan.

THE MUSIC OF CUBA: AN OVERVIEW   CHAPTER 1

in Cuba, the batá began to experience a "secularization" as musicians sought to recontextualize the drums in non-religious performances; there are documented accounts of the use of the **aberikulá** (non-consecrated) drums with the Havana Symphony and other groups dating back to the 1930s.[19] After the Revolution in Cuba, and despite a suppression of religious practice in the country as a whole, the batá drums were added to the instrumentations of several seminal groups from the late 1960s, with Irakere being the most visible and celebrated on both national and international levels. (We will explore specific batá rhythms used within some of the band's repertoire, along with several other sacred and secular styles, in Chapter V.)

The Congolese or Bantú influence in Cuba is perhaps even more ubiquitous, having penetrated both folkloric and popular music in ways that are indelibly linked to modern day culture. Cuban author and ethnographer Miguel Barnet notes that the Bantú-derived religious/spiritual traditions in Cuba are the most pervasive of all given the more "accessible" components of magic and ritual within them.[20] Known as *Reglas de Palo* or simply *palo*, this practice combines a veneration of spirit ancestors with a belief in natural (organic) powers.[21] Among the musical genres developed in Cuba of Bantú origin are **palo** (specific rhythmical variant, not to be confused with the religion), **yuka** and **makuta**. Most significant in the evolution of these traditions is the development of several percussion instruments, with the *yuka* and *makuta* drums serving as likely predecessors to the Cuban **conga** drums, referred to as the **tumbadoras**.[22] Two of the most well known genres in Cuban secular folk music of Bantú origin are **rumba** and the **conga de comparsa** (referred to as *conga* and not to be confused with the name of the instrument). The latter, a music and dance form associated with Cuba's Carnaval tradition, emerged in the early 19th century when members of the *cabildos* and other societies were given permission to display their music in public procession; the *conga* (referring to both the rhythm and the dance) remains as the principal form used in Carnaval, with distinct styles in the cities of Havana and Santiago. (More on the *conga* is discussed in Chapter V.)

• LA RUMBA

Of all secular African-derived folk traditions in Cuba, there is no more prominent genre than *rumba*. Developed during the late 19th century in the city of Matanzas, *rumba* comprises three styles: **yambú** (the oldest style, dating back to the colonial era), **guaguancó** (considered the most popular), and **columbia** (typically faster in tempo and containing a polymetric structure of 6/8 plus 4/4). The instrumentation includes vocals and a variety of percussion instruments such as the *cajones* (box drums), *tumbadoras* (conga drums), the *claves*, a metal shaker called the *maruga*, and a section of bamboo known as the *catá*, often substituted by the aforementioned *cajita china* (woodblock) in some ensembles, and which is played by two sticks called *palitos*. What makes *rumba* so compelling is its highly improvisational and interactive nature, with virtually every participant—whether drummer, singer or dancer—having a certain amount of freedom to create in a spontaneous environment resembling a jazz "cutting session," with equal parts group dynamic and individual virtuosic solos. Its structure has remained fairly consistent, usually instigated by the *claves* to establish the tempo,

---

[19] Amira, Mason, Ortiz, Orovio and others.
[20] Barnet, *Afro-Cuban Religions*, pp. 81-82.
[21] Unlike *lucumí* traditions, the *bantú* ritual practice is not inherently syncretic, often relying more on ritual and magic (aka, "spell-making") than on veneration of deities.
[22] The *tambor de conga* is similar to the *tumbadora* although much lighter, so it can be strapped on and paraded with for hours, and is associated with the genre known as *conga de comparsa* in Cuba's Carnaval tradition.

then the gradual layering in of the drums and hand percussion until the lead vocalist introduces the melody, wherein the supporting vocalists respond in call-and-response fashion, and the dancers dance. As there are no pitched instruments in the ensemble, it is the lead vocalist who establishes the key through a scat-sung melodic line, known as the *diana*. After the initial verse(s), the lead singer will initiate the *estribillo* (refrain), therein launching the most dynamic and improvisational section (for the drummers, singers and dancers alike).

Rumba's influence is felt not only throughout Cuba, but around the world, as it has spawned various interpretations—from ballroom dance, to a "round-trip" journey to West Africa.[23] As it evolved since the late 1800s, *rumba* took on the characteristics of a truly hybrid genre, representing the Spanish elements via the art of flamenco music and dance, and the African elements from prominent Bantú sources of drum and dance. Its spontaneity and complexity are almost commonplace in Cuban society, finding unique interpretations in both rural and urban communities. Its most compelling interpreters, including Los Muñequitos de Matanzas (established in 1952) and Grupo Afrocuba de Matanzas (founded in 1957), have been continually evolving and adapting the art form for decades.[24] In the early 20th century, *rumba* crossed over into the popular realm during a period of experimentation than ran parallel to the Cuban *son* (discussed shortly), and has since adopted components of varying music and dance styles. *Rumba's* "migration" from Matanzas to Havana in the early 20th century would result in numerous qualities and characteristics that distinguish it not only from city to city, but neighborhood to neighborhood. In 2016, *rumba* was officially declared "Intangible Cultural Heritage of Humanity" by UNESCO. The resurgence in *rumba's* popularity among younger generations continues to experience further innovation, exploring hybrids that draw from the wealth of Cuba's many folkloric and popular idioms. It is, without a doubt, one of Cuba's most important and influential genres, and continues its evolution today.[25]

• THE BIG FOUR: DANZÓN, TROVA, RUMBA AND SON

To attempt to summarize the significance of any of these genres is more than a little daunting, but once again, necessary to frame the essence of contemporary repertoire, in particular that of Irakere. Cuban ethnographers and musicologists agree that virtually all popular music genres heard on the island today descended from (or were influenced by) one or more of **four principal ancestors**, aka "the big four," noting the mutual as well as outside forces that would shape them over the years.[26] Identifying these genres as "ancestors" humanizes their legacy, bringing to bear the historical, cultural, musicological as well as sociological aspects that shape just about every aspect of popular—mostly dance—music. Not all Cuban popular music is specifically geared toward dancing (as is the case with *trova*), but in general, the central motivating factor in this legacy is precisely the "call to action" of dance. These primordial genres are: the **danzón** (Cuba's national dance), **trova** (guitars + poetry), **rumba** (secular folk tradition), and the **son** (Cuba's most prominent Creole genre). Since we've already covered *rumba* (above), we will explore the remaining three genres and their characteristics.

---

[23] In the 1940s, a Congolese derivative of *rumba* emerged in the Congo Basin, referred to as Rumba Lingala. Wikipedia, Washington Times, etc.
[24] In 1973, Grupo Afrocuba developed a fusion of sacred and secular styles when they created the hybrid rhythm known as *bata-rumba*, a blend of *guaguancó* (on *tumbadoras*) and Iyesá rhythms (played on the batá drums), mixed with several cowbells and other hand percussion.
[25] León, Ortiz, Orovio, Linares, Giró, Sublette and others.
[26] Ibid.

THE MUSIC OF CUBA: AN OVERVIEW — CHAPTER 1

• EL DANZÓN

The *danzón* evolved from English and French court and popular dances dating back to the 1700s, such as the *contredanse*, eventually creolized in Cuba as the **contradanza**. By the mid 1800s, further expansion and evolution would lead to the creation of the **danza** and **habanera**, the latter representing one of the most internationally known genres to emerge from Cuba during the colonial era. Among the most celebrated composers of these genres were Manuel Saumell and Ignacio Cervantes, both of whom ushered in an era of musical nationalism in the 19th century that would provide the blueprint for Cuban piano technique in the decades to follow.[27] The *danzón* was born from these predecessor forms, first composed in 1879 in the city of Matanzas.[28] Designed as a courtship dance for members of the elite social classes in Cuba, the *danzón* is structured in a **ritornello** or **rondo** form (fig. 1d), wherein the introductory or "A" section, called the **paseo**, is repeated several times throughout the piece in order to signal the dancers to change partners:

fig. 1d - Ritornello Structure

ABACAD

The *danzón* was first played by an instrumentation known as the **orquesta típica**, and later evolved into the **charanga** orchestra, consisting of flute, violins, piano, double bass, timpani, and a Cuban *güiro*. In the late 19th century, the timpani were eventually replaced by the *pailas criollas* (smaller kettle drums), and renamed as the **timbales** (which is, incidentally, the word for "timpani" in Spanish and French). In the 1930s, one conga drum was added to the *charanga*, thereby completing the instrumentation.[29]

Musically speaking, the *danzón* contains a signature rhythmical cell known as the **baqueteo** (fig. 1.2), which consists of the Haitian-influenced **cinquillo** pattern, followed by a consequent phrase:

1.2 - Baqueteo

The *ritornello* or *rondo* structure was a common attribute of many 19th century musical traditions in the Americas, but what made the *danzón* so distinct was the way in which the African influence took shape; the *paseo* (or promenade "A" section), featured multiple iterations of the *cinquillo* pattern, which served as an important cue to the dancers, signaling them to change partners. This is one of the more compelling aspects of the "Africanization" that took place within this otherwise Eurocentric genre; **the drums became an absolutely essential component of the genre**, not an embellishment or "decorative" afterthought, as with other European-derived styles.[30]

---

[27] Manuel Saumell (1818-1870) and Ignacio Cervantes (1847-1905) are the most acknowledged forbears of musical nationalism in 19th century Cuba, both having composed a body of solo piano repertoire that continues to dominate Cuban pedagogy to this day.
[28] The first *danzón* was composed in 1879 by Miguel Faílde (1852-1921), and was entitled "Las Alturas de Simpson."
[29] Most *charanga* orchestras would eventually add on an additional conga drum, for a total of two.
[30] Ortiz.

fig. 1e - Ritornello Form

ABACAD**E**

With ongoing innovations into the early 20th century, improvisational elements were added to the *danzón*, resulting in further elongation of the structure; although the style is through-composed, each subsequent section added more ad lib opportunities for the musicians, and gave dancers more choices of partners to dance with. An offshoot of the *danzón* was developed in 1929 by José Manuel Aniceto Díaz called the **danzonete**, which added elements from the *son* (see below) and included the alternation between a repeated chorus and an instrumental solo. It was not considered a fusion, but rather a variant of the *danzón*.[31] By the late 1930s, musical pioneers (and brothers) Israel and Orestes López[32] experimented with the addition of a repetitive, syncopated ostinato or "E" section to the *danzón* (fig. 1e), referring to this new part as **nuevo ritmo** (new rhythm), and enabling the ensemble members to improvise over a simple harmonic framework (usually the dominant chord of the original key).[33] In time, this added section would become known as **mambo**, and later, the **cha-cha-chá**.[34] This important lineage speaks volumes of the ongoing experimentation and creativity in Afro-Cuban music, not to mention the immense worldwide popularity of these rhythms and dances.

LA TROVA

The Spanish influence in Cuba was certainly broad, and while specific genres and styles were the result of "direct importation" from Spain early on, by the 19th century there was an explosion of creativity and innovation, with the emergence of plenty of new and distinctly Cuban genres. The early Cuban *trovador* (troubadour) was, much like her/his European counterpart, the minstrel, a free spirit and social commentator and prolific composer, similar in many ways to the great *griots* of West Africa.[35]

Over time, the evolution of this style of songwriting and spontaneous storytelling would become known as **trova**, and comprises numerous styles, including the **bolero** (romantic ballad), **guajira** (repetitive and improvisational style), **canción** (simple to complex song), and **punto guajiro** (poetic free-verse style), among others. The principal instrument used in the genre is the Spanish guitar, with subsequent guitar relatives joining in, including the Cuban *tres*, *laúd* and others, plus small percussion instruments such as the *maracas* and *claves*. Among the founders and innovators of *trova* was José "Pepe" Sánchez (1856-1918), known as the father of the genre and creator of the *bolero*, and several of its leading exponents include Sindo Garay, Rosendo Ruiz, Manuel Corona and Alberto Villalón (regarded as the "four greats"), María Teresa Vera (author of the beloved song "Veinte Años"), Francisco Repilado (aka "Compay Segundo"), Lorenzo Hierrezuelo, Ñico Saquito, and many others.[36]

---

[31] Ecured, Aniceto Diaz, Diaz-Ayala, Orovio.
[32] Brothers Israel López "Cachao" (bassist) and Orestes López "Macho" (cellist) are credited with introducing repetitive, syncopated and improvisational elements from the Cuban *son* into the *danzón*, resulting in the evolution of the *mambo* and the *cha-cha-chá*.
[33] In addition to the use of the dominant of the key, many "E" sections of *danzones* frequently utilized I-VI-II-V progressions, providing the instrumental soloists with a stable groove to contrast from the preceding through-composed material.
[34] The *cha-cha-chá* would not receive its name until 1951, when violinist Enrique Jorrín noted the scraping sounds of the dancers' feet on the floor, compelling him to come up with the onomatopoeia. Linares, Orovio, León, etc.
[35] Both European minstrels and West African *griots* (or *jelis*) serve as repositories of oral tradition and living archives of everyday life and activity, commenting on everything from the seemingly mundane to the most controversial social and political topics of the day.
[36] It is the repertoire that is the most compelling aspect of the *trova* genre, with literally hundreds of songs shared and passed on through the decades and into the 21st century. Ayala, Giró, Linares and Orovio.

The Music of Cuba: An Overview — Chapter 1

With the emphasis on the lyrics, the musical accompaniment to *trova* songs tends to be more supportive, providing harmonic colors and decorations when necessary, but not catering to the dancing public as a general rule. This would eventually change as styles such as the *bolero* and *guajira* cross-pollinated with the *son* (discussed below), becoming internationally recognized, in particular with the success of songs such as "Guantanamera,"[37] and films (and recordings) such as *Buena Vista Social Club*. Throughout the evolution of Cuban popular music in the 20th century, *trova* continued to document the social dynamic, creating a shared repertoire of beautiful ballads and colorful, often tongue-in-cheek, commentary. By the 1940s and 50s, *trovadores* (troubadours) began to explore the influences of American jazz harmony and the vocal stylings of the leading crooners of the day[38], resulting in a movement known as **filin** ("feeling"), largely relegated to the nightclubs and cabarets that were all the rage as Cuba became a hotspot for tourism as well as the playground of the Mafia.[39] Among the great singer-songwriters and interpreters of the genre were César Portillo de la Luz, José Antonio Méndez, Elena Burke, and the ever-vivacious Omara Portuondo.

After the Revolution in 1959, the lyrics in *trova* took on a socio-political angle, highlighting the themes and stories surrounding Cuba's new socialist ideology. **Nueva trova** (Cuba's "new song" movement) sought to differentiate itself from the more innocuous subject matter of the typical love song, instead focusing on the consequent social and political changes of the time. Its most ardent innovators, including Silvio Rodríguez and Pablo Milanés, reflected issues of injustice and imperialism, cultivating a new repertoire that would serve as a blueprint for much of Latin America's new song movement, known as Nueva Canción.[40]

fig. 1f - Changüí instruments

---

[37] The legendary *guajira* "Guantananera" was composed by Joseíto Fernández in ca. 1928, and is based on the verses of Cuban patriot and writer José Martí. It was made popular in the United States in 1963 by Pete Seeger, and is one of the most recognized Cuban songs.

[38] Nat "King" Cole, Frank Sinatra, Ella Fitzgerald and Sarah Vaughan not only served as inspirations for the *filin* genre, they also appeared in Cuba quite frequently at renowned cabarets such as the Tropicana and Sans Souci, as well as events sponsored by the Club Cubano de Jazz. Acosta.

[39] Acosta, *Cubano Be, Cubano Bop*, p. 167.

[40] Ayala, Diaz-Ayala, Giró, Orovio, etc.

EL SON

In Cuban music, there is a strong connection to dance primarily given the predominance of African drum-dance rituals in sacred music, and their evolution over time into secular forms. Of all of Cuba's popular dance music, there is no more influential or game-changing genre than the **son**. Considered equal parts African and Spanish rhythm and melody, the *son* originated in the rural areas of the eastern province of Guantánamo in the late 19th century.[41] Among the root forms is a style known as **nengón**, which contained call-and-response singing, wherein the lead vocalist would sing improvised verses alternating with a repeated chorus; however, unlike its descendents, it contained far less syncopation.[42] The next incarnation in the *son's* evolution was the **changüí**, which consists of a highly syncopated melody line that is both sung and doubled on the principal string instrument that developed within the genre: the **tres**. The *tres* is a guitar relative consisting of three sets (or courses) of double strings, and eventually became the signature of the *son* and its offshoots. The *changüí* instrumentation (fig. 1f) also included a *botija* (clay jug) or a **marímbula** (Congolese-derived lamellophone) used to provide the syncopated bass line, along with a prototype of the **bongos**, plus **maracas** and a metal scraper called the **guayo**.

Within the *changüí*, much of the structure in Cuban contemporary popular music can be observed, including the improvisational lead vocal style, a repetitive ostinato (known as the **montuno**)[43], a fairly moderate tempo, and a characteristic dance that became the foundation for the ensuing *son* genre. As the music and musicians migrated from the mountains to the urban areas at the turn of the 20th century, the *changüí* gave way to a more refined style, generally referred to as *son*. Changes in instrumentation included the substitution of the African *marímbula* with the European double bass, providing noticeably more tonal "stability;" the primary role of the bass in the *son* is to provide a consistently syncopated ostinato known as the **tumbao**. The addition of a regular 6-string Spanish guitar provided additional harmonic support, allowing the *tres* to maintain its melodic role and also enhance the repetitive structure with an ostinato (or *montuno*) feel, sometimes referred to as **guajeo**. It is precisely this repetitive structure in the *tres* that became the blueprint for the piano's role in popular music ensembles by the late 1930s. Another significant development in the instrumentation (in the early 1900s) was the addition of the **claves**, generally played by one of the ensemble vocalists; the unmistakable quality and timbre of the *clave* pattern (usually quite high-pitched in the early incarnation of the *son*) would permeate the early recordings of some of Cuba's most important groups, including Sexteto (later Septeto) Habanero, the Septeto Nacional de Ignacio Piñeiro, and many others. These first early *son* bands were primarily *sextetos* (sextets), and in 1927, a single trumpet was added, resulting in the *septeto* instrumentation.[44]

---

[41] Giró, Orozco, Linares, etc.
[42] Ibid.
[43] Note that in Cuban music, the term *montuno* can refer to two different aspects: it can be used to identify the repetitive section of a song containing the call-and-response singing, and also the ostinato pattern played by the piano in most dance bands post 1940. There are many who use the word *tumbao* to refer to the piano patterns in Cuban music as well as salsa, and the previously mentioned term *guajeo* often refers to the ostinato pattern played by string players. Given the ongoing evolutions with regard to popular music terminology, one can assume that there is not only one correct answer!
[44] This innovation is credited to composer, bassist and bandleader Ignacio Piñeiro (1888-1969), director of the Septeto Nacional. Piñeiro's experimentation with the *son* would lead to a multitude of hybrid styles, such as the *son-pregón*, *afro-son*, *guajira-son* and others.

The Music of Cuba: An Overview   Chapter 1

Fig. 1g - Son structure

The structure of the *son* (fig. 1g) generally consists of a brief instrumental introduction, followed by one or two verses and the *montuno* section, which features the call-and-response vocal improvisation (and tends to be the most compelling for the dancers). With the addition of the trumpet (and the augmented size of the band), increased improvisational opportunities would result from the extended *montuno* section, allowing individual solos (as well as slightly longer song lengths). Cuban *son* music was some of the first "island music" to be widely disseminated in the early 1920s, and would go on to penetrate the international market as several bands toured and recorded this music in the United States. While harmonically much simpler than the approach of its North American cousin, jazz, the *son* carried with it a rhythmical complexity and sense of groove that was universally appealing. In 1930, Don Aspiazú and his Havana Casino Orchestra introduced authentic *son* to American audiences, recording one of the biggest hits in all of Cuban music, "El Manisero" ("The Peanut Vendor").[45]

Over the subsequent decades, the four primary genres—*danzón, trova, rumba* and *son*—would not only continue to evolve on their own, they would begin to influence one another, paving the way for another explosion of creativity in what many consider to be the heyday of Cuban popular music. What follows is a simplified and semi-chronological listing of the musical and stylistic evolution that stemmed from these foundational pillars, beginning with the story of jazz in Cuba.

• JAZZ IN CUBA

As early as 1914, there were jazz bands in Cuba, although many would argue that due to the lack of any physical recordings, it might be challenging to verify that what was being played actually sounded like its American counterpart.[46] What was known was that plenty of travel took place among musicians between Cuba and the US (to places including New Orleans and New York City), and that these exchanges would invariably lead to mutual musical influence. During the 1930s, some of these early contributors to the evolution of jazz in Cuba included Jaime Prats, Moisés Simons, and Julio Cueva, the latter with whom Chucho's father Bebo Valdés (1918-2013) would work as pianist and arranger.[47] In the decade to follow, musicians such as Armando Romeu and Chico O'Farrill would contribute to the continuing presence of jazz on and off the island, in particular trumpeter and arranger O'Farrill, who would tour as a member of Armando Oréfiche's Lecuona Cuban Boys, and later travel to New York, where he would become a critical pillar (and acknowledged architect) of Afro-Cuban jazz in the USA.[48]

---

[45] Many versions of "El Manisero" have been recorded and performed over the decades, but it was first composed by Moisés Simons around 1927 for famed Cuban singer Rita Montaner. It became a huge hit for Don Aspiazú, and went on to sell over 1 million copies of printed sheet music, resulting in significant royalties for Simons. Incidentally, Aspiazú's Orchestra members included singer Antonio Machín, whose stage performance of the song included tossing bags of peanuts out into the audience, and a young saxophonist turned trumpeter who would usher in the marriage of Cuban music and jazz: Mario Bauzá.

[46] Acosta, Orovio, etc.

[47] Ibid.

[48] Ibid. O'Farrill would cut his teeth as an arranger under the tutelage of Gill Fuller, then go on to write and arrange for Machito and His Afro Cubans, Benny Goodman, Stan Kenton, and artists of Cuba's *filin* movement as well as Mexican television shows.

By the 1950s, jazz was booming in Cuba's cabarets and nightclubs, with plenty of American musicians appearing at the famed Tropicana and Sans Souci, and Cuban musicians such as Bebo Valdés leading the charge in cultivating the big band sound.

1940s & 1950s

SON-MONTUNO

Prolific composer, *tres* player and bandleader Arsenio Rodríguez (1911-1970) revolutionized Cuban popular dance music in the 1940s in multiple ways, primarily through his formation of the **conjunto** instrumentation,[49] which would serve as the blueprint for the ensuing salsa band format. Arsenio also popularized one of the most important hybrid forms of *son* that is still relevant today: the **son-montuno**. Unlike the more formal song structure of earlier *son* music, this new style cut to the chase, so to speak, beginning right at the *montuno* (call-and-response) section, primarily as a way to emphasize the improvisational opportunities for the lead vocalist as well as several instrumentalists.[50] Arsenio's *conjunto* established not only a funky and infectious sound that inspired the dancing public, he also found creative ways to infuse the music with plenty of African cultural references, and collaborated with some of *son* music's most singular and compelling artists, including singer Miguelito Cuní, pianist Luis Martínez Griñán "Lilí," and trumpeter Félix Chapotín.[51] Arsenio's prolific compositional body of work would remain a fixture in contemporary Cuban as well as salsa music, with hundreds of covers of his songs being recorded, including several by Irakere (such as "Dile a Catalina," "La Vida Es Un Sueño," and "De Una Manera Espantosa," all recorded on the 1983 album *Calzada del Cerro*).[52]

GUARACHA

A term originally used to refer to a form of late 18th/early 19th century light comic opera in Cuba,[53] the **guaracha** of the mid 1940s and beyond ushered in a more expressive, slightly faster tempo dance music derived from the *son*. Along with the expansion of the dance bands to the aforementioned *conjunto* instrumentation, many popular groups began to intensify their arrangements, featuring blazing trumpet arrangements along with a funkier, more syncopated texture, hinting at the harmonic expansion of jazz but still retaining a general simplicity, rarely moving beyond the staple I-IV-V-IV chord progression. The dancing also evolved significantly during the 1950s, bringing in elements of American popular dances (such as the jitterbug and swing), resulting in a stylized form of popular dance known as **casino**.[54] Several of Cuba's great *conjuntos* became known throughout the world for their interpretation of the *guaracha* style, notably La Sonora Matancera, featuring legendary singer Celia Cruz (1925-2003), the Conjunto Casino, and many others. As the style spread to New York and neighboring Puerto

---

[49] Arsenio's *conjunto* instrumentation added on to the already established *septetos* of the 1930s, bringing in the piano and conga drum along with three additional trumpets. This model would be adopted and later adapted by groups in Puerto Rico and New York City, with varying horn sections.

[50] This was also in direct response to the dancers' reactions, who often preferred to wait to dance until the *montuno* section had arrived.

[51] Cuní and Chappotín became heralded as bandleaders in their own right, and Lilí Martínez would establish the foundations for the stylistic interpretation of the piano in salsa music.

[52] Irakere, *Calzada del Cerro*, Areito, 1983.

[53] The word "guarachar" in Cuba is a slang term loosely meaning "to enjoy."

[54] One of the most exciting dance traditions to emerge in Cuba during the 50s is a style known as *rueda de casino* ("casino wheel"), which is essentially a round dance with multiple partners, and consists of dozens of different choreographed moves that are "called" by the lead dancer, similar to a square dance. It has experienced a resurgence in recent years and is danced by young and old alike.

The Music of Cuba: An Overview

Rico as well as Central and South America, the *guaracha* became the prototype for the eventual salsa phenomenon, both as a dance and as a musical genre, where it would experience a harmonic "boost" in texture, taking on more of a jazz sensibility in the arrangements and chord voicings.[55] Despite the use of the term "salsa" as a metaphorical description for this "recipe" of many ingredients, the roots are undeniably Cuban, and the *guaracha* is one of the most common styles played.

• BOLERO

Although developed within the genre of the aforementioned *trova* genre, the romantic ballad style of the Cuban **bolero** began to reach new heights when interpreted by some of the island's most revered singers, notably, el bárbaro del ritmo ("barbarian of rhythm") Benny Moré (1919-1963). During the 1940s and 50s, singers of the more cabaret-inspired *filin* era, as well as those in the popular dance bands (from trios to *conjuntos* to *charanga* orchestras) fully embraced this romantic ballad form that would soon spread throughout the Spanish speaking world and beyond. Many consider the *bolero* one of the most successful forms on an international level, as it spawned translations and interpretations in multiple languages. The *bolero's* musical characteristics highlight a profound lyricism and elastic phrasing, with the music essentially taking a back seat to the lyrics, although the accompaniment certainly can be expressive in its own right. The shared repertoire of *boleros* composed by some of Latin America's most celebrated singer-songwriters includes well over 200 songs, and generations later, these classic pieces are still sung in bars and on grand stages around the world. Some of the most renowned *bolero* composers include Ernesto Lecuona, César Portillo de la Luz, and Miguel Matamoros (from Cuba), Agustín Lara, María Grever and Consuelo Velázquez (from México), Pedro Flores and Rafael Hernández (from Puerto Rico), and many others.[56]

• MAMBO

A term with multiple meanings in Cuba, the word **mambo** was first publicly introduced in 1938 when brothers Orestes "Macho" López and Israel "Cachao" López composed the *danzón* entitled "Mambo," transforming the genre with the introduction of a highly syncopated "E" section (originally called *nuevo ritmo*).[57] In the early 1940s, another Cuban duo of brothers (in-law), Mario Bauzá and Frank Grillo "Machito," explored the combination of Afro-Cuban rhythms with jazz harmony and instrumentation in New York City, ushering in one of the first hybrids of jazz with Cuban music. With additional contributions by Puerto Rican titans Tito Puente and Tito Rodríguez, the New York Latin big band sound of the *mambo* was considered a truly new musical marriage.[58] In the 1950s, Chucho's father Bebo Valdés would also contribute to the landscape of this musical evolution, although his hybrid would be known as the **batanga**, a similarly jazzified big band sound, but with the inclusion of the *batá* drums in the rhythm section. However, it would be the experimentations of Cuban musician, pianist, composer and bandleader, Dámaso Pérez Prado (1917-1989), who would introduce his own unique interpretation of the word "mambo" to international audiences in the mid to late 1950s. Prado's

---

[55] Much of this cross-pollination of Cuban rhythm and jazz harmony would be pioneered by brothers-in-law Mario Bauzá and Frank Grillo "Machito."
[56] Analítica.com, Ecured, Orovio, Alén, Linares, etc.
[57] The structure of the piece broke with tradition, shortening the form to include only the *paseo* or "A" section immediately followed by the improvised "E" section. Although Orestes is credited as the composer of "Mambo," his brother Cachao contributed significantly to its arrangement.
[58] Machito, Tito Puente and Tito Rodríguez were hailed as "The Big Three," and took the Latin big band sound to the ultimate level of musicality as well as danceability. In addition, much of the music's success was due to the exquisite arranging by Puente along with pianist René Hernández and saxophonist/trumpeter Mario Bauzá (1911-1993). Bauzá is considered by many to be "the father of Afro-Cuban jazz."

concept was inspired by the American jazz band (although not as "jazzy" as the Machito or Valdés orchestras), with a blaring horn section, a high degree of showmanship, and a clever marketing strategy: virtually every song Prado composed used the word "mambo" in it![59] For many audiences, their first exposure to the *mambo* craze was by way of Prado. For decades, there were heated discussions as to who was the inventor of the *mambo*; the answer is, there wasn't just one!

Fig. 1h - Graphic timeline: danzón > nuevo ritmo > mambo > cha-cha-chá

• CHA-CHA-CHÁ

Cuban musical development seemed to explode during the 1940s and 50s, with worldwide attention garnered by the *mambo* as well as the **cha-cha-chá**. The story of the *cha-cha-chá* began with the innovations in the *danzón* by Orestes and Israel "Cachao" López, and the addition of the syncopated and repeated *nuevo ritmo* or *mambo* section (fig. 1h).[60] The new musical texture inspired the dancers to adjust and change their steps to be more in sync with the increased level of syncopation, not to mention the improvised solos during this section. Joining the López brothers in the well known *charanga* orchestra lead by flautist Antonio Arcaño (Arcaño y sus Maravillas), was violinist/composer Enrique Jorrín (1926-1987), who noticed the scraping sounds produced by the dancers' feet whenever the band would play this new rhythmical texture. Jorrín later joined the Orquesta América, and it was during his tenure there that he came up with the term *cha-cha-chá* to identify the dance (in 1951), as well as composing one of the biggest hits of the genre, "La Engañadora" (in 1953). Among the most important *charanga* orchestras to popularize the *cha-cha-chá* were Orquesta Aragón (founded in 1939), Orquesta América (founded in 1942), Fajardo y sus Estrellas (founded in 1949 by flautist José Fajardo), and the eponymous group founded by Jorrín in 1954.[61] Some of the most famous *cha-cha-chá* compositions (besides Jorrín's "La Engañadora") are "El Bodeguero" and "Sabrosona" (by flautist Richard Egües), and "Rico Vacilón" (by Rosendo Ruiz Jr.).[62]

• DESCARGA

The wealth of Cuban rhythms can seem overwhelming to anyone discovering this music for the first time, but it is precisely this embarrassment of riches that provides the musician with plenty of choices for jamming. Although the term would be cemented in the late 1950s with the seminal recordings

---

[59] Much of Prado's success would come while he lived in México, including the recording of one of his biggest hits, his rendition of "Cherry Pink and Apple Blossom White." Although not a *mambo*, this would be one of Pérez Prado's signature tunes. His *mambos* were generally characterized as "highly stylized," with plenty of dramatic breaks and stops, allowing him to utter his classic grunt numerous times throughout.

[60] Cachao affirms that the increased syncopation was in fact a direct result of the *son* and its repetitive structure, which was more enticing to the dancers. *Cachao: Como su Ritmo No Hay Dos,* (1993 documentary film produced by Andy García).

[61] Alén, Ecured, Orovio, Linares, Giró, Diaz Ayala, etc.

[62] As the popularity of the *cha-cha-chá* grew, others outside of Cuba would also contribute to the repertoire. In 1963, timbalero and composer Ernest Anthony Puente, aka Tito Puente, composed the infamous "Oye Como Va," which was based on an earlier composition of Cachao's called "Chanchullo," then later recorded by guitarist Carlos Santana in 1970. Wikipedia, Ecured, Alén, Orovio, etc.

The Music of Cuba: An Overview

by Cachao and others[63], the Cuban **descarga** (jam session) was already in full swing as a concept, with the best artists frequently engaging in spontaneous displays of musical prowess. As we will highlight in Chapter III, Chucho's father Bebo had participated in one of the earliest known examples of a *descarga* recording in 1952, which was actually considered a jazz record.[64] As with *rumba*, the *descarga* relies on a knowledge of shared repertoire, but the rhythmical possibilities are virtually limitless, drawing from everything Cuban music has to offer. The melodic and harmonic choices were generally more contained and simplified, mainly to allow for the most accessible environment for the musicians to create something cohesive on the spot; plenty of classic *descargas* center around a I-IV-V-IV progression, or even a single chord, such as a V7.[65] Whether *son-montuno, conga, cha-cha-chá, guaguancó* or *guaracha*, the art of the Cuban jam session could draw from any rhythmical or stylistic genre, and often would start off with one player initiating a groove, and the rest of the players falling in as they saw fit. As with the cutting sessions in jazz, familiarity with repertoire is important, but in Cuban music, it's more about the knowledge of the **rhythms** as opposed to complex song forms or elaborate melodies and chord changes. Over fifty years later, this tradition still holds true; while there have been plenty of new stylistic innovations since the 1950s, the concept of the Cuban *descarga* is as current as ever.

1960s – Today

MOZAMBIQUE

After the Revolution in Cuba, popular music initially responded to the changes in ideology, with emphasis on the lyrical content as opposed to any specific rhythmical or stylistic innovations. Then, in 1963, percussionist and bandleader Pello el Afrokán[66] developed a revamped version of the Cuban carnival *conga* rhythm, transforming the drum and handbell patterns, and creating a new dance step by blending Cuban *rumba* and *casino* with the American twist. While perhaps viewed more as a novelty act on the island, the style would evolve in the United States with several New York-Puerto Rican musicians such as Eddie Palmieri and Manny Oquendo creating their own renditions of it, followed by Latin rock icon Carlos Santana, who would record a cover of Pello's song "María Caracoles" in 1976.[67]

PILÓN

In the mid 1960s, an interesting hybrid of percussion-laden grooves was developed by bandleader and composer Enrique Bonne, who, inspired by the motions of workers pounding toasted coffee beans in Eastern Cuba, created a style that became wildly popular during the Carnaval celebrations around the island. Popularized by singer and bandleader Pacho Alonso, the style was named after the rustic coffee-grinding equipment known as the "pilón," and became quite well known in post-revolutionary dance

---

[63] Israel López "Cachao" was among several musicians to record albums containing largely spontaneous jam session-style albums during the 1950s, mostly for the Panart label (including *Cuban Jam Sessions In Miniature* in 1957), along with Bebo Valdés, Peruchín, Frank Emilio Flynn, Tata Güines, Julio Gutiérrez, Niño Rivera, El Negro Vivar, Walfredo de los Reyes and many others.
[64] The 1952 album was produced by impresario Norman Granz for the Mercury label and was entitled *Cubano*, under the artist name "Andre's All-Stars."
[65] Songs such as "Pa Gozar" by Tata Güines, "Descarga Cubana" by Cachao (the song is credited to O. Estivil on the album notes), and "Gandinga, Mondongo y Sandunga" by Frank Emilio are all examples of *descargas* that center around a single D7 chord (or II-V texture with the V in the bass).
[66] Pedro Izquierdo (1933-2000) was a percussionist and bandleader, whose *mozambique* style, created in 1963, was a re-vamped approach to the Cuban *conga* (music and dance for Carnaval).
[67] Orovio, Diaz-Ayala, etc.

music. Each of the instruments in the percussion section was tasked with rhythmically expressing some of the mechanical motions of the *pilón* workers, while the piano attempted to recreate the churning of the mechanical organ known as the órgano oriental, a fascinating old time instrument dating back to the mid-1800s that is still part of the musical landscape in Eastern Cuban cities such as Manzanillo.[68]

• SONGO

In 1969, bassist, guitarist and singer-songwriter Juan Formell (1942-2014) formed a group that would become known as the "Rolling Stones of Cuba," and one of the island's most legendary popular dance bands: Los Van Van. Formell's musical influences were many, and his contribution to the musical landscape included the creation of a hybrid genre known as **songo**. A blend of *son* with other Cuban textures and the forbidden sounds of American pop and rock music of the day, *songo* emerged as an evolving concept and not one specific rhythmical pattern, custom-tailored to the individual songs in Los Van Van's repertoire. In collaboration with drummers including Blas Egües and later, José Luis Quintana "Changuito," as well as pianist and co-founder César "Pupy" Pedroso, Formell developed a rhythmical style that hinted at the taboo influences of bands such as Blood, Sweat & Tears and The Monkees, combining them with a high level of syncopation and rhythmical innovation. The band's instrumentation was also novel at the time, taking a *charanga* ensemble and adding electric guitar and drum set (both seemingly controversial symbols of American rock) along with electric organs and keyboards (and by the mid-70s, trombones). Over the years, Los Van Van's sound became indicative of the balance between tradition and innovation, with *songo* representing the benchmark of danceability, and Formell's lyrics speaking to the realities of everyday life in Cuba.

• TIMBA

The word "timba" can mean many things in Cuban popular culture,[69] but it is most synonymous with the post 1990 era of intense, almost aggressive dance music, with a side order of funk and even a little rap. As with *songo*, there is not one particular or isolated pattern associated with **timba** playing; it has more to do with an **aesthetic** than a specific rhythmical structure. However, the foundations were already underway during the 1970s, when Irakere laid the groundwork for what was in store. Imagine taking everything discussed in this chapter as a whole, mixing it with American funk and rap, plus a few contemporary keyboards and synthesizers, and throwing this into a blender: that's *timba*! The rhythmical elements at play were fomented early on, when Chucho Valdés collaborated with his fellow band members, even before Irakere was founded, resulting in the combination of deep roots music of African sacred and secular origins, with jazz, rock, and classical music. Irakere bassist Carlos del Puerto began incorporating elements of funk into his playing as early as the 1970s, including slapping and pulling on the strings, and also began to strike the fretboard and slide up the neck, resulting in a sound resembling the *bombo* (bass drum) in the *conga* (Carnaval style). Chucho affirms that this was likely the first time anyone had done this in Cuban music, and the techniques are now an essential component of *timba* playing.[70]

---

[68] EcuRed, Lam, etc.
[69] Cuban *rumba* songs often refer to "la timba" as the overarching groove, and "timberos" are the ones responsible for playing and maintaining this groove. In addition, Cubans are not the biggest fans of the term "salsa" to describe their music, so it is likely that the popularity of *timba* was enhanced by the simultaneous ambiguity and "Cubanness" of the word.
[70] Chucho recounts the first time Carlos del Puerto incorporated this technique in the band, stating it was on the song "Bacalao con Pan," and later on during a section of "Los Caramelos" (a *conga* style). He recalls the audience reaction to the enhanced percussive texture, and the shift into musical "overdrive" it produced, as "locura" (craziness!). Among the contemporary *timba* bands, it was within NG La Banda that this bass technique was most developed during the 1990s, largely by bassist Feliciano Arango.

The Music of Cuba: An Overview

The rhythm section is primarily responsible for establishing a groove that is intensely syncopated and repetitive, while not over-simplified or redundant. *Timba* is a conceptual way of playing that involves a fair amount of freedom and intensity—some might say, an inherent "busyness," with a general lack of uniform pattern-playing, an emphasis on the backbeat (derived from American funk), and plenty of stops and breaks (called "bloques" or "cierres"). The basslines are perhaps the most representative of this idea, with the *tumbao* (standard syncopated bass part) tending away from the typical pattern of 2+ and 4, and instead, shifting the accents in unconventional ways. Like Irakere, most *timba* bands use the drum set in combination with congas and timbales (plus hand percussion), resulting in a much denser texture. (Of course, Irakere also used the batá drums, adding a much richer component to the rhythm section.) Another attribute of *timba* is a two-keyboard format, with one pianist playing the more traditional *montuno* patterns, and the other adding textural elements including pads, contrapuntal melodies, or doubled basslines. There are many ideas of what *timba* is, and it is certainly important to listen to the many bands who have evolved the style over the decades, so that you can truly appreciate how unique each interpretation can be. Among Cuba's top *timba* bands (since the 1990s) are NG La Banda, Charanga Habanera, Manolito y su Trabuco, Issac Delgado, Bamboleo, Paulito FG, Pupy y Los Que Son Son, and Havana D' Primera, as well as Miami based Tiempo Libre, and Swedish band Calle Real.

It must be reiterated that this mini-history in no way represents everything there is to say about Cuba and her music. With the emphasis of this book being the compositional approach of one of the island's—and the world's—most prolific and innovative musicians (Chucho Valdés), our goal is to highlight the richness and diversity of Cuban music in order to frame the significance of Chucho's place in the story.

* * *

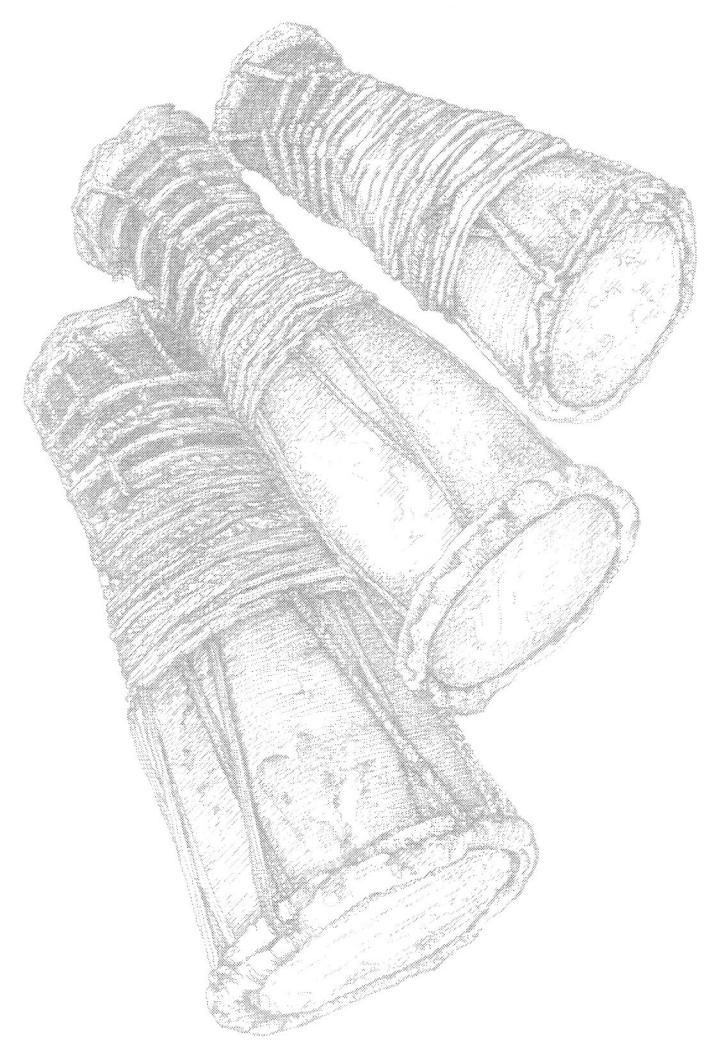

DEMYSTIFYING THE CUBAN CLAVE   CHAPTER 2

"The rules of the clave must be respected, but within limits. We (Cubans) like to think we have 'clave license,' allowing us to break the rules when musically necessary." – Juan Formell, San Francisco, 1997

• • •

If you want to understand Afro-Cuban music, it is essential to go beyond patterns and rhythms to understand its musical **language**. Among the qualities that distinguished Irakere since its founding was a deep respect for—and immersive study of—African-derived folkloric traditions, including dozens of sacred and secular rhythms, many of which were incorporated into Chucho Valdés' elaborate arrangements. At the root of nearly all music of African origin, and throughout its evolution in the Americas, is the presence of **binary** rhythmical cells or structures. These patterns affect virtually all aspects of how the music is interpreted, and in Cuban music, there is nothing more omnipresent than the concept of the **clave**. The Cuban *clave* is the lifeblood of nearly all the island's music, and in the simplest terms, can be best described as a **rhythmical pattern** (there are several varieties), an **instrument** (referred to in plural form as "claves"), and a **guide** that affects how all of the rhythmical, melodic and even harmonic components fit together. It is, therefore, imperative to have a firm grasp of the relationship between the *clave* and the music. We will begin by examining various *clave* patterns, then we will discuss the *clave's* function within popular and folkloric music, and hopefully demystify the elusive elements that tend to challenge those unfamiliar with Afro-Cuban musical techniques. Later, we will explore how Irakere's music reflected this functionality within the structures of the eleven works highlighted in this book.

First, I asked Chucho to define his concept of the *clave*, and how he would explain it to someone with no understanding or experience:

"Let me say that this question is very deep and complex. The *clave* is something we Cubans feel, and is essentially intuitive for many of us. In other words, there was never any formal 'instruction' or explanation of the *clave* at any school when I was growing up. I wouldn't know how to teach it to someone, since I never learned it from a pedagogical perspective. It's similar to flamenco musicians, who understand the most complicated structures and rhythms like *soleá por bulerías*,[1] and don't really have the tools to explain what it is they are doing. Certainly I can break down the basic elements of the *clave* such as the direction (2-3 or 3-2), etc. I'm sure my father (Bebo) could explain it much better than I can; he knew the *clave* inside and out!"

If the *clave* is such a pervasive element in Cuban music, why wasn't it "taught?" This may have more to do with cultural reasons than academic ones, but the basic reality is this: the *clave* evolved within the context of folkloric and popular music of **oral tradition**, and these folk traditions are seldom written down. As with other roots musics, Afro-Cuban music enjoys an enormous wealth of sacred and secular rhythms and songs, each of which has evolved over centuries, echoing down to us from Africa. While the *clave* concept itself is distinctly Cuban, its DNA evolved long before it became such a "tangible" element, and its essence can be interpreted in many different ways around the world. What Chucho refers to above as the "tools" needed to communicate exactly what is going on with regard to the *clave*, these have more to do with the musicological descriptors that Western music has deemed

---

[1] This is one of many *palos* (genres) of flamenco music, with myriad variations and a complex rhythmical structure.

necessary for defining a **process**. He makes it very clear that for most Cubans, they simply **feel** the *clave*; they don't need to explain it!

"During the early years with Irakere, there were times when I wrote things that were crossed with the *clave* (Chucho uses the term *montado*), and boy did Oscar (Valdés) take issue with that! There were songs where we would have lengthy discussions about what we needed to do in order to straighten out the relationship of a given phrase with the *clave*, or even a harmonic sequence, resulting in the need to insert a 2/4 measure if we wanted to change direction.[2] But doing that would then turn the harmony around, so the progression would be backwards! In these cases, I'm not really sure what is most important: the *clave* or the harmony. And therein would be the problem for us in the band, since we were trying to create music that **felt** good, and also **aligned** properly with the *clave*, but we didn't want to sacrifice the integrity of the melody or the harmonic progression. Let me just say that the king of the *clave* was (*tres* player and bandleader) Arsenio Rodríguez. He knew how to manipulate the *clave* within the melody in ways that were pure genius, and with complete intentionality. He played with it!"

Arsenio was, indeed, a masterful "manipulator" in the Afro-Cuban *son* and *son-montuno* traditions,[3] often creating clever phrases that deliberately outlined the *clave* in specific ways, some literally, and others more subtly. An example of a more deliberate approach might be Arsenio's arrangement of "Chicharronero" (the pork rind vendor), which alternates *clave* direction several times before finally settling on 3-2 direction at the *montuno* (the call-and-response section). The resulting melody of the chorus is a literal statement of the *son* clave pattern in 3-2 (fig. 2.1):[4]

2.1 - Fragment from 'Chicharronero' by Arsenio Rodríguez

In order for any of this to make sense, and before you can formulate the tools to apply these concepts, it's important to provide some background and explanation.

• THE ROOTS OF THE CLAVE

The origins of the *clave* as an instrument are certainly diverse. Alejo Carpentier asserts that *claves* were commonly in use by the seventeenth century in Havana,[5] and Fernando Ortiz notes that the origins of the *clave* as instrument reflect a people's necessity for musical expression from within the horrors of slavery and prison life early on in Cuba's history, where often the only hope or joy rested in song and dance:

---

[2] This implies that Chucho and other Cuban musicians tend to view and notate the *clave* within one 4/4 measure, and in order to turn the *clave* direction around, they must insert a 2/4 measure to adjust the direction.
[3] Please refer to Chapter I for information on the *son* and *son-montuno*.
[4] "Chicharronero" was composed around 1946 by Arsenio's pianist, Luis Martínez Griñán, better known as "Lilí," and appears on the Tumbao Cuban Classics compilation, *Montuneando* (1993).
[5] Alejo Carpentier, *La Música en Cuba,* Fondo de Cultura Económica, 1946, p. 9.

DEMYSTIFYING THE CUBAN CLAVE — CHAPTER 2

"The clave in Cuban music was born in Havana, of the marriage between the rhythm sticks used by African slaves and the tejoletas (stone pestles) used by white Andalusian indentured servants. A mulatto birth was created from within the prison cells (and labor camps), where (for a moment) blacks and whites forgot about their hard work, their pain and suffering, even without musical instruments – no drums, no guitars - far away from their miserable lives in servitude."[6]

In the various studies concerning African music and instruments, there appears to be no instrument that resembles the *claves*, nor is there any immediate "ancestor." Ortiz affirms that it was the Cuban Creole (or mulatto) who combined the elements of Spanish-derived peasant music and African-derived drumming, resulting in a "transculturation," as well as the development of the *clave* instrument itself. Perhaps the most prominent role of the *clave* in its early stages of development is in the music of the white peasant culture known as **guajiros** (descendants of Spanish farmers), in the Cuban genre known as **música campesina** (peasant music)—a direct descendant of Spanish country music. Here, in yet another musical culture born from the lower classes of society, there are no African-derived drums or polyrhythms, only the presence of the *clave* as a reminder of the humble and often painful origins of another sector of the Cuban population. Following these beginnings, the *clave* went on to "penetrate popular music throughout Cuba, by way of a 'mulattoization' and total transculturation."[7]

The foundations of the *clave* concept can be defined as a beat or pulse that is perceived or felt in a given rhythmical structure; it is something like a "timeline" to "hold on to" while the drums are played, the songs are sung, and the dancers dance. For the most part, these concepts or timelines emerged from African sacred traditions that eventually became binarized in the Americas, creating a palette of essential **rhythmical cells**. These cells, in fact, were passed down from the Africans we identified previously (the *lucumí*, *bantú* and *arará*, among others), forming the nucleus of what would eventually become known as the *clave*. These cells would travel the world and have an impact on everything from American ragtime to roots music, from the second line heard in New Orleans to the Puerto Rican *bomba*, Jamaican *mento*, and the music of Bo Diddley. Two of the most commonly heard cells in the Americas are identified (in Cuban musicology) as the **tresillo** and the **cinquillo** (fig. 2.2), and were already predominantly used in Cuban music well before the *clave* rhythm was developed:

2.2 - Tresillo & Cinquillo

Although each of these cells is a singular, one-measure pattern, the evolution of Afro-Cuban music would eventually develop a **binary structure to complete the concept of the timeline**, wherein the cell would be "answered" or followed by a consequent phrase, resulting in the *clave* as we know it today. Here is an example of an antecedent-consequent phrase using the *cinquillo* cell, known as the **baqueteo** (fig. 2.3), (the pattern played by the timbales player in the Cuban *danzón*):

---

[6] Fernando Ortiz, *Los Instrumentos de la Música Afrocubana, Vol. I*, p. 237.
[7] Ortiz, Vol. I, pp 242-3.

2.3 - Baqueteo

This pattern is clearly structured in a way that can be perceived as "tension-release," further reinforcing a condition or relationship that will define how the music "fits together." Without a doubt, the most significant and widespread Cuban musical expressions stem from the influence of African-derived folklore, and in all of Afro-Cuban music, there is no more important genre than **rumba**. *Rumba* comprises several styles, each with its own particular *clave* pattern, rhythmical structure, and dance. Irakere's incorporation of *rumba*, along with many other folkloric idioms, highlighted a reverence for authenticity combined with experimentation; a signature component of Chucho's arrangements for the Irakere band was his ability to "navigate" complex changes in structure and *clave* direction within myriad folkloric genres. To get a better understanding of the importance of the *clave* in Cuban music, let's review some of the basic aspects, and begin with some of the most common *clave* patterns.

• SON CLAVE

As the name implies, this *clave* pattern developed within Cuba's most influential genre of popular music: the **son**. Its binary structure consists of two parts in an antecedent-consequent phrase, with the first part consisting of 3 notes and 2 in the second part. Here it is notated in 4/4 meter (fig. 2.4):

2.4 - Son Clave in 4/4

It is important to state that Cuban popular and folkloric music was rarely notated during its early stages of development, and if notated, would be written in 2/4 meter (fig. 2.5):

2.5 - Son Clave in 2/4

Furthermore, it may often occur that Cuban musicians of a certain generation notate the clave in one 4/4 measure (fig. 2.6), as mentioned previously:

2.6 - Son Clave in one 4/4 measure

The terms "three-two" and "two-three" are often used to describe the relationship or **direction** of the *clave* phrase according to which measure is played first; these terms are commonly found in contemporary Salsa and Latin jazz arrangements in order to help the performer orient him/herself when playing a particular tune. In most binary phrases, there tends to be a relationship of tension and release, a natural occurrence in virtually all music. Within the *clave* pattern, the "three-side" is the syncopated measure or "tension" side, and the "two-side" is the simple "release" side (fig. 2.7):

2.7 - Son Clave (3-side & 2-side)

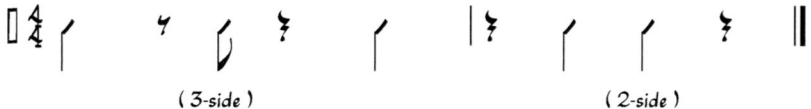

It is this binary, antecedent-consequent structure that must align itself with the **melody**. After all, the melody is the most important part of the song, and therefore determines how the rhythmical patterns will line up. In other words, **the clave direction is the result of the melodic phrase**, and in most Afro-Cuban folkloric and popular music, these melodies tend to have binary structures that coincide with the *clave* in either "three-two" or "two-three" direction. Another important component of these binary structures is the placement of accented notes within a given phrase, and where these land with the *clave*. One of the most important accents in all of Cuban music falls on the "and" of two on the 3-side, which is referred to as the ***bombo*** (fig. 2.8):

2.8 - Bombo Accent

In addition, there are many breaks and figures that have become foundational in both folkloric and popular styles, and the most common of all breaks, sometimes referred to as the *conga* break (fig. 2.9),[8] literally falls on the "and" of beat 2 and the 4th beat of the 3-side:

2.9 - Conga Break

This break is often used as a transitional element within songs, as well as a definitive ending resolving from a dominant chord to a tonic chord, and is a clear indication of the *clave* direction, primarily functioning as a song-ending or *clave-change* phrase.

To illustrate how the melody defines the direction of the *clave*, let's look at 2 simple examples. This first phrase (fig. 2.10) clearly outlines or suggests a three-two *clave* direction:

2.10 - Melody from 'Ave Maria Morena'

---

[8] Not to be confused with the instrument or rhythmical/dance style of the same name, this break is perhaps the most commonly used phrase in all of Cuban music.

And here is a classic melody composed by Arsenio Rodríguez and covered by just about everyone, including Irakere, that contains a *cinquillo*-like phrase emphasizing the 3-side of the *clave* in the second bar (fig. 2.11):

2.11 - Chorus from 'Dile a Catalina' by Arsenio Rodríguez (as played by Irakere)

One of the most important concepts in playing Afro-Cuban music has to do with the notion of a **common pulse**, regardless of the meter or style being played. Whether playing in 4/4 or 6/8, it is vital to lock into the pulse of a given rhythm, and in Cuban music, the pulse is felt on beats 1 and 3. It is vital to feel the *clave* against this half-note pulse when playing, as well as to **maintain a sense of the pulse regardless of your particular instrument or part** (fig. 2.12):

2.12 - Clave + Pulse

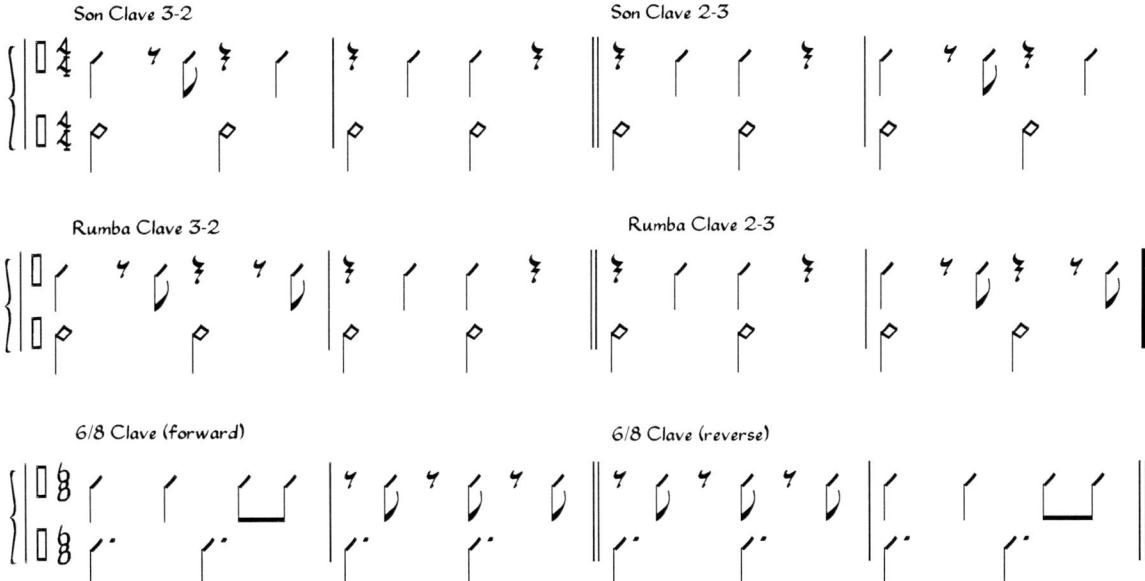

Whether or not a musical phrase begins "three-two" or "two-three," it is expected that the *clave's* direction will remain **fixed** within a song, and that the only way to change *clave* direction is to play a musical phrase consisting of an odd number of measures, thereby "turning the *clave* around" so that the next phrase begins on the other side (fig. 2.13):

2.13 - Change in Clave Direction, from "Yo Soy la Rumba" by Marcelino Guerra (as performed by Machito)

- **CLAVE-NEUTRAL PATTERNS**

Many of the rhythmical patterns played by the percussion instruments in Afro-Cuban music are structured around the *clave* in specific ways, and the general rule is that one-measure patterns are considered "neutral" with regard to *clave* direction, meaning that **they can be played regardless of clave direction**, while two-measure patterns must sit properly within the *clave's* phrase so that they are balanced. Here are several examples of *clave*-neutral or one-measure patterns (fig. 2.14):

2.14 - One Measure (Clave Neutral) Patterns

Often, percussion patterns sound "*clave*-like" so that their orientation with the *clave* seems perfectly natural, while others may seem elusive, and the only way of knowing what their *clave* direction is has to do with your knowledge of the particular genre being played. What is fairly consistent is this: **the *clave* remains fixed, and the music revolves around it**. In a moment, we will explore other ways the *clave* may "turn around."

Son clave is the main *clave* pattern heard in Cuban *son* and also in the earliest style of *rumba* known as *yambú*, as well as salsa music, Dominican *bachata*, Haitian *mereng*, and even Mexican *bolero* styles. In addition, it is not necessary to play the *clave* pattern only on the *claves* themselves. In contemporary music, the pattern will often be played by the timbales player or drummer on the woodblock (or jam block), and often during just a portion of the song. Most ensembles cannot afford the luxury of having a dedicated *clave* player! Also, the *clave* pattern really doesn't need to be consistently played in the music anyway; **the *clave* is essentially implied within all of the rhythmical structures in an ensemble, without the need to literally play the pattern throughout a given song.**

• RUMBA CLAVE

As noted earlier, Cuban *rumba* is one of the most complex and influential genres of Afro-Cuban folklore, and it comprises three distinct styles: **yambú** (the oldest and slowest of the styles, dating back to the Colonial period), **guaguancó** (the more popular of the three styles, of medium to fast tempo) and the **columbia** (the most African-flavored and rhythmically complex of the three). Each of the styles has an intricate structure, and over time, has developed unique *clave* patterns to fit its particular rhythmical characteristics. The oldest form, the *yambú*, uses the same *clave* pattern found in the *son* (shown above) and has pretty much maintained it since Colonial times. The *guaguancó* style initially used the *son* clave pattern, but changed in the 1960s with the evolution of a slightly different and more syncopated pattern originally referred to as *clave de guaguancó*,[9] and it differs by only an eighth note (when notated in 4/4 meter). Here is the pattern shown with the half-note pulse (fig. 2.15):

2.15 - Rumba Clave + Pulse

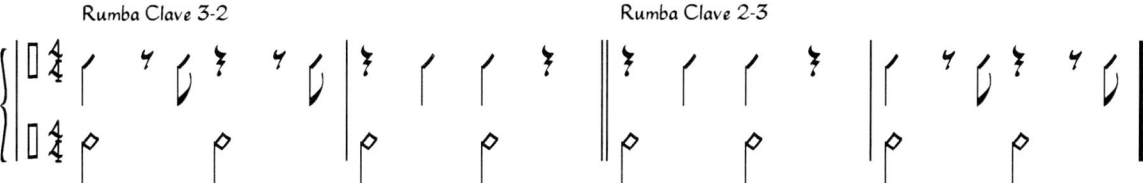

This pattern is thought to be derived from the folkloric Abakuá tradition,[10] which is typically played on a cowbell in a compound duple feel. Over time, musicians began referring to this particular pattern as *la clave de rumba* ("rumba clave") as a way to distinguish it from *son clave*, and the term has remained fairly commonplace since then. Just like the *son clave*, *rumba clave* is structured in the same binary way, with an antecedent-consequent phrase and the same notion of direction ("three-two" and "two-three"). However, what makes it more challenging to those listening or playing it for the first time is the fact that on the "three-side" of *rumba clave*, the third note is actually closer to the "2-side" measure by an eighth note, and when played by itself can be elusive (fig. 2.16):

2.16 - Rumba Clave

We find this *clave* pattern not only in the *guaguancó* style of *rumba*—where it usually initiates the songs—but also in more contemporary styles of Cuban dance music such as *songo* and *timba*. During the 1970s in Cuba, several bands began to explore a faster variety of dance music, often incorporating *rumba clave* into *son* songs as a way to make them feel more syncopated. As Irakere burst on the scene in the mid-70s, the band found myriad ways to combine traditional expressions of Afro-Cuban folklore and popular styles with jazz, funk, rock, and European classical music, often relying heavily on

---

[9] There are a number of other patterns identified by the term *clave de guaguancó,* leading one to understand the ever-evolving nature of *rumba* as a folk tradition.
[10] The Abakuá tradition is a multifaceted combination of secret society and fraternal organization, musical genre, dance, and highly influential component in African-derived culture in Cuba. The rhythmical structure of Abakuá music contains a 6/8 or 12/8 bell pattern that serves as a guide, and is reminiscent of the duple meter *clave* heard in *son* and *yambú*.

the *rumba* genre as a jumping-off point. During this time, it was equally common to use both *rumba clave* and *son clave* in popular dance tunes, as popular groups such as Los Van Van and others began to explore the hybrid possibilities of American-tinged rock mixed with Cuban *son* and *rumba*, giving way to an evolutionary style known as **songo**.[11]

By the 1990s, several Cuban bands began exploring the influences of American funk and hip-hop, creating a rhythmical feel within the percussion section that combined Cuban styles with the backbeat, all wrapped around the *rumba clave* pattern; we refer to this genre as **timba,** and it is generally accepted that the origins of this style of playing were developed during Irakere's evolution, setting the tone for the more aggressive and intense sounds to come. The general consensus was: the funkier the bass and percussion parts, the better the fit with *rumba clave* instead of *son clave*. By the time the *timba* genre was in full swing, the majority of bands tended to favor *rumba clave* precisely because of its "funkier" and more syncopated feel. Ultimately, this music has always been about feel, and the musicians who play it are also often inspired to create based on the reaction of the dancing public. Much of this experimentation with the groove had also been well underway in Irakere since the 70s, with the core rhythm section well-versed in finding a balance between musical creativity and danceability.

• 6/8 CLAVE

A bit of a misnomer, 6/8 clave is, in actuality, a 6/8 **bell** pattern of West African origin that has been around for hundreds of years. Found throughout many West and Central African nations, the pattern traveled with the slave trade, and wound up not only in Cuba but also in Puerto Rico, the Dominican Republic, Haiti, Trinidad and Tobago, and Brazil, among other countries. While in Africa it might be generally perceived as one entity or timeline that could be notated in 12/8, in the Americas it is often considered binary and is often notated like this (fig. 2.17, shown against a dotted quarter-note pulse):

2.17 - 6/8 Clave + Pulse

Just as with the *son* and *rumba clave* patterns, 6/8 *clave* also contains the same antecedent-consequent phrase relationship we discussed earlier, and serves as a guide in the music, specifically in the folkloric traditions surrounding the sacred music in Africa. As noted in Chapter I, the enslaved Africans in Cuba were able to preserve a great deal of their religious traditions by forming mutual aid societies known as *cabildos*, and over the centuries, they maintained close ties to their religion and passed down the sacred rhythms and chants to their descendants, as did the Africans and their descendants in Brazil, Haiti and elsewhere. The binary structure of these rhythms and chants can also be assigned a *clave* direction according to which measure is played first. Instead of "three-two" or "two-three," it may be easier to perceive the direction as **forward and reverse** (fig. 2.18):

---

[11] *Songo* is an evolutionary genre developed by bassist and bandleader Juan Formell in the popular Cuban group Los Van Van, stemming from the blend of Cuban dance music with American rock influences.

CHAPTER 2 — DEMYSTIFYING THE CUBAN CLAVE

2.18 - 6/8 Clave in Forward and Reverse Directions

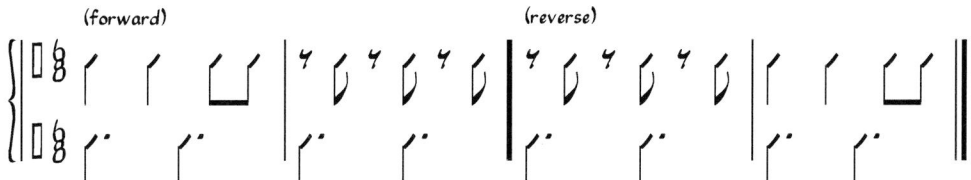

The following transcription of a Yoruban sacred chant from a portion of Irakere's seminal recording, "Misa Negra," demonstrates how the melody fits with the 6/8 *clave* pattern (fig. 2.19):

2.19 - Fragment from 'Misa Negra' – Praise Song for Yemayá

As with the melody, the various drumming patterns in the folkloric ensembles must be properly aligned with the *clave*, and in Cuba there are several African-derived forms of folklore that incorporate the 6/8 bell pattern, including Yoruban, Dahomean and Congolese genres. As mentioned earlier, the music of the Abakuá sect in Cuba contains a bell rhythm that is remarkably similar to the *rumba clave* pattern, but when notated in 6/8 can actually be understood as a streamlined 6/8 bell rhythm (fig. 2.20):

2.20 - Abakuá Bell

The most significant element in 6/8 rhythms is the polymetric feeling of three beats against two beats, also referred to as a cross-rhythm. An inherent quality of virtually all African (and African-derived) music is a complex structure that enables the patterns to be subdivided in multiple ways. Therefore, consider this as another critical hint in **decoding** the mystery of Afro-Cuban music interpretation: it is important to play rhythmical exercises that develop your capacity for **independence** and phrasing. Here are a few examples of cross-rhythms in 6/8 meter (fig. 2.21):

Demystifying the Cuban Clave — Chapter 2

2.21 - Cross Rhythms in 6/8

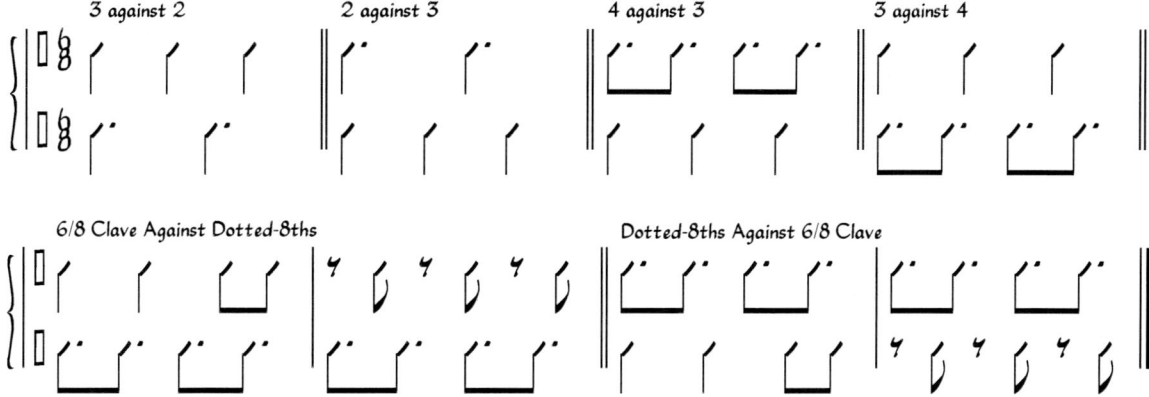

As with *son* and *rumba clave*, 6/8 *clave* can be found in more contemporary forms of Latin music, including Latin jazz and Latin rock. It is also common to hear salsa music arrangements break into brief passages of a 6/8 rhythm, if only for a moment, before returning to the primary duple feel. A solid way to navigate these changes in meter and feel is to alternate between each *clave* pattern while maintaining a common pulse (fig. 2.22); note that the pulse itself will remain fixed even though it is switching from a half-note pulse to a dotted-quarter-note pulse:

2.22 - Common Pulse

To take this one step further, an excellent exercise in navigating between these different meters involves the entire rhythm section alternating between various grooves, including switching between double-time and half-time feel. In addition, you can add swing feel to this and create a solid way for your ensemble to move fluidly between a 6/8 groove, swing, half-time and double-time Cuban styles, while maintaining a common pulse as the anchor. To make this exercise more challenging, mix up the order of the grooves, or randomly call out each one to keep the band members on their toes!

CHAPTER 2 — DEMYSTIFYING THE CUBAN CLAVE

• CLAVE DIRECTION

As mentioned earlier, the *clave* acts as a guide with regard to the melodic and rhythmical structure in Cuban music, and often it is musically necessary to create **changes in *clave* direction** to suit the melody. The most common way of doing this results from having odd numbers of measures in a phrase, thereby "turning the *clave* around" **naturally** so that the next phrase is in the reverse direction (fig. 2.23):

2.23 - Clave Turnaround

However, another scenario may occur when the *clave* turns around during a break or figure, and even though that figure may consist of an even number of measures, the next phrase begins in the reverse *clave* direction. This is known as **jumping the *clave*** (*brincar la clave*), and is generally a function of the arrangement, when it just seems natural to switch *clave* direction for the upcoming material without the need to create an odd-measure phrase. Here is a fragment of Chucho's "Bailando Así" in the transition between a break in 2-3 clave, and the chorus in 3-2 clave (fig. 2.24):

2.24 - Clave Jump – Fragment from 'Bailando Así' by Chucho Valdés & Irakere

Demystifying the Cuban Clave — Chapter 2

Chucho questions the strict adherence to consistent *clave* direction, when the music (aka, the melody), may require an "adjustment" that switches from one direction to the other:

"Why should it be necessary, that even after coming up with a transitional break that is intended to interrupt and change the feel in the groove, you should be 'dragging' along this previous *clave* direction?"

At this point, I cited an interview I had done in 1997 with the late Juan Formell, bassist, composer and bandleader of Cuba's Los Van Van, where he introduced his "*clave* license" theory, essentially justifying the "jumping" of the *clave* in order to create a different feeling, one that is more suitable to the new melodic or harmonic sequence, **regardless** of the previous *clave* direction. Chucho absolutely concurred with this statement:

"The melody should never be 'imprisoned' by the *clave* direction!"

To clarify, **the *clave* pattern itself is usually not played during these breaks**. It is important to state that this jumping of the *clave* only occurs during sections of a song where there is an **interruption in the general groove**, and never during the groove itself! In other words, changes in *clave* direction should never feel forced or awkward, and this is something that comes with the experience of really knowing the music.

• "OFF-CLAVE" – CRUZADO OR MONTADO

There is nothing more intimidating to the novice of Afro-Cuban music than the fear of being on the wrong side of *clave*! Often referred to as being *cruzado* (crossed) or *montado* (mounted), this undesirable condition occurs when an individual player is playing their particular part on the **wrong side**, meaning that their pattern—usually a two-bar phrase—is not properly aligned with the *clave*.

This doesn't affect neutral or one-measure patterns, of course, so those can be your lifesavers if you are ever in doubt as to what the *clave* direction should be. As the percussionists bear the bulk of the responsibility in the band when it comes to the *clave*, it should be understood that any player worth his/her salt must know the *clave* inside and out.

Here are two examples of patterns that are **crossed** with the *clave* (fig. 2.25):

2.25 - Crossed Patterns

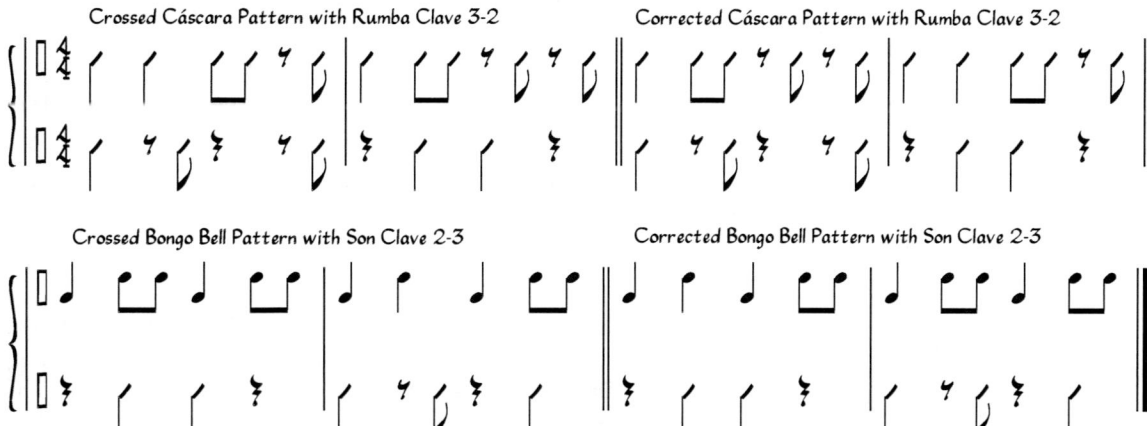

These are some very common patterns in Afro-Cuban music, and clearly, given the inordinate amount of variations that have evolved over the years, it is worthwhile to have as full a command of this vocabulary as possible.

Chucho articulates one of the primary reasons why Cuban musicians often scoff at the idea of strict adherence to the *clave*:

"I would say one of the most important concepts we came to realize, was that we were often being held captive by '*clave* correctness,' and that made the music less accessible to non-Cubans. For example, in Brazilian music, if you think about the bossa nova *clave* (Chucho refers to the accent pattern heard in bossa nova), its last note is delayed, therefore making the pattern seem **more relaxed and less rigid**."

Chucho proceeds to sing the following rhythm, which we sometimes refer to as Brazilian *clave*.[12] It is shown here in both 4/4 and 2/4 notation (fig. 2.26):

2.26 - Brazilian Clave 3-2

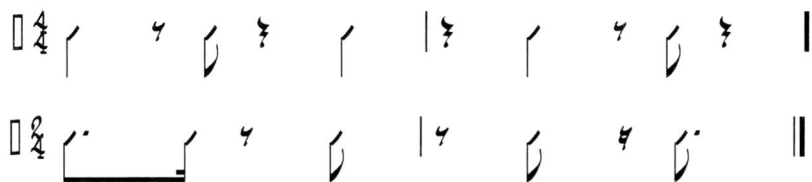

Now here, we get to an important hint at decoding the *clave* mystery: the inherent **understanding among Cuban musicians is that the *clave* is a force that is always present in Afro-Cuban music, whether it is actually played or not:**

"One of the most interesting aspects to me is that in Cuban music, the *clave* remains as an invisible force in the music, even during passages where there are breaks or riffs and stops in the groove, much like a spirit or a ghost."

● CLAVE AS A GUIDE

Much of Afro-Cuban music is the result of a vast oral tradition, and its ongoing development has experienced some dramatic changes over the years. What has remained fairly constant is a deep understanding of the *clave* as a structural guide in the music, serving as an **organizing principle**, not only for the composer and arranger, but also the improviser. Any musician wishing to fully absorb the intricacies of this music should be aware of the circumstances surrounding the *clave* and its role in the overall structure of the music. What follows are several examples of melodic and rhythmical phrases and their relationship to the *clave* (fig. 2.27):

---

[12] Brazilian musicians are often quick to point out that their music does **not** abide by this concept of *clave*, even though their music reflects similar binary phrasing and passages that alternate between syncopated and non-syncopated rhythms. The pattern listed here as "Brazilian *clave*" is actually an accented pattern that resides within the overarching percussion groove, and is also felt in "3-2" or "2-3."

DEMYSTIFYING THE CUBAN CLAVE

2.27 - *The Clave as a Guide*

• BEYOND THE CLAVE

Irakere's music was one of a select few repertoires in Cuba to cross multiple cultural as well as stylistic boundaries, and at the core of this experimentation was the notion of rhythmical freedom. While the use of duple meter seemed to anchor the majority of the band's repertoire, Chucho was certainly inspired to move beyond the realm of Afro-Cuban folk idioms as the band explored swing, rock, funk, Brazilian samba, Argentine tango, and many genres that weren't necessarily bound by the concept of *clave*. In addition, the use of odd meter was another musical tool in the Irakere arsenal, bringing to bear the distinguishing factors often used to separate dance music from concert or jazz music. Make no mistake: Cuban musicians know their audience, and when it comes to playing for dancers, the members of Irakere clearly understood the nature of the groove as first order of business! But the extraordinary diversity of the repertoire, coupled with the multilingual nature of the band's musicians, often resulted in a musical vocabulary without borders or limits.

While we will highlight a relatively small portion of Valdés' body of work in this book, it should be clear that much of Irakere's legacy as a band was Chucho's ability to frame the deep traditions of African-derived, *clave-based* folk music in ways that were unique and unprecedented. The *clave* is foundational in Cuban music, but it is not a deal-breaker. If one analyzes the aesthetic value of musical excellence, you come to realize that **the melody trumps everything, and that the *clave* is really just a result of how a particular melody is phrased.** It is, ultimately, the arranger who determines how the supporting material will highlight the tune, and what makes this music so challenging and compelling is precisely how the arrangement evolves beyond the melody. Later on in Chapter V, we will explore some of the primordial Afro-Cuban folkloric genres at the heart of Irakere's musical alchemy, and analyze the structures of an extremely complex vocabulary that reaches back to its African ancestors.

• • •

Chucho and Bebo Valdés, San Francisco, November, 1995. PHOTO CREDIT: DAVID GARTEN

Chucho Valdés: A Biography — Chapter 3

"The music from Valdés...[is] as beautiful and intense as music could be - virtuosic, soulful, filled with life and power, everything we hope that art can offer." – Jordan Levin, Miami Herald, Nov 15, 2015

"Chucho Valdés is emblematic of the evolution of Afro-Cuban jazz during recent decades, and is still at the top of his game." – Jeff Tamarkin, JazzTimes, Jan 24, 2012

• • •

To understand and deeply appreciate the legacy of Afro-Cuban jazz, it is essential to look at the role pianists have played in the repertoire dating back to the early 1800s. Chucho is part of a lineage of iconic artists who have contributed to the musical canon and whose work is perpetuated in the music education programs on the island. Anyone studying classical repertoire in Cuba must pass through Manuel Saumell and Ignacio Cervantes[1] before arriving at Lecuona, just like a jazz pianist would look first to Jelly Roll Morton or James P. Johnson before taking on Art Tatum. The legacy of the Valdés family is akin to a piano dynasty, with consecutive generations of virtuosos representing over 90 years (and counting) of music between them, so it is impossible to formulate a biographical essay on Chucho without highlighting the life and work of his father, Bebo. For a time, their careers were literally intertwined, and their mutual love and respect for one another would grow even stronger after several years apart, resulting in a series of collaborations during Bebo's twilight years, when his career experienced a resurgence. As with virtually all Cuban musicians, they are known by their respective nicknames more than their shared given name, Dionisio.[2]

• FORMATIVE YEARS

Both father and son were born in the same town of Quivicán, in the province of Mayabeque, about 22 miles south of Havana, Bebo on October 9, 1918, and Chucho on October 9, 1941. One of five children born to Bebo and wife Pilar (also a pianist, incidentally), Chucho seemed destined from the start to follow in his father's footsteps, demonstrating his musical gifts at the age of three, when Bebo noticed his son picking out melodies by ear at the piano with both hands. Bebo's career was in full swing during Chucho's formative years, when the elder Valdés was the pianist in trumpeter Julio Cueva's band while developing as a composer and arranger. In around 1948, Bebo took the helm as pianist and musical director at the infamous Tropicana Nightclub in Havana, working for nearly a decade with some of the most celebrated musicians in the world before starting his own dazzling big band, Sabor de Cuba. The Valdés family home was, as both father and son have recalled, ground zero for Cuba's musical elite, and a constant source of inspiration for Chucho growing up:

"Since I can remember, I saw my father every day sitting at the piano, practicing, playing, studying Bach preludes and fugues. He also really loved the Impressionists, including a piece by Debussy called 'The Girl With the Flaxen Hair' in G-flat minor, which he played a lot. I remember him coming home late from playing at the Tropicana Club, maybe after 2 a.m., then he'd be up early around 10 a.m. practicing! He loved playing many different pieces, especially Spanish Impressionists such as Joaquín Turina Pérez

---

[1] Manuel Saumell (1817-1870) and Ignacio Cervantes (1847-1905) were two of Cuba's most important 19th century pianists and composers, credited with the "creolization" of European-derived classical music, and ushering in the prominence of a nationalist aesthetic. Their *danzas* and *contradanzas* have become essential works in the Cuban classical canon, and are a must for all piano students.

[2] Bebo's full name was Dionisio Ramón Emilio Valdés Amaro, and Chucho's is Dionisio Jesús Valdés Rodríguez.

(1817-1870), who wrote a piece called "Orgía."[3] I remember Bebo playing this at the Tropicana as part of a choreographed dance piece...you know, the dancers would use a lot of music like this for elaborate numbers in the shows. The same thing with Gershwin's 'Rhapsody in Blue,' which he used to play at home constantly, since it was also used in the Tropicana show; he loved to practice that piece. That was magic for me...seeing those fingers, Bebo's fingers, gliding over the keyboard. I always thought to myself, 'Wow, I'll never be able to do that.' But I sure would try, picking out tunes by ear when I was left alone at the piano. As early as three years of age, my father said I was able to pick out a melody, and that's when my family realized I would probably become a musician."

At age nine, Chucho entered the Conservatorio Municipal de la Habana (now known as the Conservatorio Amadeo Roldán),[4] studying harmony and counterpoint with a contemporary of Bebo's named Harold Gramatges, who had gone to Juilliard and had also been a child prodigy. But Bebo also believed his son should also have a private teacher, and hired Óscar Muñoz Bouffartique to come to the family home. Bouffartique happened to be Bebo's solfège teacher, and Chucho recalls his lessons were a bit difficult:

"Boy, he was grumpy. He always seemed to be in a bad mood[5] and hardly ever smiled or laughed, and when you did something wrong, he let you know it right away! Oh, and by the way, he was the composer of a hit song that Celia Cruz performed with La Sonora Matancera, called 'Burundanga!'[6] He composed a lot of popular tunes, and also played violin and trumpet."

Chucho graduated from the Conservatory at age 14, and soon afterward joined his father on the bandstand, many times substituting for him and, eventually, taking over musical direction duties when Bebo left Cuba in 1960. Early on, it was clear that his most important mentor and role model was Bebo, and that the social environment in which he grew up, surrounded by many of Cuba's most prolific and influential musicians, would have a lasting impact:

"A vivid memory I have is of the amazing musicians who would visit our home on any given day. I remember Peruchín (pianist Pedro Justiz) coming over to gossip with my dad, or César Portillo de la Luz and José Antonio Méndez showing up with their guitars, working out ideas for new tunes they were composing. One day, José Antonio started to play for Bebo a song he was composing...which turned out to be one of his most famous, 'Novia Mia.' Bebo would help them by transcribing the songs and preparing the lead-sheets so they could register their copyright. Since they couldn't read or write music, Bebo would help them out—sometimes at all hours of the night. That's how it was, and I lived those moments with him. I remember my grandmother scolding Bebo, 'Bebito! How can you put up with these guys coming over and waking you up in the middle of the night?!' He would wrap the bed sheet around himself and welcome them in, working on those transcriptions...José Antonio, César, and Ñico Rojas too![7] Ñico and Bebo were great friends. I remember him asking Bebo to help transcribe one of his greatest hits, 'Mi Ayer.' He would show up with his little guitar—with no case!"

---

[3] "Orgía" is the third movement of Turina's best-known work, *Danzas Fantásticas*, Op 22 (1919).
[4] The Conservatory was free to students, thus enabling Chucho's family to provide him with excellent private teachers.
[5] Chucho refers to his teacher as having "leches muy amargas," which, loosely translated, means "extremely bad moods."
[6] "Burundanga" appears on the album *Canta Celia Cruz* (Seeco), 1956.
[7] César Portillo de la Luz, José Antonio Méndez and Ñico Rojas were all leading exponents of Cuba's *filin* movement, known for its blending of Cuban *boleros* with American jazz harmony. Like many popular musicians in the 1940s, these three were largely self-taught, and relied on professionally trained musicians such as Bebo to help document their work.

During the 1940s and 50s, Bebo's home was a nucleus of creativity, and a watering hole of Cuba's most talented and prolific musicians from all walks of life. Chucho recalls the events leading up to Bebo's tenure with the Tropicana, which began with a disgruntled diva:

"A block away from us there lived a pianist who many people never talk about, a great concert pianist named Rafael Ortega. He was the primary pianist of the Tropicana Orchestra (before Bebo came into the band), and he would come by our house to play classical pieces. Rafaelito (as we called him) was playing at the Tropicana, and Rita Montaner[8] was in the show. Well, that particular show called for some more traditional Cuban popular numbers...and by the way, Rita also happened to be a fantastic pianist herself, but the task fell on Rafael's shoulders. He was an amazing concert pianist, but he really couldn't embellish or play anything beyond the written parts, and Rita was frustrated with his lack of groove. She didn't like what he was doing, and actually threatened to quit the show because of his playing. The producers asked her what it would take for her to stay, and she said, 'Go get Bebo!' And that's how Bebo came into the Tropicana Orchestra."

With classical, popular and jazz music being constantly played in the Valdés home, the ebb and flow of musical royalty was business as usual. One of the most compelling stories Chucho tells is of the first time he recalled meeting Ernesto Lecuona,[9] one of Cuba's most prolific composers and extraordinary pianists:

"Some of Bebo's closest friends were Cuban musical icons: Ernesto Lecuona, Bola de Nieve,[10] and Rita Montaner, in particular. They were sort of a foursome, always hanging out together. Those three (Lecuona, Bola and Rita) were all from Guanabacoa (a suburb of Havana), and together they were fast friends, very close. Well, over the years, I had seen Ernesto (Lecuona) at the house many times, and remember hearing him play and thinking to myself, 'This is one of the most magnificent pianists I've ever seen!' I always heard people talking about him but never realized exactly who he was. To me, he was just another cool musician who hung out with my father. He and Bebo used to have a program on Cuban television on Channel 2, where they would play on two pianos; my dad would arrange Lecuona's *danzas* so they could perform them together on the show. One day, when I was around 14 or 15 and Ernesto was visiting the house, Bebo asked me to play 'La Malagueña.'[11] Now remember, I had seen Lecuona many times in my home as I was growing up, but I didn't really know who he was—my dad just called him Ernesto! That afternoon, my dad asked me to perform the piece 'for this man' who was visiting, and afterward, revealed who he was. I nearly fainted! In fact, there is a photograph of Bebo and Ernesto together that I recovered from my mother's home recently. It may be the only picture of them together. There was such a great love and mutual respect between Bebo and Lecuona, and all of those musicians."

In 1952, as Bebo continued in his role as pianist and musical director of the Tropicana orchestra, he would take part in a now-historic recording session produced by impresario Norman Granz, considered one of the few the jazz records made in Cuba during the 50s, called *Cubano* (on the Mercury label).

---

[8] Rita Montaner (1900-1958) was one of Cuba's most iconic *vedettes* (actress, singer and pianist), and one of the country's most popular artists between 1920 and 1950.
[9] Ernesto Lecuona (1895-1963) was one of Cuba's most celebrated and prolific composers and pianists, often called "The Gershwin of Cuba." He composed over 600 works and was a masterful pianist.
[10] Born Jacinto Villa Fernández (1911-1971), Bola de Nieve ("snowball") was renowned pianist and singer-songwriter.
[11] "Malagueña" is the sixth movement from Lecuona's 1928 *Suite Andalucía,* and one of his most well known works.

It was on this record that Bebo first performed his soon to be classic piece, "Con Poco Coco," which established the blueprint for the Cuban **descarga** (jam session), and put Bebo at the center of the cross pollination between jazz and Cuban music.[12] Author and musicologist Ned Sublette notes the significance of the year, with Bebo clearly "at the top of his game."[13] This meant, of course, that Chucho was smack dab in the middle of all of it too, literally taking the baton from Bebo on occasion when Bebo was double-booked, once he was old enough, of course. Many of the same musicians who worked with Bebo would go on to play with Chucho in various configurations over the years, and in 1957, Bebo would leave the Tropicana and go on to found one of the top dance bands of the era, Sabor de Cuba.[14] A year earlier, Chucho formed his first trio, and absorbed as much as he could from the extraordinary musicians who would come through the cabaret and nightclub scene in Havana, including the seminal jam sessions and concerts produced by the jazz association known as the Club Cubano de Jazz (CCJ).[15] But his most immersive experience as an emerging music professional would come in 1963, when he joined the Orquesta del Teatro Musical de la Habana, as we will discuss in a moment.

In his early years, Chucho learned the art of composition from his father, and was constantly surrounded by the best musicians of Cuba; what better school could one ask for? Chucho recalls his first attempt at composing, which led to an unprecedented (and undocumented) collaboration with Bebo:

"I woke up from a dream and had this fragment of a piece in my head. I remember Bebo was having breakfast, and I went to the piano and started noodling around, trying to transcribe what I had heard in my dream. Bebo came over to me and asked what I was playing, and I told him I had dreamt it. Then he said to me, 'Hey, that's pretty. We could really do something with that.' All I had was the A section, so he added the B section and wrote the arrangement, and decided to record it on his next record. So that's the first piece of mine to ever be recorded!"[16]

Meanwhile, the approaching events in Cuban history would have a dramatic impact upon the lives of the Valdés family, when Bebo decided to leave Cuba in 1960 after the Revolution, never to return. It was Chucho's task to take the helm as musical director of the Tropicana until changes in official policy would affect the lives of many working musicians, most of whom would be told that jazz was no longer an option. Fortunately for Chucho, his transition from a life in the clubs and cabarets to more "serious" music would work out fairly well.

⁕ THE ORQUESTA DEL TEATRO MUSICAL DE LA HABANA (OTM)

"In 1963, a year before I recorded my first album (*Jazz Nocturno* in 1964), I joined the Orquesta del Teatro Musical in Havana (OTM), which was a very creative group. I had been working at the Hotel Habana Riviera, playing in the club there, and had a good, steady gig. When the Musical Theater Orchestra called

---

[12] The album was supervised by renowned jazz impresario and producer, Norman Granz, and Bebo's song "Con Poco Coco" was on the b-side. Chucho recorded a version of the song on his 1998 Blue Note album, *Bele Bele en La Habana*, even throwing in a quote of John Coltrane's "Giant Steps" into the mix! Acosta, p. 170, and *OnCubaMagazine.com*, "El Arte de Bebo de Cuba," by Rafael González Escalona, April 5, 2013.
[13] Sublette, p. 586.
[14] Leymarie, p. 69.
[15] The Club Cubano de Jazz (CCJ) was serious jazz fan club established in 1958 by Cuban musicians and fiscal sponsors, who organized jam sessions and concerts with both American and Cuban jazz musicians, primarily at cabarets such as the Tropicana and the Sans Souci.
[16] The song is entitled "Cha-cha #1," and was first recorded in 1957 by Bebo Valdés & his Orchestra on the album *Cuban Dance Party*, later reissued on a French compilation. Chucho notes he didn't receive co-compositional credit since he was still unknown and only 16 years old.

me and told me this would be more of an experimental ensemble, and that guitarists Leo Brouwer[17] and Carlos Emilio Morales (Irakere founding member) were in the group, I had to join. That's when I first met and worked with Carlos Emilio. When (clarinetist and saxophonist) Paquito D'Rivera heard that we were both in this band, he joined too. He was only 15 years old! We were basically a theater pit orchestra, formed to accompany different plays, and once we settled in, a few of us got the idea to form our own group, along with bassist Kiki Hernández, drummer Emilio del Monte (who went to the same high school as me), flautist Julio Vento, valve trombonist Alberto "El Men" Giral, Paquito, Carlos Emilio and myself. I started experimenting with some arrangements and brought some things to the group to try out, and we used this as an opportunity to play the things we liked. We would hang out after the OTM rehearsals and have jam sessions, try out ideas, and see what worked and what didn't; we were serious jazz enthusiasts! At first my idea was inspired by the big band sound, but I really wanted to find a new sound, using a different, smaller instrumentation since everyone else had already been doing the big band thing. So we formed this ensemble using flute, clarinet, valve trombone and electric guitar as the main melodic instruments. We prepared enough material and in 1964, we recorded two albums: *Jazz Nocturno*, and the second with Guapachá[18] (singer Amado Borcelá). This quirky little band didn't sound like anyone else. A few years later, a few of us were chosen to join the Orquesta Cubana de Música Moderna (OCMM), and that's when I left the Musical Theater Orchestra (in 1967)."

• THE ORQUESTA CUBANA DE MÚSICA MODERNA (OCMM)

In his book *Cubano Be, Cubano Bop*, author and musician Leonardo Acosta cites the formation of Cuba's Modern Music Orchestra as the seminal post-revolutionary ensemble to preserve any semblance of jazz music on the island, during a time when any or all things American were strictly forbidden. In 1967, a decision was made to establish a band by the Consejo Nacional de Cultura (Cuba's National Culture Council, or CNC), "with the intention of creating an all-star orchestra with the best jazz musicians. The repertoire included jazz as well as Latin jazz, jazz-rock and sometimes Third Stream or symphonic jazz." Acosta poses that the workaround for the naming of the ensemble was simply to omit the word "jazz" from the title, whereby finding a loophole.[19]

"I entered the OCMM in 1967, four years after being a part of the Musical Theater Orchestra. We rehearsed at the Amadeo Roldán Conservatory, as did the Havana National Symphony Orchestra. It was during the early period of my time in the OCMM that we started to create small sub-groups from the large ensemble, mainly quartets and quintets, with Paquito, Carlos Emilio, and Oscar Valdés, who was also in the band. We started to branch out and experiment with the instrumentation, add batá drums and other percussion instruments, and as we evolved, I began to formulate the idea for Irakere — eventually adding horns, and composing some of the pieces that would become key components of our repertoire."

It would be the OCMM that would provide the fertile ground for Chucho's creative explorations, seeing as virtually all of the musicians who would go on to form part of Irakere were in the Orquesta. Among the founders of Irakere in the OCMM were Paquito D'Rivera (alto sax), Arturo Sandoval (trumpet),

---

[17] Leo Brouwer (b. 1939) is a Cuban classical guitarist, composer and conductor, and is the grandson of Ernestina Lecuona, Ernesto Lecuona's sister.
[18] The album was *Guapachá en La Habana* (Areito), 1964.
[19] Acosta suggests the OCMM's name reflected "a certain reluctance or fear of even mentioning or using the word 'jazz'." Acosta, pp. 57, 197-198.

CHAPTER 3   CHUCHO VALDÉS: A BIOGRAPHY

Carlos Emilio Morales (electric guitar), Carlos del Puerto (bass), Bernardo García (drums), Enrique Plá (drums), Jorge Varona (trumpet), and Oscar Valdés (percussion and vocals). During Chucho's tenure, there would be multiple opportunities to branch out in small group formats, and given the cadre of talented musicians in the orchestra, the combinations of instrumentation were virtually limitless. With so many of the band members having worked together over the years, there was a level of musical trust and familiarity that contributed to an absolutely top-notch and refined sound.

During the genesis of the new groundbreaking ensemble that would come to be known as Irakere, an increasing level of tension developed within the OCMM leadership, who clearly resented the sudden success of this "rogue" new supergroup. As we will explore in the subsequent chapter, Irakere's beginnings overlapped with the OCMM, and the official launch of the band would be stalled by bureaucracy. For now, we will delve into Chucho's compositional aesthetic, and the foundations for his role in the post-revolutionary Afro-Cuban jazz canon.

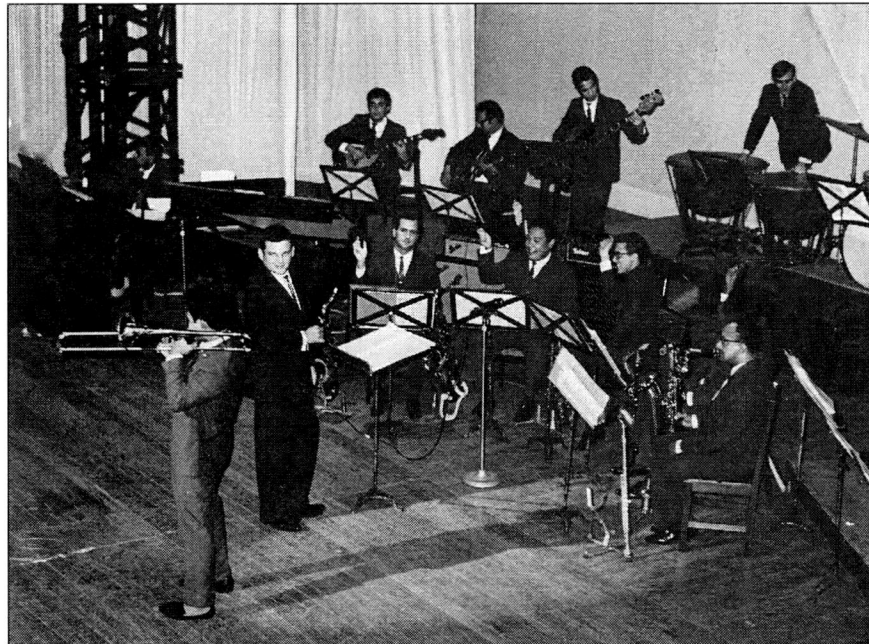

Members of the Orquesta Cubana de Música Moderna (OCMM), ca 1968. L to r: Chucho Valdés (piano), Sergio Vitier and Carlos Emilio Morales (guitar), Carlos del Puerto (electric bass guitar), Enrique Plá (tympani), Braulio Hernández and Jesús "El Chino" Lam (tenor sax), Paquito D'Rivera and Roberto Sánchez (alto sax), Julián Fellové (bari sax), Tony Taño (conductor) and trombone soloist Juan Pablo Torres.
AUTHOR'S COLLECTION

• ON CHUCHO'S COMPOSITIONAL PROCESS

"The first time I wrote anything that more or less felt logical, I must have been around 11 years old. But I didn't give it much thought. Once in awhile ideas would pop in my head and I would jot them down, but I wasn't really concentrating on composing then. I remember a time I experienced a state of dream-composing was when I was 15 or 16, and in the dream, do you know who was singing? The one and only Celia Cruz! And the tune she was singing was 'Cha-cha-chá!'[20] I woke up and said to myself, 'Wow, what a nice tune Celia was singing.' Then I realized I had never heard it before, so I wrote it down. That was really the first fully-formed composition."

---

[20] "Cha-cha-chá" debuted on Irakere's 1979 album *Chekeré Son*.

CHUCHO VALDÉS: A BIOGRAPHY CHAPTER 3

With Chucho's first two compositions utilizing the classic Cuban *cha-cha-chá* style, it was clear that the imprint of popular music was significant, in particular since the style was still in vogue. But his craft would evolve once he surrounded himself with peers and mentors who would expose him to entirely new worlds of sound. Chucho began formal composition studies in his 20s, primarily with guitarist/composer Leo Brouwer, composer and conductor Tony Taño, and Frederic Smith, who was also part of the Musical Theater Orchestra (OTM). While Chucho was a piano student of Zenaida Romeu,[21] she suggested Chucho take up a more formal study of harmony, but he seemed to do quite well in the workshop-like setting of the OTM, having access to so many advanced musicians, mentors, and diverse repertoire, while relying on his own instincts.

"Even since 1963 with Leo (Brouwer) and Tony Taño, we were exploring all kinds of harmonic vocabulary, including 12-tone harmony, serial harmony, etc. In those days, most of us thought that anything old-fashioned or traditional was B.S.! We spent a lot of time working on exercises to better understand modal thinking, trying out different progressions and scales, and creating arrangements that explored all of these ideas. Being in the Musical Theater Orchestra was really one of the highlights of my musical development; it was like an ongoing workshop in orchestration, harmony, and voicings.[22] There were a few of us who were totally captivated by this intensive study: myself, Carlos Emilio, Paquito and others. And the good thing was, we would instantly be able to try out our musical experiments with the band members. Of course we did this after-hours, once the orchestra rehearsals were over."

The same level of experimentation would continue as Chucho, Paquito and Carlos Emilio found themselves in the OCMM.

• INFLUENTIAL PIANISTS

"The first jazz pianists I heard as I was growing up—primarily because Bebo listened to them—were Art Tatum (Bebo had a great passion for him), Duke Ellington (and his band of course), Hank Jones, who for Bebo was a god, Billy Taylor, George Shearing, and of course Bud Powell—they were our world. When I started out on my own I really got into Horace Silver, and I listened to Art Blakey and the Messengers all the time. Records that really impacted me were Dave Brubeck's early albums with Paul Desmond. Brubeck really influenced me in finding new ways of improvising, of adding language beyond bebop. And of course I was very influenced by Wynton Kelly, Bill Evans, McCoy (Tyner), Chick (Corea) and Herbie (Hancock)."

• IRAKERE IS BORN

Within the atmosphere of the OCMM, Chucho and his fellow "rogue" bandmates continued to cultivate what would be the most genre-defying band in Cuban music history as they lay the groundwork for Irakere's formation. His early small-group ensembles enjoyed a fair amount of creative freedom, albeit in an after-hours scenario and out of the spotlight for a time, and Chucho's career as a bandleader and composer would begin to take off. Beginning with a few of his longtime cohorts in the orchestra, namely Paquito, Carlos Emilio and Oscar Valdés, the repertoire he developed and eventually tested in the studio and on tour would emerge. It was a fortuitous concert in Warsaw in 1970 that would

---

[21] Romeu is the grandniece of renowned Cuban composer Antonio Maria Romeu, and conductor/director of the Camerata Romeu, Cuba's all-female chamber ensemble.
[22] "Voicings" is a commonly-used jazz term referring to the selection and specific order of notes in a given chord.

serve as a turning point in Chucho's career as a bandleader, when he led his quintet in a remarkable performance at the Jazz Jamboree, eliciting the enthusiasm and advocacy of one of his musical heroes, Dave Brubeck. In 1972, Chucho participated in a concert highlighting several renowned South American artists, prompting him to come up with a name for the as yet unknown act on the bill, resulting in the birth of the faux-Yoruba term, "Irakere."

But the lightning rod that defined Irakere's undeniable popularity among the Cuban audience was a simple tune recorded in 1973 (which we will explore more in depth in Chapter VI), and of its own accord it developed as the band's first major hit: "Bacalao Con Pan." Included on the band's debut album *Grupo Irakere* (Areito 1974), the song was played live in the eastern city of Santiago de Cuba, eliciting an enthusiasm from the crowd that prompted Chucho and company to take the studio recording to a local DJ to see if they could get any traction. During this time, the band was not officially recognized by the CNC (the National Culture Council), and therefore their album was not played on Havana radio stations. But once the radio broadcast got picked up by a few stations, Cuban audiences began to request the song. As much as the more serious musicians in the band protested that the song was catering to the dancing public, "Bacalao" became a calling card for Irakere wherever they performed. With the rise of Irakere came the exodus from the OCMM, and in 1975, Irakere was an officially sanctioned group.

The chronology of the events beginning in 1977 with Dizzy Gillespie's visit to Havana for the Jazz Cruise and his recommendation of the band to Columbia Records president Bruce Lundvall, leading up to their historic signing to Columbia in 1978, their critically acclaimed performances in New York and Montreux, and their subsequent GRAMMY win in 1979—the first for any Cuban band—are detailed further in the forthcoming chapter. What was clear, however, was that Chucho's rise as one of the most recognized and heralded artists of the time was only just beginning. Irakere was an ensemble, after all, and much like Duke Ellington's orchestra, it was built on the strengths of the individual musicians. At the helm of this monster band was a musical icon who gladly shared in the successful rise of a group known for its collaborative nature. Chucho has always acknowledged the team effort required to evolve Irakere's sound, and the extraordinary artists with whom he shared the stage were, above all else, a brotherhood of musical pioneers. More on the band's evolution follows in the next chapter. For now, it is important to understand Chucho's relationship to jazz in Cuba, and the subsequent changes in how jazz education and access shaped the musical landscape.

• JAZZ IN CUBA AFTER THE REVOLUTION & BEYOND

"As you know, for many years during the 1960s and 70s, we learned jazz by listening, and listening some more. That's the only way we could really interpret jazz music, since we couldn't buy records and it wasn't played on the radio, nor was it taught in school. We transcribed solos, learned standard repertoire, and studied and applied the harmony we were hearing. Sometimes I'd spend an entire year working on one jazz recording because I was transcribing everything I heard; I was so fascinated by it. I would adapt what I learned into my playing and writing, and the most important way we learned was in jam sessions, where not only were we trying to replicate the things we transcribed, but also create variations.

As far as formal instruction, it wasn't only jazz that was omitted in Cuba, but even popular music in general. All of us who were interested in jazz or popular music at that time had to figure out a way – Emiliano (Salvador), Arturo (Sandoval), Juan Pablo (Torres), El Tosco (José Luis Cortés) and others

– it was about combining what we heard in the streets with our love of jazz and the formal study of classical music. In the 1980s there was a 'softening' if you will, and I was able to conduct a few workshops at the ISA (the Instituto Superior de Arte),[23] sharing information on the various eras or styles of American music such as blues, ragtime, swing, bebop, cool jazz and others. And of course, the students I worked with were younger people who were also interested in this music like I was, even if the teachers didn't agree! At one point they put a stop to it, which was unfortunate of course, but later on others took the torch and kept going, such as Joaquín Betancourt and Ernán López Nussa."

How was it possible, then, that jazz was alive and flourishing, albeit underground, in an otherwise hostile environment? Perhaps what was even more fascinating was the fact that listening to and playing jazz was often considered subversive; not as much as rock and roll (or rap later on) of course, but still suppressed, and more than a little frowned upon. Most aspiring jazz musicians in Cuba did what they had to do to keep up with the outside world, learning from bootleg tapes that were passed around, or better yet, buying precious recordings when on tour in Europe, then coming home to share the illicit material with their colleagues. One of the most significant events in Cuba after the Revolution, from an artistic and educational perspective, was the formation of the National Schools of Art in 1976. For the emerging generation of would-be jazzheads, the trick was to balance the state-sponsored arts education, which leaned heavily on the rigorous European (mostly Russian) classical training, with, as Chucho put it, what they learned "in the streets." The generation of Cuba's young lions, many of whom would grow up on the music of Irakere as well as famed dance band Los Van Van, were equally well-versed in Bach, Mozart and Chopin, and privately listened to and summarily absorbed the music of Miles Davis, John Coltrane and The Beatles.

At the height of Irakere's popularity during the late 1970s and into the 80s, their good fortune was the ability to travel outside of Cuba, not only exposing themselves to the international creative dialog, but also sharing with their peers the extraordinarily high level of musicianship that was somehow being cultivated during a time of cultural isolation. Following several transitional periods in the band's evolution, including the defection of two of its most prominent members, (Paquito D'Rivera and Arturo Sandoval), Irakere would continue to be the forerunners of jazz-fusion in Cuba. In the 1990s, several cultural exchange trips took place, wherein European and American artists participated in seminars and workshops at Cuba's Arts Schools (mainly, the Escuela Nacional de Arte and the Instituto Superior de Arte), paving the way for increased dialog and mutual exchange. As more and more foreigners and professional musicians began to visit the island, the formal organization of Havana's Festival Jazz Plaza (established in 1979) would be the turning point for the validation of America's most democratic art form, jazz.

"In the 90s things really began to change, especially with the trips that many American musicians made to Cuba for the Jazz Festival, and also to study our music; they ended up bringing much-needed information. I remember you and (trombonist and bandleader) Wayne Wallace coming to the ENA (Escuela Nacional de Arte) and giving those workshops on jazz theory, bringing the books, instruments and materials, and the many others who would come and set up workshops at the art schools. Perhaps the most significant moment in Cuba that got us closer to acknowledging jazz as a fundamental

---

[23] The Instituto Superior de Arte, or ISA, is Havana's post-secondary school of the arts, established in 1976.

component of our music education system, was when Wynton Marsalis and the Jazz at Lincoln Center Orchestra (JALCO) came to Havana in 2010.[24] Wynton and some of his band members (such as Ted Nash and Victor Goines) all gave fabulous workshops and masterclasses at several music schools, and this really changed the dynamic in Cuba regarding the acceptance of jazz education. During that time, I had several conversations with members of the Ministry of Culture, largely related to the exchange between the Jazz at Lincoln Center Orchestra and Cuba's music education community, leading to an 'opening' of the inclusion of jazz in the music schools and conservatories. At the end of Wynton's visit, there was a wonderful concert at the Mella Theater where this exchange was documented; it was a marvelous culmination, and a turning point for jazz study in Cuba."

Chucho Valdés is not only one of the principal architects of Afro-Cuban jazz, he was also tapped as the Artistic Director of the Festival Jazz Plaza, providing his curatorial expertise in regard to the invitation of international artists to the island. Among the most significant events in recent history was the selection of Havana as the site for the UNESCO-sponsored International Jazz Day, on April 30th, 2017, with Chucho and fellow jazz legend Herbie Hancock sharing the stage with dozens of Cuban and international artists, in a marvelous performance that was streamed live to the world. At the same time, the United States has seen a steady stream of Cuban émigrés making their homes here since Paquito D'Rivera and Arturo Sandoval first made names for themselves, garnering critical acclaim and a significantly more comfortable lifestyle while continuing to highlight the extraordinary level of artistry emanating from the island.

• PIANISM

There is no mystery that the level of technical proficiency among conservatory-trained pianists in Cuba is off the charts. Before the Revolution, attendance at the conservatory level may have been less accessible to some, or limited to those who had the means to supplement their training with private lessons. But in the case with Chucho, who was born in 1941 and attended a free municipal conservatory (the Conservatorio Municipal in Havana), he greatly benefitted from the direct access to the musicians themselves, with his father serving as his principal mentor and guide. Constantly abuzz with the highest caliber of artists from all musical walks of life, the Valdés home, as described earlier, was the ideal training ground. But there are many Cuban musicians from the pre-revolutionary era who came up in a much less structured environment, developing their chops in the trenches of bars and nightclubs and playing primarily for dancers in the famed social clubs, without the benefits of formal instruction. The trajectory of Cuba's popular dance music would develop more from this school than that of the formal institutions, and still came out just fine.

Thus, one could argue that a pianist of Chucho's caliber and familial lineage was the beneficiary of a rare and multifaceted access to a triumvirate of resources: the European classical canon (in the formal conservatory delivery model), the popular dance music of the streets and nightclubs, and American jazz. During his formative teen years, all three of these fountains of knowledge were available to him, and Bebo was a living blueprint of this phenomenon as well as a conduit for his son. After the Revolution in Cuba, the focus of the Conservatory would continue to omit or exclude jazz and Cuban popular music from the curriculum, this time reinforced by the Russian, or more precisely, Soviet influence. Training continued

---

[24] JALCO's first of several visits to Cuba was coordinated in part by the efforts of Horns to Havana and our mutual friend, Susan Sillins. The work of Horns to Havana includes music education, instrument repair and donation, and the training of luthiers (instrument technicians) to ensure the longevity of the few precious instruments on the island.

to be rigorous, but immediately after 1959, jazz was a four-letter word and clearly unwelcome in the formal music education system. If you wanted to learn jazz, you learned from recordings, transcribed and imitated what you heard, and never brought it up in school. And if you wanted to learn Cuban popular music, the closest you came was via the repertoire of Ernesto Lecuona and other early 20th century composers. But the brotherhood that was Irakere, and many groups before and since, would delve into the deep roots of their shared African heritage, further enriching their musical palette with sacred and secular expressions steeped in oral tradition, driven underground for decades. And herein is the "secret" recipe: the preservation of hundreds of years of African ritual music in Cuba, as in Haiti or Brazil, is precisely what contributed to the extra something special that makes Afro-Cuban jazz what it is.

Chucho describes a bit about his access to jazz recordings before and during the 1960s, and how it was that he and his colleagues were able to learn so much without any direct resource:

"During the late 50s when Bebo was directing the Sabor de Cuba orchestra, there was an American named Andrés who all of us musicians knew, and he had a record store in Havana with tons of jazz records - an amazing collection of big band records, quartets, everything! I bought records from him in 1958 and 59. He even played a little trombone and would always let us know what was coming out next, but that all came to an end in 1960. Then in 1963, I discovered shortwave radio and the program called 'Voice of America Jazz Hour' with Willis Conover.[25] There was a show from 2:15–3pm called 'Music USA' that played popular American music, with singers like Carmen McRae, Peggy Lee, and Nina Simone. Then, from 3:15 to 4pm there was the jazz program. This was the only access to this information and repertoire that we had during those years, and of course I shared this with Carlos Emilio, Paquito and others. I became an expert at finding the right radio frequency! This was my first exposure to Miles Davis' Quintet, and also the first time I ever heard McCoy (Tyner) was because of this program; listening to him gave me goosebumps! Later I bought a tape recorder so I could try to capture the broadcasts and study the music. This is how we all learned."

Listening to Chucho improvise, you will at once experience a liturgy of musical dialects, from Bach and Boulanger to Brubeck, to a sprinkle of Thelonious Monk and a hint of Bill Evans; the voicings of McCoy Tyner coupled with the relentless Afro-Cuban *montuno* grooves inspired by Peruchín; the rich harmonic palette of French and Spanish Impressionists with the powerful drum beats of the Yoruba and Bantú nations. And yet there is total fluidity in this approach, with nothing trite or derivative. There is honesty and immense history in Chucho's playing and his writing, and in order to even come close to being able to replicate his aesthetic, you will need to experience total immersion into the entire musical canon between the 19th and 21st centuries! **Decoding Afro-Cuban jazz requires multiple lifetimes, and even then you may not have all of the answers. But that is precisely the point of the challenge in taking on such an immense topic; the joy is in the journey, not the destination.**

• THE ART OF COLLABORATION

There are many artists with whom Chucho has worked over his extraordinary career, certainly far too many to name here. Perhaps his most indelible relationship is the one he developed and nurtured over his lifetime with his own father and mentor, Bebo Valdés. From musical tutelage to the passing of

---

[25] The "Voice of America Jazz Hour" was a broadcast begun in 1955 that reached over 30 million listeners via shortwave radio transmission. It's host, Willis Conover, was heralded as "the disc jockey who fought the Cold War with cool music." NY Times obituary, May 19, 1996; Wikipedia.

the torch, Bebo is clearly the primordial link in defining Chucho's artistic sensibilities, as is evident from the many times they shared the stage or recorded together. Among the later works they collaborated on was an appearance in Fernando Trueba's critically acclaimed documentary, *Calle 54* (2000), and the moving father-son GRAMMY-winning album, *Juntos Para Siempre* (2008). During Bebo's career resurgence in the 2000s, he went on to garner multiple awards and accolades. The father and son spent more quality time together as Chucho made the decision to relocate to Spain, enabling him to stay close as Bebo's health waned. Bebo's passing in 2013 marked the end of an incredibly prolific era in Cuban music, leaving a legacy that has rarely been matched in popular music. And with the void left behind, Chucho has carried forward with the exuberant spirit instilled in him since those magical years watching Bebo's fingers glide over the keyboard. His body of work reflects an ongoing search for new sonorities, with a purposeful, highly creative and openly collaborative work ethic. What follows are several of his favorite musical alliances over the years.

• GREAT SINGERS

Some of the key experiences that have shaped Chucho's development not only as an artist, but also as a composer and producer, are well worth mentioning. Among his more recent projects outside his solo work and relaunching of Irakere, are stunning collaborations with acclaimed vocalists Omara Portuondo, Pablo Milanés[26], and Afro-Spanish sensation Concha Buika.[27]

"I used to accompany Omara with the OCMM—we recorded several albums with her during the 60s and I always admired her, but I thought it would be nicer to do something with just piano and voice. We always dreamed about doing an album together, and finally did in 1997 (with the album *Desafíos*, and later in 2011 with *Omara & Chucho*). The project with Buika (*El Ultimo Trago* in 2009) took some time to put together, because they had sent us old versions of the Chavela Vargas[28] material as arrangements for guitar and voice, and I only had one week to transcribe those parts! Imagine, one week to make a miracle happen and transform those Mexican *rancheras* into something more Afro-Cuban. We did a live performance in Havana right after we had recorded the album, and the audience loved it."

• SILVIO RODRÍGUEZ

"Silvio had been working with Grupo Afrocuba (in 1990), with all of those fantastic arrangements by Oriente López[29], and I had just returned from a very long and exhausting European tour with Irakere. I came home late one evening, and early the next morning at around 7am, Silvio's manager Tito Márquez is knocking on my door. Of course I was half asleep and groggy when I answered, asking him what he could possibly want at this hour of the day. He said it was very important, so I let him in. He told me Silvio was offered the opportunity to perform a grand showcase concert in the Estadio Nacional in Chile (Chile's largest stadium in Santiago) in April of 1990[30], and since Afrocuba had recently disbanded, Silvio wanted me to help him arrange the music for the concert, which was quickly approaching. Tito told me

---

[26] *Nueva trova* icon Pablo Milanés and Chucho recorded an album together in 2009 called *Más Allá de Todo* (Wrasse Records).
[27] Chucho collaborated with Afro-Spanish singer Concha Buika on the critically acclaimed *El Último Trago* in 2009, and with Cuban vocal icon Omara Portuondo on the albums *Desafíos* (1997) and *Omara & Chucho* (2011).
[28] Chavela Vargas was a Costa Rican-born Mexican singer, known for her interpretation of *rancheras*. She received a GRAMMY Lifetime Achievement Award in 2007. Wikipedia.
[29] Grupo Afrocuba was an experimental ensemble under the direction of flute player/composer/keyboardist Oriente López, and served as the supporting band for Silvio Rodríguez's 1986 album, *Causas y Azares*.
[30] This was an historic occasion marking the end of Pinochet's rule in Chile, and also the end of a previous ban prohibiting Silvio Rodríguez from performing in the country. A live recording was made of the concert entitled *Silvio Rodríguez en Chile*.

that Irakere's musicians were really the only ones who could do this, given we were all excellent sight readers, and also since I was known for writing out charts rather quickly. I was so tired that morning I turned him down, but Tito was insistent and returned soon after with Silvio himself. Silvio tried to persuade me, saying this was going to be an historic occasion, so I agreed and asked him to hand me the Afrocuba charts so I could create the new arrangements. However, it turns out almost all of their repertoire had been memorized, and never fully written out! I asked Silvio, 'What are you trying to tell me?' And Silvio says, 'Well, I need you to transcribe everything. Oh, plus I need you to write some new arrangements too.' I asked him how much time he had before the concert so I could prepare, transcribe and arrange everything, not to mention rehearse, and he says to me, 'About three weeks.' You can imagine how I felt! But how could I say no and pass up an opportunity like that? I remember doing one of the arrangements (for 'Venga La Esperanza') in one night, and writing out all the parts so I could bring everything to rehearsal the next day. Looking back, I'd have to say it was one of the most incredible concerts of my life, with over 80 thousand people in the audience. Silvio told me later on, that if we hadn't agreed to do the concert with him, he would have turned it down."

• IVAN LINS

"I had long admired Ivan's music, and I love his compositions. We actually met at a festival in Portugal around 1981 and he loved hearing Irakere. But we didn't work together until February of 1996, when I received a call from Rio de Janeiro saying he was coming to Cuba to do a performance, and asked if I wanted to accompany him with the band, so of course I said yes! We had just one rehearsal at La Tropical, and recorded the show at the Casa de la Música. (The live recording was released as *Ao Vivo* in 1996 on both Cuban and Brazilian record labels.) Ivan came with a brilliant cellist and arranger, Mario Manga, and we played a program of mostly his pieces, plus one Irakere piece ('La Explosión') as an instrumental interlude of sorts. Our next collaboration was in 2010, when I invited him to perform with me and my Quartet for a festival at the Grand Theater of Havana (now named after prima ballerina Alicia Alonso), and joining us for that concert was the great Portuguese *fado* singer, Mariza."

• WYNTON MARSALIS AND THE JALCO

"I've had the amazing opportunity to collaborate multiple times with Wynton and the Jazz at Lincoln Center Orchestra (JALCO). The first was in 2010, when Wynton and the Orchestra made their historic trip to Havana (as noted earlier), and the visit culminated with an incredible concert at the Mella Theater (where Wynton and Chucho played an exquisite duo rendition of Gershwin's 'Embraceable You'). The second was when I was invited as a pianist to perform at a Duke Ellington tribute at Jazz at Lincoln Center in New York, followed by another invitation to perform at a Dizzy Gillespie festival there the following year. And most recently, in 2014, I was invited to perform for the Lincoln Center's season opening celebration, on an Afro-Cuban suite that Wynton wrote celebrating *orisha* culture, where I participated as a special guest along with Pedrito Martínez."

• LEO BROUWER

"In 2014, Leo was producing an annual chamber music festival that takes place every October in Havana, culminating on the National Day of Culture (celebrated on October 20th), and he invited me to perform a symphony for piano and orchestra he had composed in my honor, 'Concierto de los Ancestros.' We played it on October 15th at the Karl Marx Theater. Leo has always been such an important part of the Cuban musical landscape, and we have known each other since our time together in the Orquesta del Teatro Musical de la Habana back in the 1960s."

• LANG LANG

"On October 9th, 2015 (Chucho's birthday!), I had the great honor of performing with celebrated classical pianist Lang Lang, the Havana Symphony, and guest conductor (and Director of the Baltimore Symphony), Marin Alsop.[31] The stage was set up in front of the grand cathedral, and the plaza was completely packed. It was a remarkable moment for many reasons, not only because we received the first new Steinway piano to arrive in Cuba in over 50 years, but also because of the variety of repertoire that was performed. Lang Lang played Tchaikovsky's Piano Concerto No. 1 in B-flat minor, we performed Gershwin's 'Fantasia Cubana,' as well as my original piece, 'Claudia,' a ragtime piece by James P. Johnson, a two-piano arrangement I did of 'Tres Lindas Cubanas,' that included (the composer) Antonio María Romeu's original solo that I transcribed, and we ended the program with a rousing rendition of 'Cumbanchero' (composed by Rafael Hernández) with the orchestra. That arrangement was wild, opening with a fragment of Rachmaninoff's Concerto No. 3 and even including a fragment of Rimsky-Korsakov's 'Flight of the Bumble Bee'—it was insane! We started with the first part, and slowly built it up as we went mano-a-mano until breaking out the theme of 'Cumbanchero.' The crowd went crazy with emotion, people were in tears, and we nearly tore the roof off the church with that last number! I'll never forget it. This was one of the first Cuban-American productions to take place in Cuba since 1959; it was truly impressive." (I asked Chucho how long they took to rehearse and prepare, and his response was, "Well, Lang Lang arrived that same afternoon.")

• GONZALO RUBALCABA

"Back in 2012, I was asked to host a Latin jazz piano summit at Carnegie Hall (part of the *Voices of Latin America* series, on December 4th), so I invited Gonzalo along with Egberto Gismonti (from Brazil), and Danilo Pérez (from Panamá), and we did a four-piano concert of solos, duos, and a quartet. Each one of us played our own thing, then we would play together in different configurations, each bringing some of the traditional repertoire from our respective countries, mixed with jazz. Ay, yay, yay...it was beautiful! This led to another exciting opportunity, when a film company from Tenerife, Spain, reached out to me, Gonzalo, and Dominican pianist Michel Camilo to do a musical documentary project in tribute to the great Ernesto Lecuona called *Playing Lecuona*.[32] I was in Cuba at the time, so I recorded a few pieces, one with my Quartet, one solo piece, and one with Cuban folklore group Los Muñequitos de Matanzas. Gonzalo was in Spain at the time, so he did his pieces with a flamenco ensemble, and Michel recorded his pieces partly in New York and the rest in Spain. Even though we never played together, it was a great way to each showcase our own interpretations of Lecuona's music.

I'd also like to mention my most recent collaboration with Gonzalo. Since we worked on the *Playing Lecuona* project, we had talked about doing something together; as you know, we never got to play the Lecuona repertoire together until we came to San Francisco (in 2015) to perform along with Michel Camilo.[33] Gonzalo and I have different musical approaches, of course, given we represent two different generations (Gonzalo was born in 1963, and Chucho in 1941), so for us to play together, it's almost like speaking the same language with two distinct dialects, although we understand each other perfectly!

---

[31] This historic concert was in celebration of the City of Havana's 500th anniversary.
[32] *Playing Lecuona* is a 2015 musical documentary and a soundtrack recording highlighting the music of Cuban composer Ernesto Lecuona, featuring Chucho Valdés, Gonzalo Rubalcaba and Michel Camilo.
[33] The SFJAZZ organization presented Chucho, Gonzalo Rubalcaba and Michel Camilo together in an all-acoustic performance of solo, duo and trio pieces, highlighting the repertoire of Cuban piano genius Ernesto Lecuona in the summer of 2015, and again in May of 2017.

We knew we would really need to find a way to come together; he would need to come closer to my style, or I to his. Gonzalo represents a more contemporary approach, and it would be very challenging to create a hybrid of our styles, so we decided to meet in the middle, and it has worked. Gonzalo is truly one of the most important pianists of our time, and of the planet! And do you know how this all got started? Well, it turned out that we now live a few blocks from each other (in South Florida), and I invited Gonzalo over one afternoon since I have two grand pianos set up in my home studio: a Yamaha C7 that I use to 'work out' and practice, and a Steinway that I use more for 'play.' We started jamming that day for fun, and our wives said, 'Hey, why not do something together since you're neighbors?!' Well, we realized their suggestion made a lot of sense, and decided to create this project together."[34]

The two maestros are, without a doubt, embarking on yet another remarkable path in their highly influential and groundbreaking careers, and it will be a joy to see where they go from here.

• • •

Among Chucho's many awards and honors are an Honorary Doctorate of Music from Berklee College of Music in 2011, 6 GRAMMY Awards and 3 Latin GRAMMY Awards. Please refer to Appendix B for an Annotated List of Works composed by Chucho.

---

[34] In 2017, Chucho and Gonzalo decided to launch a duo project called *Trance* and go on tour, and as of this writing, are slated to record their first album together in 2018.

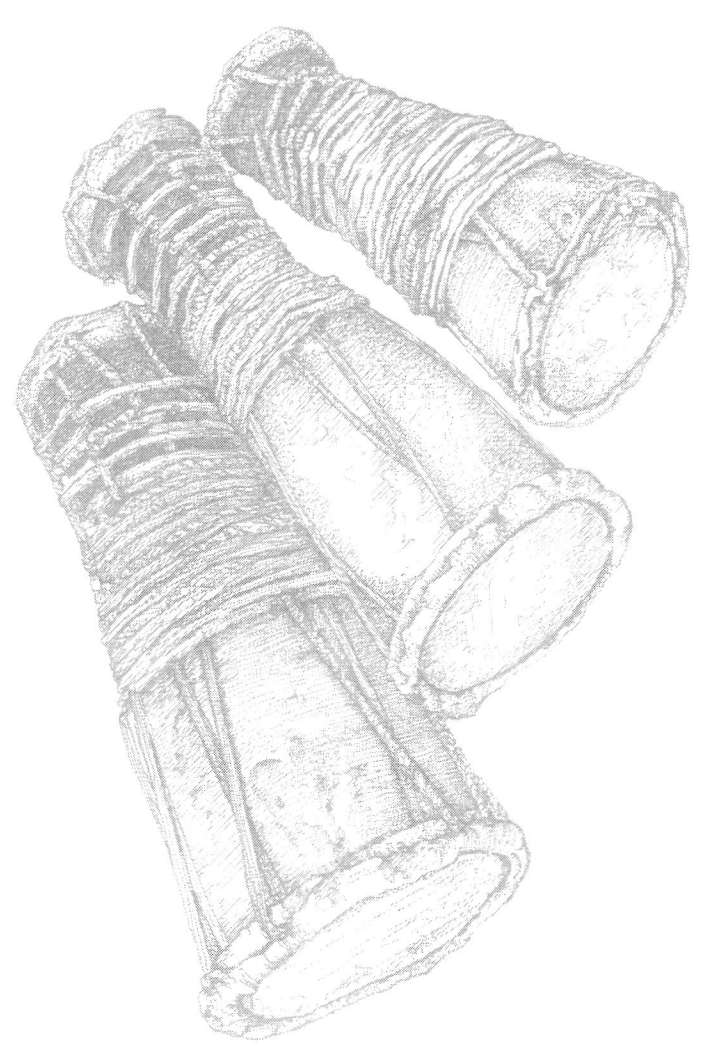

A Brief History of Irakere   CHAPTER 4

"There really is a brotherhood in music which, like love, needs no translation, merely improvisation."
– Arnold Jay Smith, DownBeat Magazine, 1977

"Irakere was, for me, a point of departure that opened new doors, new horizons, from the African roots to a fusion of jazz and popular dance music." – Chucho Valdés

• • •

1977 was a pivotal year in music around the globe, with rock and disco surging in the charts[1], the death of Elvis, and the increasingly electrified sounds of jazz blurring both creative and commercial lines with artists including Miles Davis, Herbie Hancock, Weather Report and others taking jazz to another level. The year also proved to be a seminal moment for one of Cuba's most genre-defying bands, as was witnessed by Arnold Jay Smith from *DownBeat* magazine, when he and a team of music journalists embarked on a brief journey to the island in May for a historic series of jam sessions and concerts as part of the now-famed "Jazz Cruise." Among the noted artists arriving on the island were Dizzy Gillespie, Stan Getz, Earl "Fatha" Hines, David Amram and a host of others.[2] Irakere, the eleven-member powerhouse ensemble directed by pianist/keyboardist Chucho Valdés, soon learned that Dizzy would become one of their fiercest advocates after hearing the band perform. But to appreciate this moment, it is essential to go back a bit and uncover the trajectory that led to this point.

• THE OCMM

Before Irakere was a band, the musical machinations were already well underway as Chucho cut his teeth in the Orquesta Cubana de Música Moderna (OCMM), developing the conceptual ideas for the supergroup as he continued to break out on his own with small subgroups of the OCMM members. While the word "jazz" may have been omitted from the orchestra's name, there was certainly the intention of framing much of the repertoire around a hybrid concept of classical, popular and jazz music, as can be heard on one of their classic recordings, "Ay Mamá Inés," wherein the arrangement opens with a statement of Tchaikovsky's *Piano Concerto No 1* in B-flat minor, superimposed over the original melody (composed by Eliseo Grenet) and structured as an Afro-Cuban *rumba*![3] In an excellent synopsis of Irakere's evolution, jazz writer Chris May notes that the repertoire of the OCMM was often "relentlessly portentous," often sacrificing the strengths of the individual soloists in favor of a more derivative and often cheesy sound.[4]

Despite the bombastic nature of the ensemble's repertoire, the OCMM was, in effect, a training ground for Cuba's future Afro-Cuban jazz stars, including Chucho, Paquito D'Rivera, Arturo Sandoval, Carlos Emilio Morales, Orlando "Cachaíto" López, Carlos del Puerto, Juan Pablo Torres, Jorge Varona, Enrique Plá, Guillermo Barreto, and so many others. While musical direction and conducting duties belonged mainly to Armando Romeu and Rafael Somavilla (respectively), Chucho, along with trombonist Juan Pablo Torres, were occasionally tapped to bring in arrangements for the orchestra. However, it was increasingly clear that smaller subsets of the orchestra were a more viable model for consistent work,

---

[1] The Eagles' "Hotel California" and Donna Summers' "I Feel Love" were (respectively) the top number one hits worldwide, and *Saturday Night Fever* had just hit theaters. Wikipedia, *1977 In Music* and *1970s in Jazz*.
[2] Acosta, Leonardo. *Cubano Be, Cubano Bop*, pp 214-215.
[3] "Ay Mamá Inés" (composed by Eliseo Grenet) is included in the OCMM's eponymous compilation, originally recorded between 1967 and 1970, directed by Armando Romeu and conducted by Rafael Somavilla. Virtually all of the founding members of Irakere can be heard on this unusual orchestration.
[4] Chris May, "Chucho Valdés and the Birth of Irakere," *All About Jazz*, May, 2007.

especially out of the country. Chucho reflected on these seminal years, recalling a historic trip to Warsaw in 1970 for the Jazz Jamboree when he was 29:

"I went to Poland with my Quintet (the Quinteto Cubano de Jazz, which included Paquito D'Rivera, Oscar Valdés, Cachaíto López and Enrique Plá). We were second-to-last on the bill, right before the Dave Brubeck Quartet with Gerry Mulligan! The Polish audience went crazy, screaming and pounding on the floor, and gave us a standing ovation. I was so moved, I nearly died. Then I learned that Brubeck had been in the wings watching us the entire time. After his set, he came to our dressing room, gave me a hug, and I'll never forget what he said: 'Never stop!' All of us in the band cried like babies that evening; what an unforgettable moment."

Upon returning to Cuba and resuming rehearsals with the OCMM, Chucho would also find further creative inspiration away from the Orquesta, and see his own work gain notoriety:

"These were mainly quartets and quintets, with Paquito, Carlos Emilio, and Oscar. We started to branch out and experiment with the instrumentation, added batá drums and other percussion instruments, and as we evolved, I began to formulate the idea for Irakere, eventually adding horns, composing some of the pieces that would become key components of our repertoire. We would wait until after the OCMM rehearsals would finish and work on the Irakere ideas afterward...at some point we could tell that the Orquesta director was more than a little bothered by us, especially once we recorded 'Bacalao Con Pan' (in 1973) and it became a hit![5] That's when Irakere needed to move to another rehearsal space."

Several Irakere founding members were also members of the OCMM, but the tension between the two bands became more apparent when Irakere would appear with the Orchestra in a double bill, and the audience would shout out requests for Irakere to play instead:

"There was an overlap between the OCMM and Irakere during my last two years in the orchestra... it was a bit of a challenge since Irakere was gaining in popularity, and it took a while for us to receive official approval to strike out on our own, so to speak. Let's just say that the CNC (the Consejo Nacional de Cultura, which was the official entity that would need to provide its approval) put up some 'resistance,' and that struggle lasted nearly two years. They didn't want to jeopardize the OCMM by having so many of us leave, and essentially tried to block Irakere's recognition by the Ministry of Culture, so I quit the OCMM (in 1975). It was very difficult, but we prevailed!"

WHY "IRAKERE?"

There are likely several conflicting stories floating around surrounding the origins of the name "Irakere" and who came up with it first. Despite the point of contention between several former members, Chucho asserts that the name for the band predates the group's formation, resulting from another of his many "side-gigs" as a leader:

"In 1972, there was an event that was produced at the Amadeo Roldán Theater called the 'Encuentro Latinoamericano.' This was right after we had recorded *Jazz Batá* (with Oscar Valdés and bassist Carlos

---

[5] "Bacalao Con Pan" appears on Irakere's debut album, *Grupo Irakere* (1974).

A Brief History of Irakere — Chapter 4

del Puerto that same year), which was a critical experimental phase for us as we were forming what would be Irakere, and this concert was the perfect opportunity for us to come up with a name for the band. I recall that someone named Mr. Rizo from the Dirección de Música (a precursor to the Culture Ministry, responsible for the formal organization of all live musical events), called to invite me to put a band together for this concert, which was going to highlight South American music and important artists, including Victor Jara. In fact, I thought it would be important to write something with a South American spirit, so I wrote an Andean theme in a Latin jazz vein, using a *huapango*[6] style alternating with a Cuban *tumbao*, etc. Rizo liked it and agreed to have us perform, and when he asked me for the name of the band, the first thing that popped in my head was the word 'Irakere,'[7] which he promptly rejected, saying it didn't sound commercial enough. I insisted that this was the name of the band, and that's how it all started! Others claim to have come up with the name, but this was the first time we used it."

• THE ORIGINAL GROUP (FOUNDED IN 1973)

Simply put, Irakere was the only band in Cuba to successfully champion a repertoire that straddled the line between instrumental jazz and popular dance music, and do so at an optimal level, achieving national and international acclaim. The sound of Irakere may defy genre, but the quintessential element that made it tick was precisely the blending of many disparate musical languages, so to speak. The term "fusion" was still fairly fresh during the 1970s, and from a purely semantic perspective, it literally described what the band was: a fusion. Rock and funk, Afro-Cuban sacred and secular rhythms and chants, European classical music, jazz, and a host of world rhythms, melded together in innovative ways by expert musicians, almost all of whom were conservatory-trained and at the top of their game.

Irakere publicity photo, ca 1976. L to r: (standing) Enrique Plá, Carlos Barbón, Arturo Sandoval, Chucho Valdés, Carlos Averhoff; (seated) Paquito D'Rivera, Jorge Alfonso "El Niño," Carlos Emilio Morales, Carlos del Puerto, Oscar Valdés. AUTHOR'S COLLECTION

Irakere's founders were mostly members of the OCMM, with some of the players joining within a

---

[6] The *huapango* is a Mexican folk dance of Aztec origin, played in 6/8 time.
[7] The word *irakere* is referenced as "faux-Yoruba" and thought to symbolize the word "forest" or "vegetation," although it is not listed in any official linguistic record. It is likely a hybrid interpretation of the *lucumí* dialect spoken in Cuba by descendants of enslaved Africans from Western and Central Africa.

year due to completion of military service. Virtually all of the members had worked with Chucho in some form or another since the 1960s, the longest being Carlos Emilio and Paquito. Much like Duke Ellington, Chucho crafted a repertoire for the band that was tailored to the individual strengths of the players, emphasizing their virtuosity as soloists. The challenges of breaking away from the OCMM were many, but the accolades Irakere received before they were even recognized as an official entity spoke volumes of the direction they were headed. The first incarnation of the group consisted of the following members:[8]

> Chucho Valdés, (piano, organ)
> Paquito D'Rivera, (alto sax)
> Carlos Averhoff, (tenor sax, who joined in 1974)
> Arturo Sandoval, (trumpet)
> Jorge Varona, (trumpet)
> Carlos Emilio Morales, (electric guitar)
> Carlos del Puerto, (electric bass)
> Bernardo García, (drums, who was soon replaced by Enrique Plá)
> Enrique Plá, (drums, who replaced Bernardo García)
> Oscar Valdés, (vocals and percussion)
> Armando Cuervo, (vocals and percussion, who entered in 1977 and left in 1980)
> Lázaro Alfonso "El Tato," (congas and percussion, who was soon replaced by his brother Jorge Alfonso "El Niño" several months later)
> Carlos Barbón (the roadie, who played hand percussion on occasion and left in 1977)

Upon the band's debut in 1973, it was clear that the bar had been raised by the very same members of the OCMM once they stepped into their role as "Irakeres." Those who witnessed the first performance, including journalist, saxophonist and author Leonardo Acosta, immediately knew that this band was on an entirely different level, citing "their superb technique, the virtuosity of their soloists, the driving swing that they maintained in any rhythm and at any tempo, and the intelligent recovery (preservation) of our cultural heritage combined with experimentation. Also significant is the excellent way they fuse Afro-Cuban elements with jazz."[9]

Acosta also points out that Irakere was not the first popular group in Cuba to incorporate the African-derived batá drums into a contemporary setting, noting that guitarist Sergio Vitier utilized them in his ensemble, Grupo ORU (founded in 1968), which featured renowned folkloric singer Merceditas Valdés, and her husband, drummer and timbalero Guillermo Barreto (also from the OCMM), along with a cadre of excellent *bataleros* (batá drummers).[10] However, it is clear that Irakere's amalgam of electric bass and wah-wah-laden guitar, Farfisa organ, trap set and Cuban percussion, and a stellar horn section to rival those of Chicago, Blood, Sweat & Tears, or Earth, Wind & Fire (all major influences, incidentally),

---

[8] A few members joined soon after being released from military service, including Arturo Sandoval (trumpet) and Enrique Plá (drums, who replaced Bernardo García). Carlos Averhoff came a year later, in 1974, having previously played with seminal group, the Grupo de Experimentación Sonora del ICAIC, and also had to complete his military service. However, Averhoff is considered a founding member, and remained in the band until 1994. The horn section in this first iteration consisted of 2 trumpets and 2 saxes: Arturo, Varona, Paquito and Averhoff. Armando Cuervo is also considered a founder, although he entered in 1977.
[9] Acosta, p. 213.
[10] Vitier was also a member of Cuba's Grupo de Experimentación Sonora del ICAIC, another of Havana's important experimental ensembles. Acosta, 212-213.

was far beyond what anyone on or off the island was concocting at the time. Chucho shares some of the technical and musical influences that were critical in shaping the band's sound:

"Over the years I used a variety of keyboards and organs, based on what was available or what was in vogue. Early on and through most of the 1970s, my setup included a Fender Rhodes (which was a gift from Columbia Records), a Farfisa organ, and a Roland Jupiter-8. In the 80s I used a Yamaha CP-70, a Solina String Ensemble (also called the Arp String Ensemble), a Yamaha organ that the Ministry of Culture provided, a Vocoder, and while we were in Switzerland, I bought a Hohner Clavinet. Back then we were totally listening to Blood, Sweat & Tears, as well as the incredible Chicago horn section, and of course Herbie Hancock, especially the *Head Hunters* album (1973). I basically 'lifted' Herbie's 'Chameleon,' changed a few notes, and created a variation of it for Irakere's opening theme! And songs we did like 'Aguanile Bonkó' were greatly inspired by Earth, Wind & Fire, with those disco-like horn riffs."

Dizzy Gillespie and Chucho Valdés, ca 1990. AUTHOR'S COLLECTION

• 1977, DIZZY GILLESPIE & THE JAZZ CRUISE IN HAVANA

Irakere's first major European tour would take place in 1976, including stints in Finland, Italy and Germany, but it would be a fortuitous week in 1977 that would prove to be a game changer in the band's trajectory. Chucho recalled this significant moment in Irakere's early years:

"In May of 1977, a cruise ship stops in Havana, and we found out that Dizzy Gillespie was on board, along with Stan Getz, Earl 'Fatha' Hines, David Amram, Billy Hart, Rob McClure (bassist) and an amazing pianist who was playing with Stan, Joanne Brackeen. Two days before the concert at the Mella Theater, we had a jam session in the Hotel Habana Libre (in the Salón Caribe room) with all those folks; this was the first time that Dizzy heard Irakere. At the concert at the Mella afterward, we all ended up playing together, along with Los Papines, where we did a tribute to Chano Pozo and played 'Manteca.' That was historic, unforgettable, and the beginning of the turning point for the band. It was Dizzy who recommended us to Bruce Lundvall (of Columbia Records), who eventually brought us to the Newport Jazz Festival in 1978 and signed us to a record deal."

Irakere's repertoire was certainly well-suited to the individual members of the band, and it was quickly apparent that a few individuals would stand out whenever the band took to the stage, among them Chucho, of course, as well as trumpeter Arturo Sandoval, and saxophonist Paquito D'Rivera.

It may have been perceived as jazz-rock or fusion, but it was also extraordinarily Afro-Cuban at its core, celebrating the most profound African-derived sacred and secular rhythms and themes, while avoiding any adherence to traditional norms or conventions. Vocalist and percussionist Oscar Valdés played a critical role in shaping the rhythmical explorations of the repertoire, bringing in his immense wealth of knowledge on the Afro-Cuban folk idioms. In addition, Acosta noted that Irakere's strength was in defining the Cuban element "not just in the percussion, but also in the phrasing, the attack, and the soloists' sense of rhythm, as well as in the ensemble passages."[11]

What was less obvious was the binary nature of the material, with half focusing on ornate and musically complex pieces for international jazz-lovers, and the other half invoking the inherently more danceable material that the Cuban public couldn't resist. This duality or bifurcation would eventually come to a head in the band; but for now, let's explore the next important phase in Irakere's history.

• 1978, BRUCE LUNDVALL, & THE 1ST GRAMMY

In April of 1978, a small private jet arrived in Havana with a contingent of American music industry folks, including producer and CBS A&R Director Jay Chattaway, Jerry Masucci (co-founder and president of Fania Records), and Columbia Records president Bruce Lundvall. They had all come to hear Irakere upon the recommendation of Dizzy Gillespie, following the momentous occasion of the Jazz Cruise in Havana the prior year. The goal was to "audition" and then contract the band to play at the Newport Jazz Festival in New York that June at Carnegie Hall, record the performance, and sign them to the label:

"After a ton of meetings with Cuban state officials, we did a show at the Bellas Artes Theater, which the executives loved, followed by a jam session at Egrem Studios. Bruce was the important link in taking Irakere to the next level, hiring us for the Newport gig and the show at Carnegie Hall, then taking us to Switzerland for the Montreux Jazz Festival. Both of those concerts (Carnegie Hall and Montreaux) were recorded and released as a compilation, eventually resulting in our first GRAMMY Award (in 1979). In reality, the best versions of the material were all done at Montreux, since the sound was much better, so every song on that record was from that second show."

Released in 1978, the phenomenal Columbia album *Irakere* (subsequently reissued in 1994 as *The Best of Irakere*) featured all live material from the band's Montreux appearance, and resulted in Irakere's 1979 GRAMMY Award for Best Latin Recording.[12] Lundvall's advocacy for the band continued when he and Fania president Jerry Masucci collaborated on the production of a historic festival called "Havana Jam" which took place in March of 1979 at the Karl Marx Theater.[13] The unprecedented encounter between Cuban and American musicians was an oasis of cultural and artistic exchange during an otherwise challenging time.

---

[11] Acosta, pp. 217-218.
[12] Grammy.com.
[13] The historic three-day festival (from March 2-4, 1979) featured a host of top-tiered American and Cuban musicians, including Billy Joel, Kris Kristofferson, Weather Report, Stephen Stills, Rita Coolidge, the Fania All-Stars, the Trio of Doom (John McLaughlin, Jaco Pastorius and Tony Williams), Tata Güines, Pablo Milanés, Orquesta Aragón, Frank Emilio, Elena Burke, Los Papines, Sara González, and of course, Irakere. Two live double albums of the festival were released on Columbia Records in 1979, followed by an album featuring the Fania All-Stars performance on the Fania label. There was also a documentary film made of the festival, aptly named *Havana Jam 1979*.

A Brief History of Irakere — Chapter 4

"Later that year, in November, we flew with Bruce and his delegation back to New York to begin a two-month US tour, and also to a record our next album for Columbia (a studio album), *Irakere 2*, which received a GRAMMY nomination. The tour was also very successful. But as you know, with the changing political situations and the increasing tension between the US and Cuba, it was difficult for a time."

Unable to pick up their GRAMMY Awards during the ceremony, Chucho and the rest of the band would wait until 1991, when Lundvall would return to Cuba once more with the long-awaited awards, and sign both Irakere and Chucho (as a solo artist) to Blue Note Records. After ending his tenure with the Blue Note label, Chucho remained close friends with Bruce, and considered him a dear friend. Lundvall passed away in 2015, but was, without a doubt in Chucho's mind, one of the most influential and visionary personalities in music.

• IRAKERE VERSION 2: THE 1980s

Irakere embarked on an ambitious (or perhaps breakneck) touring and performing schedule, and managed to record a number of studio albums during the 1980s, although recording in Cuba often meant inferior sound quality and the fact that a given project might not see the light of day until an international label would distribute it. Fortunately, many of these recordings have since been reissued, although not necessarily in the original context, with untold compilations often containing duplicate versions of songs. For Irakere, opportunities to record took them to Europe in the late 80s (mainly Germany and England), with some of the better-sounding albums recorded live at Ronnie Scott's in London.

Musicians of the caliber of Irakere were clearly in a league of their own, finding themselves traveling the world — albeit much of that world limited to Soviet bloc countries. But living and working in Cuba during the post-revolutionary era was increasingly challenging for many excellent players who longed for greater opportunity, as well as personal freedom. With the only choice being defection, many Cuban artists and others made the difficult decision to leave family and country behind. Within Irakere, one of the sore subjects had always been the notion of the band's bifurcated repertoire, with members including Paquito D'Rivera and Arturo Sandoval expressing their displeasure at having to resort to playing dance music.

They were serious jazzheads, and the split-personality of the band soon began emerge as a wedge that eventually drove them away, not to mention the promise of more lucrative opportunities outside of Cuba. Upon the exodus of Paquito D'Rivera in May of 1980 (while Irakere was on tour in Europe), and Arturo Sandoval the following year, the second iteration of the band brought in a revamped format and a fresh new sound. The evolving membership eventually led to a 6-piece horn section with three trumpets and three saxes, including a baritone. In addition to top-notch new players Germán Velasco (sax), Juan Munguía and José Miguel Crego "El Greco" (trumpets), flautist and bari player José Luis Cortés joined the new lineup. Better known as "El Tosco," Cortés would eventually leave in 1988 along with other recent additions to form the seminal dance band, NG La Banda.[14] It was El Tosco's influence that marked a transitional phase in Irakere's sound, evolving a precursor to the impending *timba* craze that would take shape in the 90s.

"Jorge Varona said he wanted to leave to start his own family band, but his project fell apart and he returned, so by adding him back in, the horn section was now 3 trumpets and 3 saxes. 'El Duke' (recorded in Germany in 1986 on the Messidor album *Misa Negra*) was a great example of that sound. I

---

[14] During the 1970s, Tosco had also been a member of Cuba's celebrated popular dance band, Los Van Van.

remember how hard it was when all those horn players left to join Tosco in NG La Banda. I had the task of trying to adopt my previous arrangements for a crazy new instrumentation!"

Despite the dramatic changes, many critics, and even Chucho himself, felt this particular version of the band was even tighter and more unified as an ensemble than the first. While the first incarnation of Irakere was largely built on the virtuosity of the individual soloists, the second felt more like a coherent ensemble.

> Chucho Valdés, (piano, keyboards)
> Germán Velasco, (alto sax, until 1988)
> Carlos Averhoff, (tenor sax)
> José Luis Cortés "El Tosco," (flute, bari sax, until 1988)
> Jorge Varona, (trumpet, until his death in 1988)
> Juan Munguía, (trumpet, until 1988)
> José Crego "El Greco," (trumpet, until 1988)
> Carlos Emilio Morales, (electric guitar)
> Carlos del Puerto, (electric bass)
> Enrique Plá, (drums)
> Oscar Valdés, (vocals and percussion)
> Jorge Alfonso "El Niño," (congas, percussion, until his death in 1987)

- **VERSION 3: THE LATE 80s & EARLY 90s**

El Niño died tragically in 1987, and there followed a period of mourning with the death of Jorge Varona a year later. However, many acknowledge this iteration as an example of Irakere's multigenerational phase, when young musicians, fresh out of Cuba's music schools, were recruited for the coveted spots in the band. The third iteration of Irakere added Manuel Machado (trumpet & flugelhorn), and later, Adalberto Lara "Trompetica" (tpt), Carlos Álvarez (trombone), César López (alto), Javier Zalba (bari, soprano, flute), Orlando Valle "Maraca" (flute, keyboards), Oscarito Valdés (Oscar's son, on drums, perc, drum machine) and Miguel "Angá" Diaz (congas).

Irakere publicity photo, ca 1981. L to r: Enrique Plá, Carlos Averhoff, Jorge Alfonso "El Niño," Juan Munguía, Chucho Valdés, Oscar Valdés, José Luis Cortés "El Tosco," Carlos del Puerto, Germán Velasco, Jorge Varona and Carlos Emilio Morales.
AUTHOR'S COLLECTION

> Chucho Valdés, (piano, keyboards)
> César López, (alto sax, from 1988 until 1996, then again in the 2000s)
> Carlos Averhoff, (tenor sax, until 1994)
> Manuel Machado, (trumpet & flugelhorn, until 1989)
> Adalberto Lara "Trompetica," (trumpet, joined in 1989)

A Brief History of Irakere

Chapter 4

>Juan Munguía (trumpet, returned in 1988)
>Carlos Álvarez, (trombone)
>Javier Zalba, (bari, soprano, flute)
>Orlando Valle "Maraca," (flute, keyboards, from 1987 until 1994)
>Carlos Emilio Morales, (electric guitar)
>Carlos del Puerto, (electric bass, until 1996)
>Miguel "Angá" Díaz, (congas, percussion, until 1994)
>Enrique Plá, (drums)
>Oscar Valdés, (vocals and percussion)
>Oscarito Valdés, (drums, perc, drum machine)

During this era, Chucho was also exploring solo piano work. An excellent example is the acclaimed album *Lucumí Piano Solo* (Messidor, 1988), which was recorded in Germany on a Bösendorfer piano, and completed in only one hour!

"In 1993 I was starting to explore smaller group formats when I was invited to perform on a solo piano concert tour in Canada with other major jazz artists, including Keith Jarrett. Actually, I was *'cagao'* (shit-scared)! But fortunately it was a success, and came out better than I had imagined. I was thrilled to receive excellent reviews after a performance in Montreal, and that was the moment that convinced me the solo piano thing just might work."

• VERSION 4: MID TO LATE 90S

This period was perhaps the most difficult era of Irakere, with another significant shakeup in the structure of the band that Chucho recalls as a time of great "disorientation." Several additional members of Oscar Valdés' family band, Diákara, were inserted, for a time resulting in a two-drummer and two-guitar format, plus plenty of experimentation with sequencing and drum machines (largely handled by Oscar's son Oscarito, who had been playing with Grupo Afrocuba). It eventually unraveled on its own, proving that the crazy new format would not work, leading to the exodus of Oscar Valdés and his offspring. Other members followed suit, launching solo careers or leaving the island, including Angá, Maraca and César López.

Joining the fourth incarnation of Irakere were Andrés "Negrón" Miranda (conga player and a student of Angá's), bassist Jorge Reyes (replacing Carlos del Puerto, who relocated to Finland in 1996), Jorge Luís Valdés Chicoy (guitar, who joined Carlos Emilio in a 2-guitar format), followed by a variety of horn players, including Román Filiú, Irving Michel Acao, Julio Padrón, Mario Hernández "El Indio," Basilio Márquez and Alfredo Thompson. Guitarist Carlos Emilio Morales, who died in 2014, stayed with Chucho until his health no longer allowed him to play (around 2006). All told, Carlos Emilio had the longest musical relationship with Chucho at over five decades, second only to Bebo, of course. From time to time, Chucho's sister, singer Mayra Caridad Valdés, would join the band for brief stints on tour, but she was more of a featured guest as opposed to a member of Irakere. In addition, with the success of Roy Hargrove's *Crisol* project (including the GRAMMY-winning 1997 album *Habana*), Chucho was spending more time away from Irakere. Chucho's record deal (as a solo artist) may have kept him away from the band, but it also led to unprecedented success and critical acclaim. In under a decade he recorded over a dozen albums and toured constantly either as a soloist or in small group settings. It was increasingly clear that Irakere might not last long into the 21st century, although the band did manage to record a few more albums while Chucho juggled his solo career. However, the demands of his contract with Blue Note Records, and his subsequent relocation to Spain, seemed, for a time, to put the iconic band on the back-burner.

CHAPTER 4 — A BRIEF HISTORY OF IRAKERE

• CHUCHO REFLECTS ON IRAKERE'S KEY PLAYERS OVER THE YEARS

"(Jorge Alfonso) El Niño's footsteps were never really replaced, even after Angá came in (RIP to both of them). What he brought to the band was unique, magical. The same thing for Arturo and Paquito; each one was one of a kind!! Both of them are such extraordinary musicians, true maestros. Oscar Valdés not only contributed his significant knowledge of the African and Afro-Cuban folkloric traditions, he was an extremely organized and capable band manager, good on the business side of things, and certainly an important advocate for popular music. His sound was, in many ways, the signature for Irakere, especially in terms of the danceable repertoire. Carlos Averhoff (who died in 2016) was perhaps the most devoted member of the band, and an excellent section leader. He really cared about the details, the phrasing, dynamics, making sure the horn section had everything down perfectly. Sometimes while we were on tour, he'd gather the players at all hours in his hotel room to go over parts! He was also a gifted educator, a brilliant saxophonist and sax teacher, and an advocate for the band's repertoire in the schools.

Carlos Emilio was, I think, overlooked as a player, and in my opinion was the greatest Cuban jazz guitarist of all time. He was modest, discrete and a little shy, but what I admired about him was his diction on the instrument (his ability to speak the jazz language), as well as his approach. Two of his all-time favorite guitarists were Tal Farlow and Barney Kessel. And wow, what can I say about Carlos del Puerto?! Without him Irakere wouldn't exist! He was the backbone of the band, supporting the group but also bringing immense creativity and innovative ideas. He is such an excellent musician, and he also made important contributions to the arrangements over the years, helping us improve the work and make it better. Carlos is one of the greatest musicians I have ever known."

Nearly 20 years would pass between del Puerto's departure from Irakere in 1996 and their meeting before a performance in San Francisco in 2014, with Carlos surprising him backstage before an Afro-Cuban Messengers show. Chucho called him on stage for a lovely *descarga*, which was the first time that they had played together since the 90s.

"Enrique Plá had this Tony Williams-inspired sound that everyone loved, and he adored Tony's playing. In 1964 I remember Plá bringing back Williams' album (*Life Time* on Blue Note) from Paris to share with everyone; this was probably the first Tony Williams record in Cuba! Plá's playing, especially those breaks and fills he did, were essential to the arrangements; without them the tunes wouldn't be the same, and we wouldn't have sounded like Irakere! Plá was like our signature, as Chappotín was to Arsenio;[15] you take Chappotín's trumpet out of that band, and it wasn't the same. One of the mistakes I made (during the 90s) was replacing him (briefly) in the band."

• VERSION 5: FROM THE MESSENGERS TO IRAKERE 40

Beginning the new millennium with a GRAMMY Award for his 2000 Blue Note album *Live at the Village Vanguard* (with a quartet format), Chucho created an offshoot version of Irakere with no horns[16], then in 2006 he dissolved the band, focusing on his smaller group and eventually naming it the Afro-Cuban Messengers. The Messengers line-up included Juan Carlos de Castro Blanco "El Peje" (drums), Lázaro Rivero Alarcón "El Fino" (bass), Yaroldy Abreu (percussion), and Dreiser Durruthy Bombalé

---

[15] Chucho is referring to trumpet great Félix Chappotín and his longtime association with *tres* player and bandleader Arsenio Rodríguez.
[16] Chucho notes that he was able to record one final album with a reduced format of the original band, but has yet to release this material.

A Brief History of Irakere

Chapter 4

(vocals & perc). Eventually he added two horns: Reynaldo Melián Álvarez (trumpet), and Carlos Miyares Hernández (sax). With this ensemble he recorded *Chucho's Steps* (on the Four Quarters label), winning the 2011 GRAMMY Award for best Latin Jazz album.

What is undeniable is the role of each of his bands as a training ground or musical academy, of sorts, for every single member who came on board, no matter how brief their tenure. The parallel between Chucho and Art Blakey is a fine example of this, given the importance of their contributions to their respective fields, and the many excellent musicians who have come and gone through each ensemble over the years.

So how was it, then, that the idea to rekindle the Irakere repertoire came about? In 2012, Chucho transformed his ensemble once again, with a new line-up that brought in Gaston Joya (bass) and Rodney Barreto (drums), both of whom had studied music in Havana's conservatories since elementary school, and remaining were Dreiser Durruthy Bombálé (percussion and vocals),[17] and Yaroldy Abreu Robles (perc), all of whom form the rhythm section of the newest incarnation of Irakere. It was this particular group of young lions who suggested that Chucho reform the band, mainly to resurrect the classic repertoire that had served all of them so well as students in Cuba's music schools over the years. In Barcelona in 2014, Chucho launched the 40th anniversary edition of the band, Irakere 40, adding on a cadre of horn players who had all studied the entire Irakere canon, and some who had memorized now-classic solos by former members. Rounding out the newest iteration are Ariel Bringuez (tenor sax), Rafael Aguila "Paco" (alto), Manuel Machado, Carlos Sarduy and Reynaldo Melián Álvarez (trumpets). The 2015 recording, *Tribute to Irakere: Live in Marciac,* won the GRAMMY for best Latin Jazz album in 2016, and the subsequent tour throughout the USA and Europe received critical acclaim, signaling a revived spirit of the band that has not only transformed the musical landscape of Afro-Cuban jazz, it has endured and reinvented itself.

• • •

---

[17] Chucho compares Dreiser to iconic Cuban folklore singer Lázaro Ros, bringing to the ensemble not only an authentic African aesthetic, but remarkable abilities as a batá drummer and dancer.

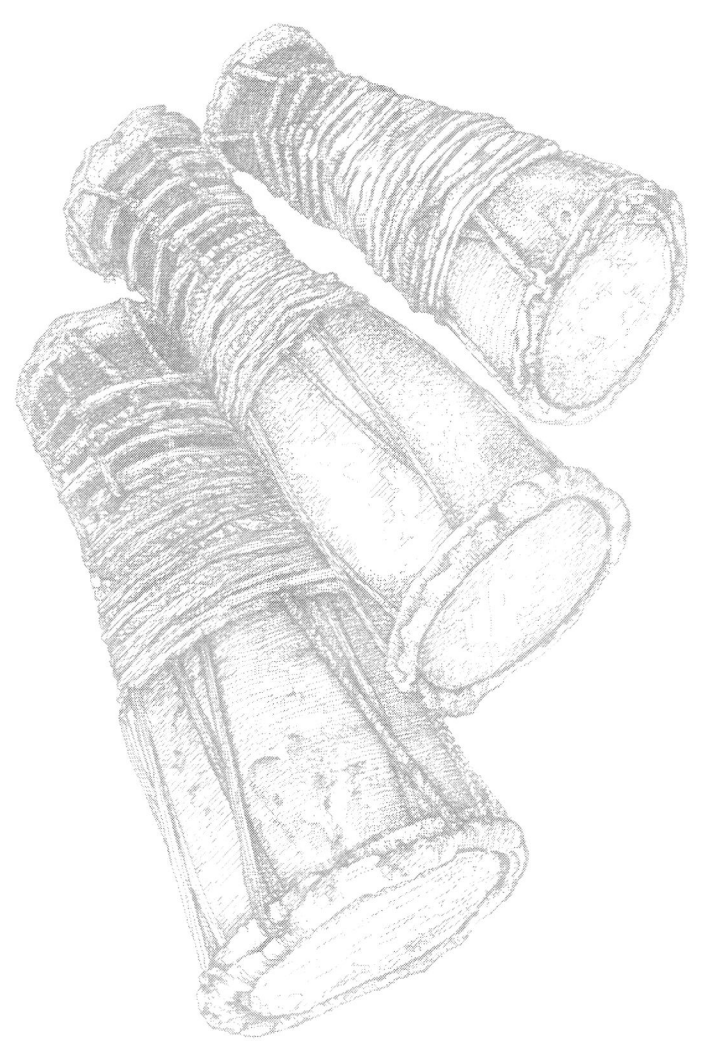

Afro-Cuban Folk Genres — Chapter 5

"Folklore is the heritage of the people." – María Teresa Linares

"In traditional African society the sacred and the secular are inseparable." – S.A. Adewale

"Where I come from we say that rhythm is the soul of life, because the whole universe revolves around rhythm, and when we get out of rhythm, that's when we get into trouble." – Babatunde Olatunji

• • •

The legacy of Afro-Cuban folklore is extraordinarily diverse and complex. In order to deeply understand even a fraction of its many genres, sub-genres, stylistic evolutions, variations and so on, one would need to spend at least an entire lifetime in full immersion, and we realize this may not be the most practical advice! As noted previously, it is precisely the richness and diversity of Cuba's cultural lineage that played a critical role in defining the music of Irakere, not only from a musicological standpoint, but from a deeply personal one as well. Chucho Valdés, and all of the musicians who passed through the band, developed within the context of these traditions because they grew up in Cuba and were exposed to dozens of rhythms, songs, dances, spiritual practices and other creative expressions. They were (and are) the beneficiaries of a great wealth of knowledge—a combination of formal pedagogy and oral tradition—that is seldom "taught" in the practical sense of the word. Yes, there is no denying the extraordinary conservatory training that most of these musicians received since early childhood; but without a doubt, the lessons of the "streets and nightclubs," the spiritual centers of worship, the illicit jazz recordings heard on shortwave radio, the exposure to music from foreign lands, and the ancient wisdom passed down from elders, were of even greater significance in defining the evolution of this music.

In order to provide some insight into Irakere's process of drawing from so many broad cultural traditions, we will lay out a "liturgy" of sorts of Afro-Cuban folkloric styles, and include basic transcriptions of their inherent rhythmical structure as a frame of reference. This list is by no means comprehensive, nor is it intended to provide a detailed analysis of how each genre or sub-style may have evolved over the generations.[1] Think of each of the following examples as an individual snapshot of a much larger "moving picture," one that continues to develop and transform as that particular rhythm or tradition is shared with others, and is molded into something entirely new. That is what folklore is after all: a tradition made by the people for the people; a living art form, a continuum, and an ongoing conversation. Furthermore, many of these genres can be considered as foundational "mother musics" in Cuba, given that everything heard and played today has both direct and indirect links to at least one of these traditions.

In the history of the slave trade in Cuba, there were (and still are) many different African ethnic groups represented, although their specific numbers were often miscalculated in various census reports, with improper classifications given to significant subgroups of larger, mostly regional, populations. As noted previously, there is general consensus that Cuba's afro-descendant population is made up of three primary West and Central African nations or ethnicities (in order by size of population): the

---

[1] For those styles and genres not represented here, including the traditional/popular styles highlighted in Chapter I, please consult the *Salsa Guidebook* (Sher Music Co), and other sources noted in the Bibliography.

bantú (Congo), ***lucumí*** (Yoruba)[2] and ***arará*** (Dahomean). Others argue that the ethnic makeup stems from four principal groups, defining the third largest group as Ibo (or Igbo), and the fourth most representative group as Ewe-Fon. But many ethnographers point to a much broader and culturally diverse lineage, highlighting the erroneous assumption that members of varying nations could somehow be lumped together as one. In his dissertation on the *lucumí* culture in Cuba, noted scholar Miguel Ramos states that it was precisely the distinct and unique cultural aspects of each ethnic group that contributed to the rich expressions of folklore on the island, and that these expressions were primarily manifested through the survival of religious practice:

"Congos, Lucumís,Ararás, Mandingas, Gangás, Carabalís, and others were lumped together as Africans, and their ethnies' distinctive contributions to Cuban music, cuisine, aesthetics, and other areas were subsumed under an inauthentic category. The uniqueness of each cultural group's influence was retained only in their religious systems and the cultural practices that have evolved from these. Had it not been for these, individual ethnic identity would have been minimized, possibly beyond recognition, or simply forgotten."[3]

He further emphasizes that the survival of religious practice was, and still is, a form of cultural resistance:

"The mere fact that African religions continued at all in the Americas, despite the many impediments they encountered, is a testament to their ability to resist, adapt, and thus endure."[4]

This is critical to understanding the foundational elements of folk traditions in general; by the very nature of its survival in Cuba and elsewhere in the Caribbean and Latin America, African cultural practice can be viewed as the ultimate expression of defiance. While this topic may seem more sociological or philosophical, it is nonetheless an important reminder that the vestiges of folkloric dance-drum traditions carry a deep significance and should be honored and respected. That said, let's explore some of the many extraordinary folk rhythms that permeate Afro-Cuban music.

We will divide this chapter into three main sections, beginning first with **sacred rhythms**, followed by **secular folk styles** that are commonly used in popular music, and finally, the **adaptations** used in the musical fusion pioneered by Irakere. The goal here is to illustrate how Irakere's rhythm section transformed or adopted the aforementioned traditional styles, and distributed the parts among the instruments. For the most part, the majority of the styles represented here focus on folkloric music developed in Havana; however, we felt it important to included several of the folk traditions of Matanzas as well.[5] While this work is not intended as a reference guide on Cuban folk idioms, we must acknowledge the absence here of many Eastern Cuban folkloric genres that are clearly worth investigating. If Irakere had chosen to incorporate the Franco-Haitian styles of *tumba francesa* or

---

[2] A common alternative spelling for this term is "lukumí."
[3] Ramos, Miguel. "Lucumí (Yoruba) Culture in Cuba: A Reevaluation (1830s-1940s)," pp. 65-66.
[4] Ibid, p. 11.
[5] One exception is the *conga santiaguera* (from the Santiago province), which is presented here to illustrate the differences between it and the *conga habanera,* and also to emphasize its multicultural origins (with African, Chinese and Spanish roots).

Afro-Cuban Folk Genres

Chapter 5

gagá into its repertoire,[6] we would certainly include them here. Furthermore, it must be stated that the fragments represented here should not be considered "complete" or definitive; they are brief statements of a much larger vocabulary. Think of Afro-Cuban music as a language containing many dialects, accents, parts of speech, slang, double-entendre, metaphor, etc., and you will get the idea; there is no way to succinctly boil each genre down to a two or four-measure phrase! Regardless, you should begin to get some idea as to the intricacies of these rhythms by examining their interlocking components, and also, their relationship to the *clave* (when pertinent).

The following sections in this chapter consist mainly of percussion transcriptions, and in some cases, are notated to represent some of the varying tones produced by a single drum (please refer to the drum key that precedes each section of examples). Many of the styles include bell and hand percussion patterns as well, and these too can be nuanced. However, there are subtleties to percussion performance that are beyond the scope of this book. To gain a better understanding of the intricacies of Afro-Cuban percussion techniques, we recommend a number of resources listed in the Bibliography, and better still, a private instructor with thorough knowledge of these traditions. To those readers who may not be experienced with drumming or percussion, we can only stress the obvious: to fully understand and interpret Afro-Cuban music, you **must** understand the drum.

Sacred Music

• LUCUMÍ TRADITIONS

While the population of Yoruban Africans brought to Cuba was not as large as that of Bantú groups,[7] their sacred dance-drum traditions have permeated the national culture and identity in far-reaching ways. In the practice of Regla de Ocha or Santería, there are multiple manifestations of musical liturgy depending on the particular **cabildo** (religious and mutual aid society) from which it emerged, as well as the town or neighborhood where it developed. For centuries, more than a quarter million descendants from varying regions of Nigeria managed to retain primordial elements of "their most precious possessions: their language, customs, music, oral literature, and ethos of life, morality and religion. In that struggle—a kind of cultural underground-movement—religion served as the hard core of cultural resistance."[8] It is also important to note the principal role of Yoruban drumming traditions and their relationship to trance, with the drums themselves, as author Amanda Villepastour points out, acting as "instruments of speech surrogacy, mimicking and coding natural language into musical talking."[9] We will look at three primary forms of religious music of *lucumí* (Yoruba) origin, as well as some of the specific **toques** (rhythmical patterns) within them.

Toques de Batá (Batá Rhythms) – The Nigerian-derived two-headed batá drums reemerged in no other colony except Cuba, despite the fact that millions of Yoruban Africans were dispersed throughout North and South America as well as the Caribbean. It is commonly thought that the origins of the drums date back over 500 years in Africa, and were likely introduced in Cuba around the early 1800s

---

[6] Both *tumba francesa* and *gagá* are cultural manifestations of Haitian influence that penetrated Eastern Cuba following Haiti's Revolution in 1791. *Tumba francesa* emerged as a hybrid form, inspired by the runaway slaves (maroons) who led the successful rebellion against the French in Haiti, and *gagá* music has direct connections to vodou ceremonial traditions.
[7] By several accounts, the numbers of enslaved Africans of Bantú origin in Cuba was nearly twice that of the Yoruba.
[8] Mirtha Fernández, *Cuba Review,* 2005.
[9] Villepastour, p. 3.

(by some accounts, the 1830s). The Cuban batá ensemble consists of three hourglass-shaped drums: the **Iyá** (the largest drum), the **Itótele** (the middle drum), and the **Okónkolo** (the smallest drum); the larger of the two drum heads on each instrument is referred to as the *enú*, and the smaller head is the *chachá* (see drum key below, fig. 5a). In the religious tradition known as Regla de Ocha (or Santería), the ceremonial context where the consecrated batá (*fundamento*) are used is known as the *guemilere* (loosely translated, meaning "party for the *orishas*"). Within the ceremony, the batá are played for the *oru del igbodu* (unaccompanied drumming), and the *oru del eya aranla* (drumming, singing and dancing). During the liturgy, specific *toques* (rhythms) are played for each of the *orishas* (deities); some of the *orishas* require the playing of several distinct rhythms and variations, as well as dozens of praise songs.[10] The unconsecrated drums, such as those used by Irakere and other popular music groups, are known as *aberikulá*, and were first publicly played in Havana in the early 1930s.[11]

fig. 5a - Batá Drum Key

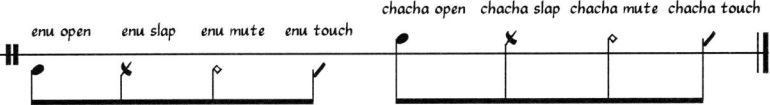

- **BATÁ EXAMPLES**

The following excerpts (figures 5.1 – 5.8) represent a few of the more than 100 known *toques de batá* used in Cuba, and of significance to this work, those adapted by Irakere in several of their most important pieces:

5.1 - Alaró (or Aro) – for Yemayá

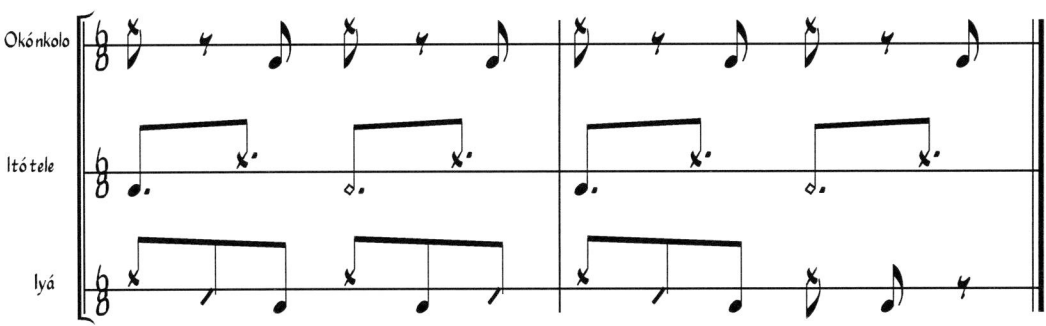

The Iyá part is generally fluid and varied

---

[10] Author Kenneth Schweitzer refers to the *toques* as "multi-sectional compositions." Schweitzer, p. 66.
[11] In 1936, Cuban ethnographer Fernando Ortiz commissioned the first unconsecrated set of batá drums, known as *aberikulá;* these are the drums that are used in secular, popular contexts (such as the music of Irakere).

Afro-Cuban Folk Genres — Chapter 5

5.2 - Bariba Ogé De Ma for Babalú Ayé (Clave 3-2)

This toque follows an AAB, 12-bar form (1st X only)

5.3 - Chachálokpafúñ for multiple Orishas (clave 3-2)

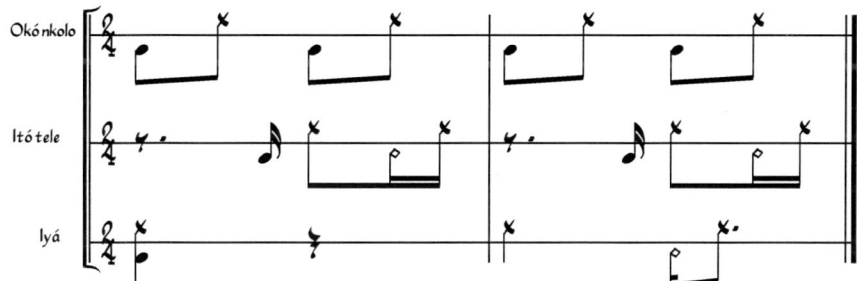

5.4 - Iyesá for multiple Orishas (Clave 3-2)

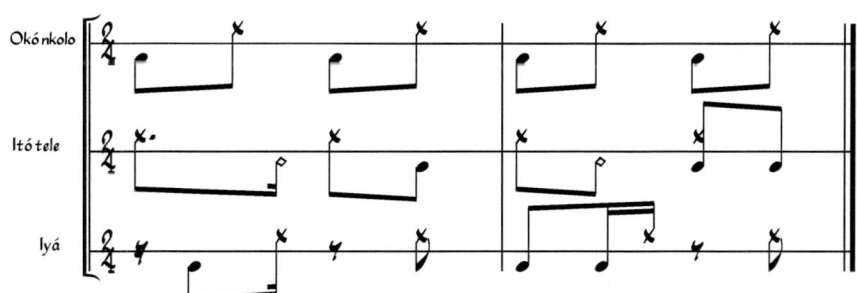

5.5 - Latokpa ~ Toque for Eleguá (Clave 3-2)

5.6 - Rumba Obatalá (Clave 3-2)

5.7 - Yakotá for multiple Orishas

5.8 - Yeguá – toque for Babalú Ayé (or Asojano)

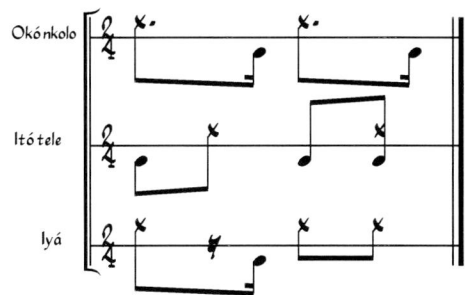

Afro-Cuban Folk Genres — Chapter 5

Toque de Güiro (Chékere ensemble + single drum and cowbell) ~ The word *güiro* has multiple uses in Cuba, and in this particular case, refers to another form of musical liturgy in the *lucumí* tradition. Unlike the bàtá, which encompass over one hundred complex rhythmical patterns and variations, the *toque de güiro* consists of one general style or pattern that is used to accompany the same praise songs in the Regla de Ocha ceremony. The ensemble includes 2 or 3 beaded gourd *chékeres* (sometimes referred to as *güiros*), one conga drum, and one cowbell or *guataca* (garden hoe blade). (See drum key, fig. 5b.) The drum tends to have the most improvisational freedom, while the *chékeres* and the bell maintain more static or fixed parts (fig. 5.9).

fig. 5b - Toque de Güiro Key

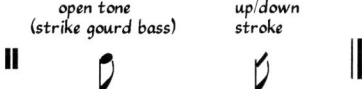

5.9 - Toque de Güiro (bell + 2 chékeres)

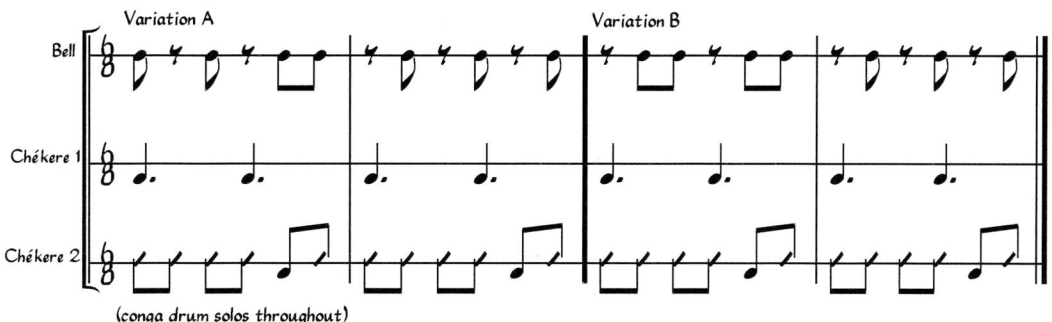

Bembé (3-drum Ensemble with cowbell) ~ The term *bembé* can sometimes be used to describe the Afro-Cuban 6/8 styles often heard in secular music,[12] but the original context in Cuba is another of the most commonly used forms in *lucumí* liturgical music. In comparison with the bàtá drumming ensemble, the *bembé* style is more "accessible" in that it does not require such rigorous training or complex initiation, although there are several styles and interpretations used throughout Cuba.[13] The ensemble consists of three drums: a high-pitched drum and medium-pitched drum that preserve a more steady pulse, and the lead, lowest-pitched drum, responsible for most of the improvisation.[14] There is often a chékere or maraca added, plus a metal *guataca* (garden hoe blade) or regular cowbell used in the ensemble (see drum key, fig. 5c). The drums can be played with hands, or with a hand/stick combination, and the bell rhythm that is used is the standard 6/8 bell pattern, as introduced in Chapter II (fig. 5.10).

fig. 5c - Bembé Key

---

[12] It may be common to come across the term *bembé* on song style descriptors or album liner notes; the traditional form is specifically associated with *lucumí* religious music in Cuba.

[13] While traditional *bembé* utilizes its own special drums, the style is often played using regular conga drums.

[14] The denominations of the drum names varies from city to city in Cuba. In Matanzas, the names are associated with the Bantú *palo* or *yuka* traditions: *caja*, *mula* and *cachimbo*.

5.10 - Bembé (bell + 3 drums)

Iyesá Music (from Matanzas) ~ While Iyesá music is also a component of the *lucumí* tradition of liturgical music, it is exclusively from the province of Matanzas, stemming from the various *cabildos* founded in the region by direct descendants of the Iyesá people from Nigeria. Iyesá drumming comprises two distinct patterns: one called Oshún (in 4/4 time), and the other known as Ogún (in 6/8) time. These two *toques* are used to accompany praise songs for all of the *orishas*. Iyesá music is typically played using four cylindrical drums and two cowbells; three of the four drums are played with sticks, and the lead drum (the *caja*) is played using a hand/stick combination (see drum key, fig. 5d). Like the batá, Iyesá drums are also consecrated.[15] We will highlight here an excerpt of the 4/4 (Oshún) style (fig. 511):

fig. 5d - Iyesá Key

5.11 - Iyesá for Oshún (2 bells + 4 drums)

[15] Lameca.org.

Afro-Cuban Folk Genres — Chapter 5

• ARARÁ TRADITIONS

The descendants of the Ewe-Fon from Dahomey (present day Benin) are, by many accounts, the fourth largest African ethnic group in Cuba. Referred to as *arará*, the *cabildos* they established in Western Cuba (mostly in the Matanzas province) date back to the 17th century,[16] and the religious system is similar to that of the *lucumí*, with the veneration of deities known as *foduces*. The music comprises drumming, singing, and body percussion elements, with a complex system of rhythms containing 4 and 6-bar phrases, as well as odd measure lengths. The ensemble typically consists of four drums: three smaller drums played with sticks, and the largest drum (the *yonofó*) played by a hand/stick combination, a hoe blade or bell, and (sometimes) a maraca or rattle (see drum key, fig. 5e). Ethnographer Fernando Ortiz and several musicologists have noted similarities between the Afro-Cuban *arará* music and that of the vodou traditions in Haiti.[17] Here is a fragment of this style (fig. 5.12):

fig. 5e - Arará key

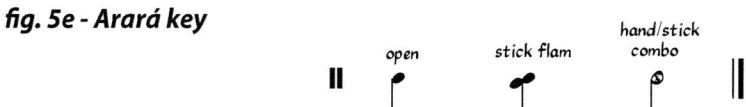

5.12 - Arará (bell + 3 drums)

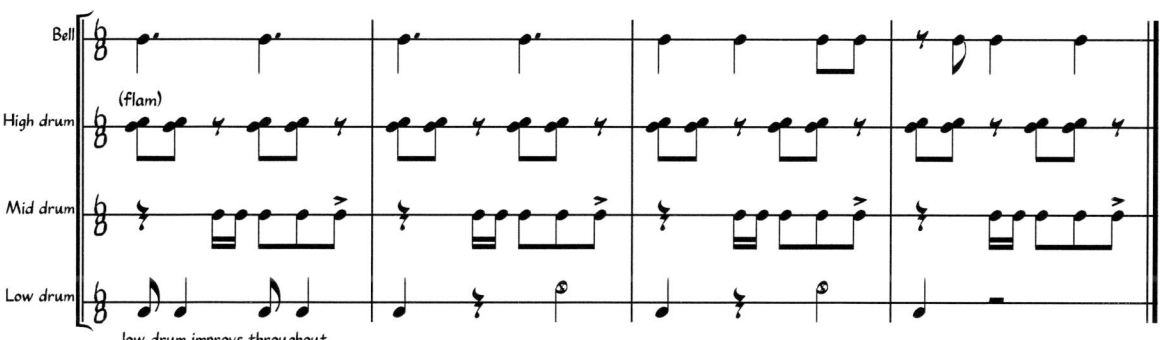

• BANTÚ TRADITIONS

Without a doubt, the influence of the largest Afro-descendant group in Cuba can be felt across both folkloric and popular music genres—from rural to urban communities—and this influence extends throughout the island in various sectors of the arts and culture. Although classified together and identified as "Congos" in Cuba, Bantú descendants from Central Africa encompass several specific cultural groups or regions,[18] and their musical traditions comprise both sacred and secular forms, directly impacting the development of **rumba** and **son**, among other genres. The Bantú religious tradition runs deep, stemming from the formation of the *cabildos* throughout Cuba, and includes musical styles such as **palo** and **makuta**. There are several denominations of Bantú religious practice in Cuba, known as *Reglas de Palo*, that incorporate the veneration of nature spirits and ancestor

---

[16] Among the active *arará cabildos* in the province of Matanzas are: Ojún Degara, Arará Dahomé, and Arará Savalú (or Sabalú).

[17] Ortiz, *Los instrumentos de la música afrocubana*, various.

[18] Fernando Ortiz noted several ethnic sub-categories of Bantú nations, including Motembo, Mumbona, Musumdí, Mumbala, Mondongo, Cabenda, Mayombe, Masinga, Banguela, Munyaka, Loango, Musungo, Mundemba, Musoso, and Entoterá, which, according to him, referred to Kongo or Bantú regions or peoples (Ortiz 1975, 45).

worship, as well as the belief in natural powers,[19] and include forms of dance-drumming traditions as well as the practice of "spiritism." The instruments used in the percussion ensemble include drums, sticks (called the ***catá***), and bells (see drum key, fig. 5f), with the tall cylindrical *makuta* drums serving as likely predecessors to the modern day *tumbadora* (conga drum). Among the most influential of the secular music and dance styles is **yuka**, which also contains its own specific drums and is representative of the pelvic movements of the dancers in the *guaguancó* style of *rumba*. Many folklorists refer to these three styles—*palo, makuta* and *yuka*—as being part of a "cycle" in the Cuban Bantú tradition (referred to as ***ciclo congo***). Here is a fragment of the *toque de palo*, representing the way it is played in Havana (fig. 5.13):

fig. 5f - Palo Key

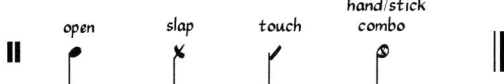

5.13 - Palo (bell, catá + 3 drums)

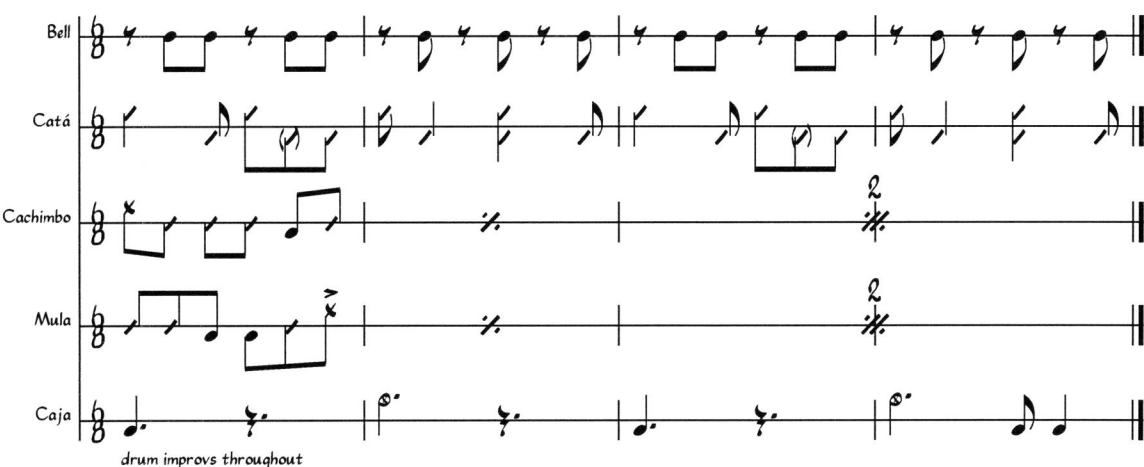

ABAKUÁ MUSIC

Africans descended from the society known as the Ékpe, who originated in southeastern Nigeria as well as parts of Cameroon (near the region of the Calabar River), are known as Carabalí in Cuba. Bringing their own unique language (Efik) as well as distinct dance-drumming traditions and quasi-religious spiritual practices, they formed secret male fraternal (or mutual aid) societies known as **Abakuá**, the first known society dating back to 1836 in a suburb of Havana.[20] The ritual practices of the ceremonies (known as *plantes*) incorporate a complex system of drumming, singing and dance, with a level of mystery and secrecy that although not widely "documented," has permeated virtually

---

[19] Religious syncretism in Africa had been prevalent since the 15th century, when the Kingdom of Kongo adapted the Catholic religion and developed a hybrid form.
[20] Linares, Miller, Sosa, etc.

every aspect of popular culture in Cuba, including many linguistic elements and expressions.[21] With its own set of drums, Abakuá music is structured in 6/8 or 12/8 patterns, and its signature timeline is a bell pattern that in many ways resembles the Cuban *clave* (see drum key, fig. 5g). Groups such as Irakere have drawn from the wealth of songs, improvisational techniques, and phrases that have been widely disseminated through recordings since the 1920s, and it is not uncommon to hear references to Abakuá culture in many styles of folk and popular music.[22] Here is a fragment of two commonly played patterns, one from Havana and the other from Matanzas (fig. 5.14), that can be heard in many recordings:

fig. 5g - Abakuá Key

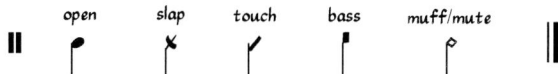

5.14 - Abakuá (bell+3 drums)

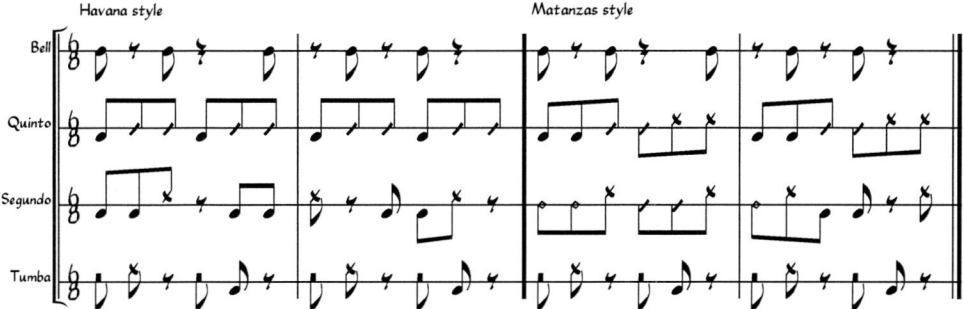

Secular Music

While the line between sacred and secular music may seem obvious at first glance, it is clear that Afro-Cuban music has found a way to blur this line beautifully without diminishing the importance or the character of either. In some cases, the evolution of secular music came out of the sacred and/or spiritual traditions that, while seemingly suppressed or pushed underground, were able to be remarkably well preserved. The profane in African-derived folklore is not always clear cut, but of all of Cuba's music, there are no two more important genres than those of the **conga** (music for Carnaval), and **rumba**.

• CONGA DE COMPARSA

The **conga** style of music and dance developed within the *cabildos* and was directly associated with

---

[21] Abakuá words are a "creolized" form of Efik language, sometimes referred to as *bríkamo*, and can be heard in everyday slang in Cuba. *Bríkamo* generally refers to all people from the Calabar region in Africa.
[22] Among the most pervasive of Abakuá influences is that of the movements adapted in *rumba* dance technique, especially the style of *columbia*.

the Catholic calendar, when Spanish colonizers "allowed" the Africans to display their music and dance in processional style. The word "comparsa" refers to the specific contingent or ensemble that participates in Carnaval, and each group contains numerous costumed dancers, drummers, and floats/decorations. Originally coinciding with colonial era Catholic celebrations such as patron saint festivities, or during the Epiphany (January 6th), Carnaval in Cuba would later take place during Lent, and as in most Latin American countries, was celebrated on the two days before Ash Wednesday. Since the Revolution (in 1959), Carnaval typically takes place during the summer months, with Santiago's in July, and Havana's in August.[23] While its religious origins are historically acknowledged, the ways in which Carnaval traditions are manifested today seem far from religious in appearance, although many *comparsas* do integrate sacred musical themes, songs and dances. Over the centuries, two specific stylistic variations emerged, one from the city of Havana and the other from Santiago de Cuba, each with its own unique characteristics and instrumentation.

With the arrival of thousands of indentured Chinese workers to Cuba, a particular double-reeded horn instrument known as the *suona,* and referred to as the *trompeta* or *corneta china,* was adapted by the Santiago variant called the **conga santiaguera**,[24] where its nasal, high-pitched tone is the only voice capable of cutting through a battery of bass drums (*bombos*, played with mallets), *tambores de conga* (lightweight conical conga drums), and brake drums, among other percussion (see drum key, fig. 5h). The rhythmical structure (fig. 5.15) places the heaviest accent of the bass drum on the "and" of the fourth beat of every other measure (when notated in a 2-bar phrase), resulting in a highly syncopated feel (and a contrasting accent compared to that of the Havana style). The Havana style (fig. 5.16), known as **conga habanera**, features a bass drum pattern more heavily accented on the "and" of the the second beat of the measure (again, in a 2-bar structure), and typically uses multiple cowbells or frying pans called *sartenes* instead of the brake drums, plus traditional brass such as trumpets or trombones instead of the *trompeta china*. Both are highly improvisational, featuring a constant soloing role for the lead *quinto* drum. All combined, the instruments are intended to provide a "relentless" groove for participants in the procession, as thousands of costumed dancers and revelers literally march to the beats of the drums for hours on end. Here are two snapshots of each style (shown in 4/4 meter):

fig. 5h - Conga Key

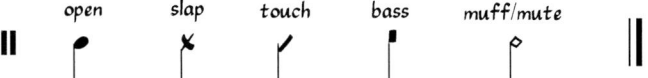

---

[23] EcuRed, Granma, Ortiz, etc.
[24] The instrument is thought to have been adapted in the *conga santiaguera* style around 1916. EcuRed.

Afro-Cuban Folk Genres — Chapter 5

5.15 - Conga Santiaguera (sartenes, congas + 3 bombo drums)

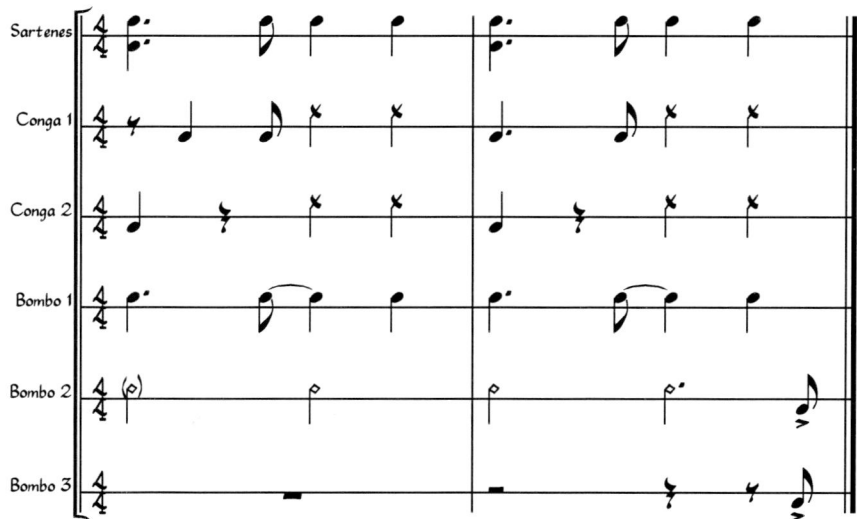

5.16 - Conga Habanera (cowbell, sartenes, 3 congas, snare + bombo drum)

bombo ad libs freely

RUMBA

Author and musicologist María Teresa Linares encapsulates the essence of Cuba's most ubiquitous folkloric genre when she states that *rumba* "is the purest expression of Cubanness."[25] Since it first emerged around the 1880s in the city of Matanzas, **rumba** became a synthesis of many cultural influences—from diverse African sources including Bantú *and* Abakuá forms—to elements of Spanish flamenco and more, coalescing into an ever-evolving tradition that has since spread around the world. Now an acknowledged part of Cuba's cultural patrimony,[26] *rumba* has come to symbolize the identity of the entire nation. Authentic *rumba* emerged during a time of transition from colonialism and slavery, and over time developed as a blend of African and Spanish rhythms, melodies, and colloquial expression. As with many of the African-derived sacred and secular drum-dance genres, *rumba* features a drum "hierarchy" of sorts, providing a foundational bass drum part and a secondary "answer" to complete the phrase that serves as the primary rhythm, with a third lead drum taking the improvisational (or "talking") role. Author Ned Sublette notes the appearance of this structure in many forms of folk music in Cuba, emphasizing this aspect as "a fundamental concept in West and Central African percussion."[27]

The first *rumba* style to take shape during the colonial era was the **yambú**, which is thought to be derived from the Bantú *yuka* style, and is typically the slowest in tempo and most "elegant" in its dance interpretation. It was originally played on box drums known as **cajones** that were readily accessible to workers on the docks in the port city of Matanzas, and are combined with the **claves**, **palitos** (two sticks striking a piece of bamboo known as the *catá*), and a metal shaker called the **maruga**. The adaptation of the Bantú *yuka* as well as *makuta* drums eventually led to the creation of the Cuban **tumbadoras** (conga drums), resulting in the three denominations of **tumba** (bass), **salidor** or *tres-dos* (second or middle drum), and the highest pitched **quinto** (lead solo drum). Sublette further emphasizes that the function of the *quinto* is "generally florid and melismatic."[28] Over time (by the late 19th century), two other styles of *rumba* would develop: the **guaguancó**, and the **columbia**. Often, the three styles are identified as a cohort or "complex" (as in *complejo de la rumba*), and each style may be further identified using the term "rumba" as a sub-heading (such as *rumba-guaguancó*).

The structure of *rumba* songs has remained fairly consistent since it first evolved from earlier choral ensembles known as **coros de clave** (large vocal groups with small percussion instruments that performed in ambulatory fashion). In a typical *rumba* ensemble, the song begins with the *claves* to establish the tempo, followed by the gradual layering in of the drums and minor percussion to stabilize the rhythm (see drum key, fig. 5i), wherein the lead vocalist will "scat" sing a vocalized melody (called the *diana*), providing the key for the other vocalists in the ensemble.[29] The lead singer will then sing one or two verses, sometimes in harmony with another vocalist while the drummers maintain a fairly steady, repetitive pattern and the *quinto* punctuates around the vocals. Once the lead vocalist arrives at the *estribillo* (the refrain), the ensemble kicks into overdrive, with the primordial element of call-and-response setting up an extraordinarily complex layering of improvisations by the lead singer,

---

[25] "La rumba es la más pura expresión de la cubanía." Linares, *LaJiribilla.com*, 2001.
[26] *Rumba* was officially declared "Intangible Cultural Heritage of Humanity" by UNESCO in December of 2016. ECN.cu.
[27] Sublette, *LaMeca.com*.
[28] Ibid.
[29] Since there are no pitched instruments in the ensemble, the vocalist scats in order to establish the key to be sung. This is also where the Spanish influences were most pervasive early on, given the flamenco-like qualities of the singing during the late 19th century and into the earliest 20th century.

Afro-Cuban Folk Genres — Chapter 5

lead drummer, and the dancers, who now take to the center of the "stage" or circle to engage in one of Cuba's most influential dance traditions.[30] It is here where the elements of African deep-roots culture come to the forefront, showcasing the Bantú or Abakuá elements mixed with more subtle Spanish flamenco-infused flourishes. We should state that while *rumba* may represent a "bi-cultural" heritage on the surface, deep down it is inherently African, highlighting the previously mentioned musical characteristics (polyrhythm, syncopation, improvisation, call-and-response, and repetition), as well as the cultural lineage preserved and cultivated within the various *cabildos* in both rural and urban areas. For well over a century, *rumba* has come to represent the fomentation of Cuban cultural authenticity, and it continues to evolve in the hands of the next generation.[31]

What follows are musical fragments demonstrating each of the three styles (figs. 5.17, 5.18 and 5.19), including the distinction between the *guaguancó* style developed in Matanzas and that of the Havana variant. As noted earlier, there is no justifiable way to isolate a given fragment of this music; there is simply too much going on—in a highly improvisational environment—to reduce this complex genre into meaningful "chunks." Furthermore, as musicians continue to adapt and adopt other musical forms and expressions, *rumba* has undergone a range of hybrid interpretations, including the **bata-rumba** genre developed by Grupo Afrocuba de Matanzas in the early 1970s, and the more recent **guarapachangueo** style, featuring a heightened degree of syncopation and a redistribution of the parts among the *tumbadoras* and the *cajones*.[32] Within contemporary ensembles (such as Irakere), the percussionists in the band need to find ways to represent the patterns and ongoing conversations that tend to happen in the more authentic ways of playing, and this is no small task.

fig. 5i - Rumba Key

---

[30] Traditional *rumba* dance is performed by male-female couples in the *yambú* and *guaguancó* styles, while the *columbia* is typically danced by a solo male dancer, although there are several well known female dancers of the style. The *guaguanó* features a particular pelvic move known as the *vacunao*, which represents the "courtship" element or simulation of copulation between rooster and hen, a common characteristic of African-derived dance aesthetics. Often, the *quinto* player will mimic the steps of the dancer's feet on the drum, highlighting the extremely interactive nature of this complex genre.

[31] Among the most important ensembles to develop the *rumba* genre are Los Muñequitos de Matanzas, Grupo Afrocuba de Matanzas, Los Papines, Grupo Clave y Guaguancó, Rumberos de Cuba, Osain del Monte and others.

[32] The emergence of the *guarapachangueo* initially stemmed from the need to interpret *rumba* with fewer than the normal number of drummers, wherein one drummer would morph two different roles into one.

CHAPTER 5 — AFRO-CUBAN FOLK GENRES

5.17 - Rumba Yambú (clave, palitos, maruga, 2 drums)

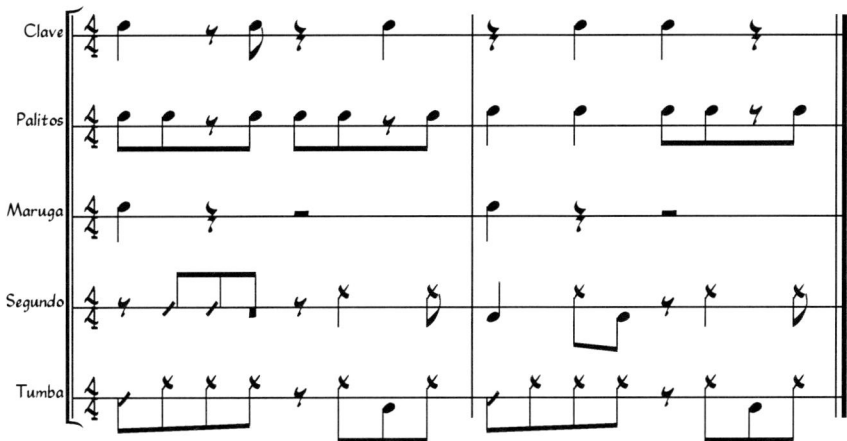

5.18 - Rumba Guaguancó (clave, palitos, maruga, 3 drums)

the quinto drum solos throughout

5.19 - Rumba Columbia (bell, palitos, maruga, 3 drums)

the quinto drum solos throughout

Afro-Cuban Folk Genres — Chapter 5

• MOZAMBIQUE

As noted in Chapter I, the **mozambique** was an adaptation of the Cuban *conga* rhythm used for Carnaval, and was developed in 1963 by percussionist Pedro Izquierdo, better known as Pello el Afrokán. Stylistically it has many similarities to the *conga* in pattern types as well as instrumentation, but provided just enough variation to come up with something long-lasting and catchy. Interestingly enough, many New York salsa musicians first heard the style over shortwave radio broadcasts or rustic recordings, and ended up developing an interpretation that, although noticeably different, would also become standardized in Latin music performance. Now an added component to the genres represented in Cuba's Carnaval, the *mozambique* has a percussion-heavy texture featuring two distinct bass drum patterns, varying conga parts, and a unique bell rhythm. Here is a snapshot of the traditional Cuban style (fig. 5.20):

5.20 - Mozambique (clave, bell, congas, 2 bombos)

• PILÓN

A hybrid form of popular dance music developed in Eastern Cuba around 1964 by percussionist and band leader Enrique Bonne, and later popularized by Santiago-born singer Pacho Alonso, the *pilón* style combined the percussion-driven sounds of Carnaval rhythms with the fascinating *órgano oriental* (mechanical organ) tradition commonly heard in cities such as Manzanillo. The premise of Bonne's mixture was inspired by the movements of coffee plantation workers pounding or grinding coffee beans in a large device (the *pilón*), coupled with the carousel-like rhythms of the *órgano* cranking away. For over two decades, this style inspired countless television appearances by Alonso and others, and a very particular dance that also mimics the mechanics of the *pilón*. Here is a breakdown of the style played on timbales and one conga player using two drums (see drum key, fig. 5j), as demonstrated by José Luis Quintana "Changuito" (fig. 5.21):

fig. 5j - Pilón Key

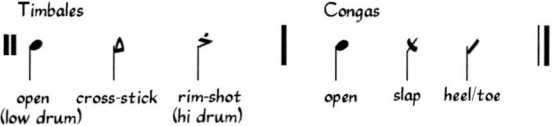

5.21 - Pilón (clave, bell, congas, timbales)

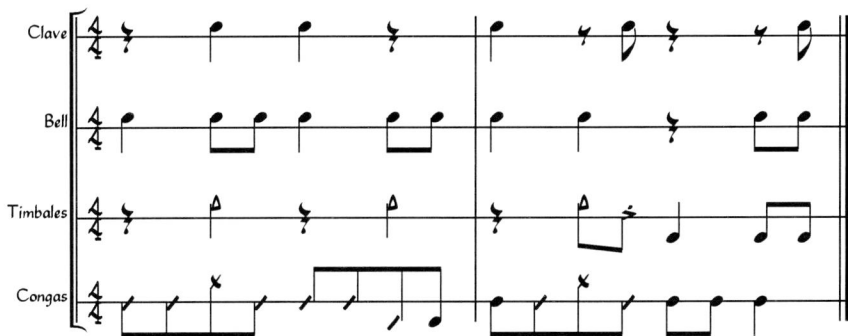

Adaptations

• CREATIVE BLENDING OF FOLK IDIOMS IN IRAKERE'S REPERTOIRE

The brilliance of Irakere (and certainly the vision of the group's leader, Chucho Valdés) is the artful combination of traditional folk and popular rhythms, classical genres, jazz, funk, rock and fusion, all melded into a cohesive expression that in many ways still defies categorization. What follows here is an attempt to isolate fragments of Chucho's arrangements on three select compositions referenced in this book, where he and the musicians adapted particular elements of the aforementioned folk genres and distributed the parts among the band, primarily the rhythm section (see drum key fig. 5k). In some cases, folkloric styles are performed as completely or authentically as they would be in the sacred context (even though it is absolutely clear that they aren't intended that way), and in others, we will demonstrate how the arrangements reflected or hinted at the traditional styles within a less rigid framework.

• COMPOSITION: "MISA NEGRA"

Folk styles used: *toque de güiro* (fig. 5.22), *bembé* (fig. 5.23), and *Iyesá (toque de batá* but only with Iyá drum, fig. 5.24).

Fig. 5k - Drum Key

Afro-Cuban Folk Genres — Chapter 5

5.22 - Misa Negra – Güiro fragment

5.23 - Misa Negra – Bembé fragment

5.24 - Misa Negra – Iyesá fragment

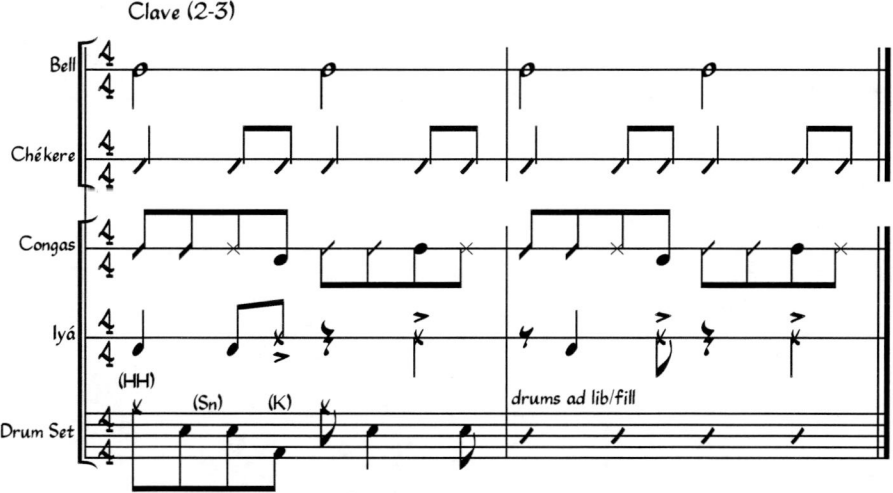

COMPOSITION: "BACALAO CON PAN"

Folk styles used: *Iyesá* (see fig. 5.4 above) featuring batá drums mixed with traps, congas and cowbell. The studio recording includes all three batá drums, resulting in a thicker texture than would typically be played live. The drum set plays a "boogaloo-style" groove with a backbeat played on both the snare drum and an open hi-hat (fig. 5.25).

5.25 - Bacalao Con Pan – Iyesá + Boogaloo groove

COMPOSITION: "EL TATA CIMARRÓN"

Folk styles used: *toque de Yeguá* (see fig. 5.8) with added 6/8 bell; *chachálokpafúñ* (see fig. 5.3) with Iyá drum only (with the congas creating the "response" to the Iyá calls) while the drummer marks the time in a more supporting role (fig. 5.26), and a *palo* hybrid (see fig. 5.13) during the breakdown section with the chorus, "Sarabanda Changó" (fig. 5.27).

5.26 - El Tata – Chachálokpafúñ with Iyá drum only

5.27 - El Tata – Palo hybrid during breakdown chorus

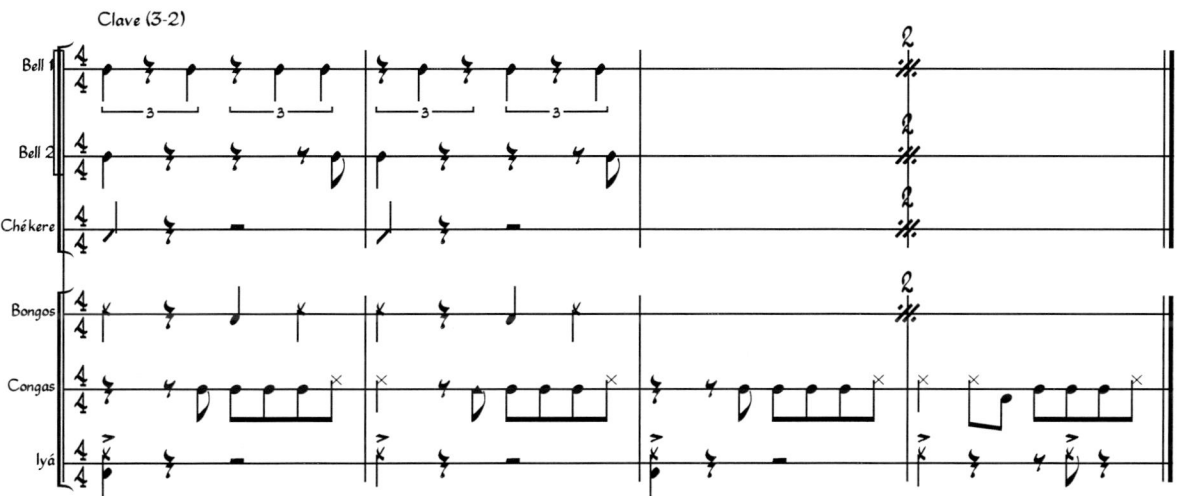

Two significant works that are also worth mentioning here (the first of which is also referenced in Chapter VI), demonstrate Irakere's use of multiple *toques de batá* (batá rhythms) and other sacred styles, often structured as medleys. While not every interpretation of these *toques* is necessarily "authentic" as it would be in a liturgical context, for most Cuban audiences, it was as close as you could get to the real thing. "Juana 1600" (composed in 1976) opens with a medley of various *toques* for at least three different *orishas*. First released on the album *Grupo Irakere* in 1976, the definitive recorded version was performed live in 1979 at the Capitol Theater in New Jersey (subsequently released on several compilations), and judging from the audience reaction, was akin to an explosion! The opening medley includes the following *toques* shown earlier: *aro* for Yemayá (see fig. 5.1), *baribá oge de ma* for Babalú Ayé (see fig. 5.2), and *rumba Obatalá* (see fig. 5.6).

"Changó" was composed in 1988 and appears on Irakere's second live album at Ronnie Scott's in London (released in 1989 and reissued as *Exuberancia*) and was also recorded in 2004 for the 30th anniversary of the band (with the fourth iteration of the ensemble). An example of Chucho's epic suite writing, this piece highlights the orisha Changó using a series of *toques* played in a sacred context, followed by a series of rapid-fire horn/percussion solis in mixed meter. The primary groove is a fast 6/8 that highlights the standard bell rhythm. Following a mesmerizing conga solo by Miguel Angá Díaz on the original recording, the band launches into a full fledged Abakuá groove (see fig. 5.12), followed by what can be best described as the Irakere signature groove "on steroids" (fig. 5.28 below), before returning to a sacred chant for Changó over a *bembé* style (see fig. 5.10). The final finish is a unison soli with the entire band.

IRAKERE'S "SIGNATURE GROOVE"

It might be possible to synthesize the blending of traditional folkloric and popular styles that resulted within Irakere's trajectory as a band, but in reality, each rhythm section iteration over the years contributed such distinct elements that it would require multiple volumes like this one to fully appreciate the scope of what went into this mix. It is clear that the "morphing" of many styles and genres early on produced a conceptual way of playing in the band—and with many groups since—that has more to do with phrasing and individual chops than specific patterns or styles.[33] Taking a snapshot of any Irakere tune with an uptempo feel, and you find a blend of multiple genres all existing at once. To finalize this chapter, we present the best attempt at summarizing Irakere's signature groove from its early incarnation (in the early 1970s), that led to the sound eventually acknowledged as *timba* (fig. 5.28):

5.28 - Primordial Groove (Rumba Clave 2-3)*

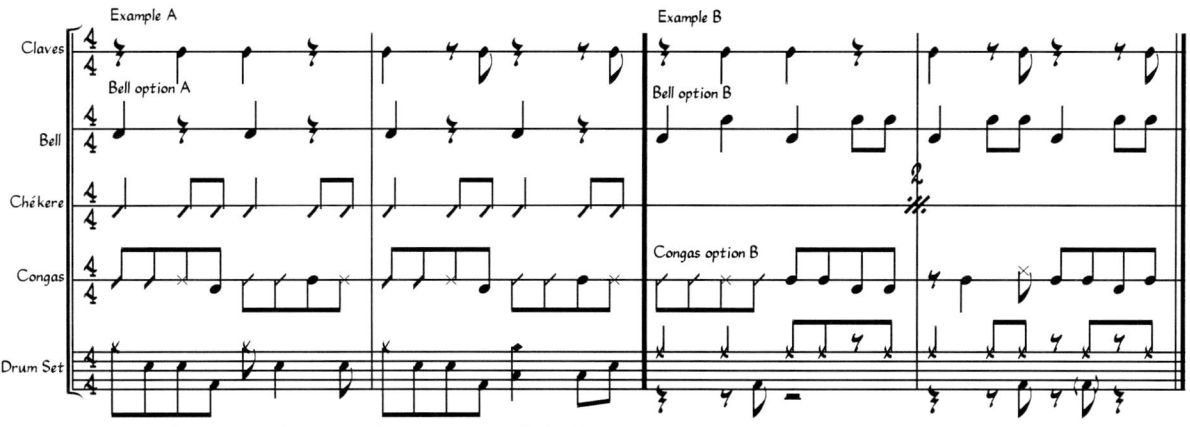

*As with most folkloric and popular styles, the drumming patterns are fluid and highly improvisational. The drummer may mount a cowbell to the bassdrum and play either pattern notated above.

The next chapter highlights analyses of eleven compositions and arrangements penned by Chucho Valdés, some dating back before the emergence of Irakere as an ensemble. After the summation and analysis of these works, we present condensed scores of the arrangements as performed by the band, enabling further study and exploration.

• • •

---

[33] As noted previously, the musical amalgam of styles that became Irakere's signature groove combined elements of *son, rumba, guaracha,* and *songo,* and could be justified as an early example of *timba*. Many times, the stylistic classification given to certain songs using this mixed groove was noted as *son-batá*.

The Songs   Chapter 6

"It is a rare event indeed where one experiences a true artist speaking pure music. Such [is] the work of Valdés." – Yochanan Sebastian Winston

"(Valdés') mastery as composer and player is on full display: an encyclopedic vocabulary of Afro-Cuban rhythms and an expansive palette that includes all manner of modern jazz as well as traditional classical repertoire." – Boston Globe

• • •

In this chapter we present eleven of Chucho's compositions, three of which predate the formation of Irakere, but were later included in the band's repertoire. The goal here is to provide context and useful information on each piece so that it might be interpreted (as well as appreciated) with a high degree of authenticity, and also provide anecdotal references that will hopefully inspire and enlighten. After a brief summation, Chucho adds his commentary and provides fascinating backstory on the work, followed by a mini analysis with essential details, including rhythmical style(s) used, clave direction, form, tempo, and other pertinent information. Specific recordings are cited, including those with versions by other artists, and all of these can be found in Appendix C ("Referenced Audio Recordings").

"Mambo Influenciado" (1963) was composed while Chucho, at age 22, was a member of the Orquesta del Teatro Musical de la Habana (OTM), and recorded with his Combo in 1964 on the album *Jazz Nocturno*, his first recording as a leader. The instrumentation was also dramatically different from the combo or big band ensembles of the time. It was during the many jam sessions and open workshops after the OTM rehearsals that Chucho and his fellow band members would experiment and try out new repertoire, so when he was offered the chance to record his first album, he selected his fellow "jazz-heads" from the orchestra to form the combo, including Paquito D'Rivera (alto sax & clarinet), Julio Vento (flute), Alberto "El Men" Giral (valve trombone), Carlos Emilio Morales (electric guitar), Enrique "Kiki" Hernández (bass), Emilio del Monte (drums), and of course, Chucho on piano. The original tempo was fairly moderate, and over time, as the tune was adopted as a standard, it began to be performed at much faster tempi.

An excellent solo piano rendition was recorded for Finnish label Love Records in 1977, and released by the Cuban Egrem label in 1979 as *Piano 1*. Perhaps the most beautiful rendition is the version recorded for the Messidor label on the album *Lucumí Piano Solo* (1988). The tune has been covered quite a bit, including a lightning-fast version by Arturo Sandoval and Chucho on their Quartet album *Straight Ahead*, and a sizzling 2006 big band arrangement by Cuban pianist Hilario Durán on the album *From the Heart* featuring Paquito D'Rivera and Horacio "El Negro" Hernández. The bop-infused melody is a definite departure from the *clave* based *son* styles of the day, and could easily be swung, but holds its own perfectly well in the straight-eighth feel as a minor blues. A favorite played at virtually all Latin jazz jam sessions, "Mambo Influenciado" was one of the first post-revolutionary hybrids of jazz and Cuban music to be recorded on the island, and as such, did not receive much "official" attention (meaning, it was not played on the radio). However, five decades later it has endured as one of Chucho's greatest gifts to the Afro-Cuban jazz canon.

"When I brought it to the band, it felt new and different, innovative and refreshing, and definitely necessary for us to create our own sound (apart from the OTM). It became a favorite among the band members as well as others who heard it and also started to play it. Eventually, students at the Escuela

Nacional de Arte[1] started to use it for applied lessons in improvisation, and it became something of a local standard. My most important inspiration for this song was actually Horace Silver's 'Soulville' (from *The Stylings of Silver*, Blue Note, 1957) —check out the end of that tune and you'll see I ended up borrowing a little fragment of that for the end of my piece! It wasn't a conscious thing; Silver's tune was definitely stuck in my head as I was developing my song, but it sure worked out well."

Basic Analysis:
- Form: minor blues
- Key: D-minor
- Solos: over form
- Rhythmical style: *guaracha*
- Clave direction: 2-3
- Tempo (bpm): ranges from 145 to 190
- Notes: four-measure intro is sometimes repeated two times
- Cited recordings: Chucho Valdés y su Combo. *Jazz Nocturno* (Areito, 1964); Chucho Valdés. *Piano 1* (Egrem, 1979); Chucho Valdés. *Lucumí Piano Solo* (Messidor, 1988); Arturo Sandoval & Chucho Valdés Quartet. *Straight Ahead* (Jazz House, 1988); Hilario Durán, *From the Heart* (Alma, 2006).

"Misa Negra" (composed in 1969), is known by many for the recording from the Montreux Jazz Festival in 1978, which, as author/musician Leonardo Acosta put it, is "17:36 minutes of Afro-Cuban polyrhythm, brilliant horn passages, and impressive solos, particularly the extended acoustic piano solo by Chucho."[2] Certainly one of the band's most dramatic and epic suites, "Misa Negra" was composed well before Irakere was formed, while Chucho was a member of the Orquesta Cubana de Música Moderna (OCMM). A recording of its debut in Warsaw in 1970 with his Quinteto Cubano de Jazz (an offshoot of the OCMM) may be lurking about on hard-to-find vinyl, but the definitive performance was the groundbreaking concert at Montreux, which was subsequently included on the band's Grammy-winning album for Columbia Records, (reissued in 1994 as *The Best of Irakere*). Irakere recorded a studio version in Germany for the Messidor label in 1987 (*Misa Negra),* but the live performance from Montreux is unquestionably the definitive version.

The "Black Mass" is a masterful combination of sacred and secular elements, highlighting Chucho's hard-bop tendencies wrapped in powerful African rhythm, and features every weapon in the Irakere arsenal, from spellbinding and torrid grooves to lilting and moving melodies, and exquisite solos by Chucho as well as Paquito D'Rivera (alto sax), Arturo Sandoval (trumpet), Carlos Emilio Morales (guitar), and Jorge Alfonso "El Niño" (congas). Much of the transcription included here leaves significant passages open for musical experimentation and creativity, as this was a cornerstone of Irakere's methodology when they were evolving the piece from its original, scaled-down form. Among the highlights of the piece is a praise song to Yoruban goddess Yemayá, one of several climactic moments, featuring the powerful lead vocals of Oscar Valdés and virtually the entire band singing the choral response. It is precisely the collaborative nature of the band that contributed to the success of this work and so many others.

---

[1] Cuba's National School of Art, also known as "la ENA."
[2] Acosta, Leonardo. *Cubano Be, Cubano Bop*, p. 217.

The Songs — Chapter 6

"I was always interested in the fusion of sacred African chants with jazz, and blending those ideas with Cuban percussion, especially the batá drums. Going back to Bebo, in the late 1940s/early 50s he had created a new fusion of Cuban *son* with the batá, called the *batanga* (considered a precursor to the *mambo*). My dad created this amazing Afro-Cuban band, and he worked with one particular batá drummer named Trinidad Torregosa who played with him; Torregosa was the one who added the sacred rhythms to the rhythm section, and Bebo's band was one of the first popular groups to do that.[3] Jumping ahead to the conceptual idea for Irakere, I thought I could reinvent this notion and make it my own. As I began developing my vision, I had listened to several spiritual masses, in particular a praise song known as 'La Luz Redentora' (Redemptive Light),[4] which I really loved. At the same time, I was greatly inspired by an album of Charles Lloyd's called *Forest Flower* (recorded live at Monterey Jazz Festival in 1965) that was so free, so inspiring. My goal was to blend all of those influences together, and that is when I composed 'Misa Negra.' The first version didn't have the batá drums, but it did have the free jazz feeling, and an instrumental adaptation of the spiritual. Once Irakere was formed, I worked with Oscar (Valdés) to adopt the African chants, and combine them with free jazz and the sacred batá rhythms. Since we had a drummer and two other percussionists, Oscar suggested we use all three batá drums.[5] Oscar had great knowledge of the Afro-Cuban religious traditions, the many rhythms and chants. I didn't have all of that information, so Oscar was really the one who enriched the concept of the group by bringing in all of these traditions. We collaborated together and experimented. Our rehearsals were constant explorations; in the beginning we never came into the rehearsals with fully conceived arrangements. For example, Carlos (del Puerto) would come up with a bass line that complemented the batá rhythm, and I would create harmonic voicings that would support and enrich the melodies of the chants, but all of the horn arrangements I would usually write out. In reality, every member of the band contributed something, even later on when the arrangements were more fully formed. And when we threw in those African sacred chants for Yemayá, the entire crowd would go nuts! The combination of all of those elements together was very moving, very powerful, especially for the Cuban audience."

Basic Analysis:
- Form: suite in four movements: I. *Rezo* (prayer) II. *Acercamiento* (approach) III. *Llegada y Desarrollo* (arrival and development) IV. *Despedida* (farewell)
- Key: F-minor
- Solos: alto sax, piano, guitar, congas, trumpet (plus lead vocal feature at letter 'G')
- Rhythmical style(s): 'A' section is a *son*; 'E' section is a fast 6/8 *bembé*; 'I' section is *Iyesá*; 'J' section is fast *guaracha*
- Clave direction: multiple, using both 6/8 and *rumba clave*
- Tempo (bpm): ranges from 115 to over 230
- Notes: the semi-rubato intro simulates an Afro-Cuban spiritual and is often conducted; the praise song at letter 'E' is for the *orisha* Yemayá, goddess of the sea, and begins with a *rezo* (prayer or invocation), followed by the chant: "Awoyó a e, awoyó."
- Cited recordings: *Irakere* (Columbia, 1978 - reissued as *The Best of Irakere* (Columbia, 1994); *Misa Negra* (Messidor, 1987).

---

[3] One of the first documented uses of batá drums in a popular context is thought to have taken place in 1936 at the Tropicana Night Club with Gilberto Valdés, no relation to Chucho.
[4] "La Luz Redentora" is something akin to a Cuban spiritual, often used in masses combining Christian hymns with African drumming and spirit ancestor worship.
[5] *Conguero* Jorge Alfonso 'El Niño' and either drummer Enrique Plá or percussionist Armando Cuervo would play the smaller drums, the Itótele and the Okónkolo (respectively), while Oscar played the lead Iyá drum.

CHAPTER 6 — THE SONGS

"Neurosis" (1972) — Originally recorded with Chucho's trio in 1972 on the album *Jazz Batá*, (with Carlos del Puerto on bass and Oscar Valdés on percussion), "Neurosis" is based on the "A" section of the Gershwin tune "I Got Rhythm." The sparseness of the trio version is evident, primarily due to the absence of a drum set, resulting in the more experimental sound of Oscar's playing around with various percussion instruments within the tune. Chucho's blues-tinged bop lines are flawless, even if the sound quality—and the piano upon which he played them—were not. *Jazz Batá* has been out of print for some time, but is certainly an important document of Chucho's pianistic as well as compositional evolution.[6] Subsequent versions featured an extended the A section during solos, with the incorporation of the B section (bridge) often on cue, alternating between fast *son* and swing feel. "Neurosis" changes *clave* direction multiple times, and the 'A' section can also be played using a *clave*-neutral, almost *bomba* or *makuta*-like groove.[7] On the live recording at Ronnie Scott's, Chucho quotes Sonny Rollins' "Oleo" and Joe Zawinul's "Birdland" during his piano solo, much to the thrill of the jazz-loving audience.

"The first recorded version of the tune was on *Jazz Batá* with Carlos and Oscar. This was a drummer-less trio, and since we were only three, Oscar put together sort of a 'percussion rack' of multiple instruments and 'toys' so he could create more variety of textures. This might have been the first time this had been done in Cuba, as far as I can tell. I told him, 'Let's create a trio without drums but add one batá drum, congas and other hand percussion,' so we could find another sonority. The song was basically just the main riff over an 8-bar vamp, similar to the A section of 'I Got Rhythm' but with more of a bluesy feel or spirit, although not a 12-bar blues idea either. On that first recording, I played the head (after a layered intro of congas and bass line), and the second time through I banged out clusters on the piano like a drummer, which basically serves as a bridge. There was something about the tune that also had a New Orleans feel to it. Then, in later versions, I decided to add the bridge from 'I Got Rhythm,' using that harmonic progression to create more contrast, ultimately resulting in an AABA form, and making it more satisfying compositionally. At the same time, I still wanted it to feel free and loose, so Carlos (del Puerto) started to create more bass variations to break away from the standard *tumbao* rhythm, and I would have the horn players solo over the extended A section, sometimes letting them go 'out there.' In my head, I was trying to create something like free jazz, but I called it 'free *son*' instead! This was a time when I was seriously into Keith Jarrett and Charles Lloyd, and looking back, even the first recorded version was pretty ahead of its time for a Latin jazz record. On later recordings, I would throw in a quote here and there during my solo of different standards, such as 'Oleo.' Actually, for the Ronnie Scott's recording, we started off with a bass vamp (over a dorian minor chord) and got into this elaborate break and horn riff before introducing the main theme. (This is the version represented here.) Over the years since I first recorded it, I made several modifications, but the aspect I most want to preserve is the free-*son* idea."

---

[6] The contents of *Jazz Batá* are included in a 2017 Apple Music compilation reissued as *Lo Mejor de Chucho Valdés*.
[7] The *bomba* is an Afro-Puerto Rican style and the *makuta* is Afro-Cuban folk music, both of Bantú origin.

The Songs CHAPTER 6

Basic Analysis:
- Form: modified "Rhythm changes" (AABA, but the 'B' can be on cue)
- Key: F-Major
- Solos: over form, or over open 'A' with 'B' played on cue, or free over tonic chord
- Rhythmical style(s): hybrid of fast *son* or *guaracha* alternating with swing
- Clave direction: multiple
- Tempo (bpm): half-note = 122 or faster
- Notes: 'A' section can be played over a clave-neutral feel, such as *makuta* or calypso style, alternating with swing for the 'B' section
- Cited recordings: Chucho Valdés Trio. *Jazz Batá* (Areito, 1974); Irakere. *The Legendary Irakere in London* (Jazz House, 1988); Irakere. ¡Afrocubanismo Live! (Bembe, 1996); Chucho Valdés. *Lo Mejor de Chucho Valdés* (Apple Music, 2017).

"Bacalao Con Pan" (1973) is considered Irakere's first major hit, and was originally credited on the album notes to Raúl Valdés (Chucho's brother), even though Chucho is the author. Appearing on the group's debut album, *Grupo Irakere* (1974), the genre is listed as a "son batá" —most Cuban releases indicate the specific rhythmic style of the tunes on the liner notes, but this particular term was actually something Chucho and the band members agreed on since the fusion of *son*, *rumba* and *batá* rhythms was brand new. Chucho views the rhythmical groove they came up with as a critical predecessor to the contemporary *timba* developed during the 90s. Another important innovation with this tune was the effect of the **breakdown** midway through, with the piano vamping on an extended *montuno* while the percussion stops, followed by a complex break, in Cuban music referred to as a "cierre." The transition from the breakdown back to the basic groove serves as an energy boost, akin to shifting into overdrive...in a high-performance vehicle! This was unprecedented in Cuban music until this piece came about. Furthermore, bassist Carlos del Puerto began to play a percussive figure on the electric bass during the breakdown that simulated the bass drum (known as the **bombo**) in a Cuban *conga de comparsa* rhythm, striking all four strings on the fretboard, then sliding up the neck to create a glissando effect. As noted in our overview of Cuban music in Chapter I, this too, would become an essential technique of modern-day *timba* performance practice.

"I started experimenting with the idea for 'Bacalao Con Pan' in late 1972, and it was recorded at EGREM Studios in Havana in 1973 (and released in 1974). Since we were still not an 'officially sanctioned' group by the Ministry of Culture, they wouldn't play the song on the radio. Meanwhile, we went to Santiago de Cuba on a brief tour and played it there, and people went crazy for it. We took the original recording to a radio DJ there named Rodulfo Bayán, and he played it as part of a program highlighting the *carnavales*, making it sort of an official theme song. When a Havana radio DJ heard that broadcast, he decided to play our recording, and that's when 'Bacalao Con Pan' became a hit, even though people didn't know who we were! Now, I have to say that the original intention of the song was to please the dancing public, and when I first brought it to the rehearsal, the band members seemed fine with it. But once we went into the studio to record it, that's when some of the members reacted negatively, saying we were placating to the dancing crowd instead of playing more serious music. Even the engineer (Tony López) suggested erasing it! He said, 'How can serious musicians like you play this kind of thing?'[8] The rejection of the tune by some of the players, especially Paquito (D'Rivera), was understandable of course. But for me, the proof was in the crowd's reaction. No matter where we played and what we played, this was the tune that got the biggest reaction, especially at venues like the Salón Mambí of the Tropicana. 'Bacalao' was the hit, and we had to play it. The best barometer of success for our repertoire was when Paquito and Arturo (Sandoval) would reject a given song; if they hated it, I pretty much knew it would be a hit!

The structure of 'Bacalao' started out as a simple groove, with the instrumental melody, the bop riffs, the batá rhythm (specifically, the *Iyesá* rhythm), and that funky Blood Sweat & Tears kind of sound. The original title of the instrumental piece was 'Habaneco,' but we realized we needed some kind of simple chorus so Oscar could improvise and reach the crowd, so Carlos (del Puerto) says, 'Just make up anything simple, it doesn't matter what we say; how about 'bacalao con pan?!' And that's how the tune came together. By adding those extended *montunos* and the breakdown, with Carlos hitting on the electric bass guitar like a drum, then the band coming back in even stronger, that was incredibly powerful. Of course in the long run, we realized it was precisely this combination of experimentation, high level arranging and playing, and danceability, that created the perfect recipe for Irakere. I certainly didn't enjoy seeing Paquito and Arturo suffer when we focused on playing the more danceable stuff, since their suffering affected me as well. But the will of the people was clear, and we needed to find a balance between all of those sonorities. We had a series of dance tunes that were very successful. Sometimes we rehearsed at neighborhood high schools, and we knew that if the students stopped to listen to what we were playing at any given moment, that tune was probably going to be our next hit. The jazz fans appreciated the bebop riffs we would throw into the middle of these dance tunes, the classic lines of Dizzy's, for example, so they could latch onto that. The secret link, of course, was finding a balanced repertoire that could satisfy both the dancing crowd and the more intellectual, jazz-loving crowd."

Basic Analysis:
- Form: ABC, followed by extended *montuno* section
- Key: G-minor
- Solos: over *montuno* section
- Rhythmical style: *son-batá* (this piece is considered the first *timba* prototype, and uses the *Iyesá* batá rhythm throughout most of the song)
- Clave direction: 2-3 *rumba clave*
- Tempo (bpm): ranges from 145 to 190
- Notes: the breakdown often features the piano by itself, or can be combined with a minimal percussion groove known as *bota*[9]
- Cited recording: *Grupo Irakere* (Areito, 1974).

---

[8] Chucho refers to the comments made by the engineer and some of the band members citing this "lightweight" repertoire as "musiquita," literally meaning "little music."
[9] The *bota* technique was developed by Los Van Van percussionists Changuito and El Yulo, wherein the conga player marks the time with a pattern that emphasizes the heel-toe movements, and the drummer usually plays a pattern highlighting the bass drum. This technique became a main staple of contemporary *timba* playing.

THE SONGS

CHAPTER 6

Chucho Valdés with vintage gear, ca 1980. AUTHOR'S COLLECTION

"Aguanile Bonkó" (1978) — Recorded live both for its debut in May of 1978 in Havana (at the 12 y 23 Theater), as well as the subsequent performances at the Newport Jazz Festival in New York and Montreux Jazz Festival in Switzerland[10], this piece is, perhaps, the ideal representation of the musical amalgam that is Irakere. The title is a hybrid of Yoruba (*lucumi*) and Efik words: "aguanile" or "awá ni'lé" in Yoruba roughly translated means "we arrive," and "bonkó" is a term from the Abakuá society meaning "friend" or "brother."[11] With a combination of gritty synths, disco-tinged horn lines, Afro-Cuban *rumba* vocals, crackling percussion grooves laden with a backbeat, and a blazing free-jazz tenor saxophone solo by Carlos Averhoff, this is one of Chucho's most frenetic and grooving works for the band. The influence of American supergroup Blood, Sweat & Tears is clearly present throughout,[12] not only for the sonorities of the now-vintage gear and Chucho's post-bop Fender Rhodes voicings, but the epic and relentless musical roller coaster ride of emotions for the listener. The principal chorus, structured within a *rumba-guaguancó* style, features constant call-and-response improvisation by the vocalist (Oscar Valdés), and provides the perfect tapestry for Averhoff to take things well outside. The main chord progression centers around a Phrygian cadence, a common feature of many Afro-Cuban *rumbas*, but the tenor solo section stays in one modal space, allowing the soloist to explore uncharted territory.

---

[10] Chucho asserts that the Montreux recordings were superior in sound quality to those from the Carnegie Hall performance, and thus were the ones chosen for the GRAMMY-winning Columbia recording. He also notes that the debut performance of "Aguanile Bonkó" at the 12 y 23 Theater was well-received by the public. That version can be heard on *Selección de Éxitos 1973-1978* (Areito), reissued by Egrem as *Recital en Teatro 12 y 23*.

[11] The Efik term *bonkó* is the name for the lead drum in the sacred Abakuá tradition (the *bonkó enchemiyá*), but the word has evolved in a more colloquial sense, and is typically accepted as a fraternal salute meaning, "brother." Mason, p. 90, Miller, p. 23, and Vaughan, p. 153.

[12] Chucho notes his inspiration of the horn-drum break in the Blood, Sweat & Tears classic song "Spinning Wheel."

Chapter 6 — The Songs

"I can't remember which song came right before 'Aguanile' during the Montreux Jazz performance, but the audience was giving us an ovation and clapping in such a perfectly steady tempo, that we used that to count off the tune. It was marvelous! The opening keyboard and bass line feels just like a Blood, Sweat & Tears groove, and I even incorporated that initial drum break from their song 'Spinning Wheel' into the first section of the tune. 'Aguanile' was totally meant for Oscar to sing. The song would have never worked without him, and in fact, we never played it once he left the band. And once Averhoff started soloing, we just let him run free. He had been listening to a lot of Michael Brecker in those days, and even in a tune that attracted the dancers, we still were able to 'get away' with a little free jazz! What is interesting is that the first live performance we did of the song was also a pretty decent recording (it is featured on a recent reissue of *Recital en Teatro 12 y 23*), and the crowd embraced it right away. It was like a magnet...so catchy."

Basic Analysis:
- Form: disco head with *rumba* style refrain
- Key: D-minor
- Solos: over *montuno* section
- Rhythmical style(s): disco-funk, *songo-timba*
- Clave direction: 2-3 *rumba* clave (notated 1 clave per measure, 16th-note subdivisions)
- Tempo (bpm): 136
- Notes: sax solos over tonic minor chord in free-jazz style
- Cited recordings: *Irakere* (Columbia, 1978 - reissued as *The Best of Irakere* (Columbia, 1994); *Selección de Éxitos 1973-1978* (Areito, 1981 - reissued as *Recital en Teatro 12 y 23*, Egrem, 2011).

Claudia (1978) — Another standard in Afro-Cuban jazz, and a beautiful *bolero* composed during a time where the romantic genre was certainly not in vogue among younger Cubans, "Claudia" was actually a commission of sorts by one of Chucho's friends who worked in the Ministry of Culture, and was released on Irakere's second Columbia recording, *Irakere 2* (1980). Its melodic simplicity and harmonically rich texture was the perfect platform to showcase Arturo Sandoval's masterful trumpet playing, and it has since been covered by a number of artists, including Sandoval as well as fellow Irakere alumnus, Paquito D'Rivera. There is a written rubato introduction that is seldom played, but was recorded by Sandoval on his first solo album *Turi* (1981) shortly before he left Irakere, with Chucho's exquisite arrangement. There are a few subsequent studio and live versions by Chucho with Irakere as well as smaller ensembles, and two excellent versions of "Claudia" appear on the Arturo-Chucho Quartet album *Straight Ahead* (Jazz House,1988), as well as Irakere's 1993 recording, *Live at Ronnie Scott's*.

"When we were getting ready for our first US tour in 1978, a friend of mine, Vice Minister of Culture Emilio Quesada, was a serious music collector and fan, and very knowledgeable about all kinds of music. He was recently married, and he and his wife had a 3-year-old daughter named Claudia. He asked me one day to write something for her, and I really didn't want to do anything like a lullaby. As I conceived the melody, I was really thinking more about the image of a woman, with a more romantic mood. So a *bolero* made perfect sense to me, using a simple melody over some nice chords. I brought it to the band and we tried it one evening while Emilio was there, and I told him I'd name it after his daughter if he liked it. Well, he did! The tune was really a great feature for Arturo (Sandoval). There is a lovely introduction that hardly anyone ever plays, mainly because it has some seriously high notes. Arturo recorded it on his album *Turi,* that I arranged for him (in 1981). I actually like the intro

The Songs   Chapter 6

better than the main melody! When Irakere first recorded it while we were in New York, we didn't use the intro, and the producers also added a string section to the tune after we left the studio. We also recorded it in 1991 at Ronnie Scott's in London (on the album *Live at Ronnie Scott's*, released in 1993), and used the intro part, and Paquito (D'Rivera) and Arturo played it together on their Messidor recording, *Reunion* (1992), which is also very nice; but I think Arturo's version (from *Turi*) is the best, quite frankly. Many years later, I ran into Emilio and his daughter, and I sat down at the piano and played the piece for her."

Basic Analysis:
- Form: AAB
- Key: G-minor
- Solos: over form
- Rhythmical style: *bolero* (the live version morphs into a funky double-time groove during the vamp out)
- Clave direction: N/A (*boleros* are usually *clave*-neutral)
- Tempo (bpm): 95-100
- Notes: piano often begins with rubato solo, followed by trumpet melody intro (also rubato), before piano initiates intro groove.
- Cited recordings: *Irakere 2* (Columbia, 1980); Arturo Sandoval. *Turi* (Areito, 1981); Arturo Sandoval & Chucho Valdés Quartet. *Straight Ahead* (Jazz House, 1988); Paquito D'Rivera & Arturo Sandoval. *Reunion* (Messidor, 1992); Irakere. *Live at Ronnie Scott's* (World Pacific, 1993).

Calzada del Cerro (1983) — The name of a the three-kilometer boulevard in the Havana neighborhood where Chucho resided for over 17 years, the Calzada del Cerro is listed on the World Monuments Fund watchlist for its historic characteristics, citing the district as "a one-time summer retreat for Havana's Creole aristocracy (where) the elite built classical-styled mansions along the thoroughfare, each more Italianate than the next."[13] In complete contrast to this analysis of 19th century Havana idealism, the grit of the now dilapidated Cerro neighborhood was what Chucho loved the most, equating it in some ways to the streets of Harlem. His tune was inspired by his years spent walking the streets, soaking up the sounds and the local colors, and is at the same time a tribute to another pianist who marked a critical place in the Latin jazz lexicon, Clare Fischer, and his standard cha-cha-chá, "Morning." Chucho's tune is, virtually, a sound-alike in structure and texture, although without the AABA form of "Morning," but the melody is equally catchy. On the song's debut recording (*Calzada Del Cerro*, 1983), there is an exquisite guitar solo by Carlos Emilio Morales, often heralded as the "Wes Montgomery of Cuba," although his personal favorite was Tal Farlow.[14] Among the characteristics of this period in Irakere's repertoire was Chucho's use of the Yamaha CP-70 electric grand piano, and on this tune, he also breaks out a Vocoder and takes a remarkable chordal-voice solo, which may be the first time in Cuba that anyone had used that particular piece of equipment.

---

[13] "Calzada Del Cerro." World Monuments Fund. Web. 21 June 2017.
[14] Carlos Emilio was also a huge fan of Barney Kessel. Chucho considers Carlos the greatest Cuban jazz guitarist ever.

In 1990, Tito Puente recorded a version of it on his Concord Picante release, *Goza Mi Timbal*, and opted to change the title of the song to "Cha-cha-chá" given his concern that the non-Spanish-speaking audience might not get it.[15] Irakere's recording featured the second iteration of the band, with recent addition Germán Velasco on the alto sax. But original altoist Paquito D'Rivera would eventually record "Calzada" in 1995 (at Fantasy Studios), after a fortuitous reunion in San Francisco prompted RMM Records to document the historic gathering of not only the former Irakere band mates, but Chucho's father, Bebo Valdés, as well. The song was featured on the album entitled *Paquito D'Rivera Presents Cuba Jazz*, and later reissued on a compilation called *¡Con Mucho Ritmo! The Very Best of TropiJazz* on the Verve label in 2005.[16]

"The Cerro neighborhood was my home in Havana for over 17 years, and Calzada del Cerro is the main boulevard, where I spent many hours walking. I didn't have a car during those years, so I walked everywhere! And on this tune there is a tremendous influence from Clare Fischer, with a very similar structure to his song 'Morning.'[17] I actually bought Clare's book with all of those amazing transcriptions.[18] It's super interesting, written both in traditional notation and with chord symbols, which is extremely helpful. Now the Cerro neighborhood was, of course, my main inspiration for writing this piece. Cerro is a very lively and popular neighborhood in Havana, with plenty of 'street culture,' humor and intensity, working class, down-to-earth people. Plenty of popular slang comes from this neighborhood, what we refer to as 'cubanía' when they talk; in many ways it feels like Harlem to me. Those folks are major music-lovers and Irakere fans!" (Chucho uses the clever phrase, "irakerísticos" to accentuate his point.)

Basic Analysis:
- Form: AB
- Key: G-minor
- Solos: over form
- Rhythmical style: *cha-cha-chá* (the feel is more of a *son-montuno*)
- Clave direction: (*cha-cha-chás* are generally in 2-3 *clave*, but the pattern is implied)
- Tempo (bpm): 125
- Notes: Chucho's use of a Vocoder was fairly groundbreaking in Cuba in 1983
- Cited recordings: Irakere. *Calzada del Cerro* (Areito, 1983); Tito Puente. *Goza Mi Timbal* (Concord Picante, 1990); *Paquito D'Rivera Presents Cuba Jazz* (RMM, 1995 - reissued as *¡Con Mucho Ritmo! The Very Best of TropiJazz*, Verve, 2005).

---

[15] From the author's conversation with Mr. Puente in studio during the recording of *Goza Mi Timbal* in 1990.
[16] The author was among the co-producers of a reunion concert featuring Chucho and Bebo Valdés, Carlos Santana, and several members of Irakere entitled *Irakere West* at San Francisco's Great American Music Hall in November of 1995. This concert marked the beginning of a rekindling between Chucho and Bebo, and led to a series of recordings and documentary films produced in the US and in Spain, among them, the album with Paquito for RMM Records.
[17] The song was first recorded on Fischer's 1965 album *Manteca* for Pacific Jazz Records.
[18] Fischer, Clare. *Harmonic Exercises for Piano*, Advance Music, 2010.

The Songs

Chapter 6

Miguel "Angá" Díaz, Carlos Santana, and Chucho Valdés at the Great American Musical Hall, San Francisco, November, 1995. PHOTO CREDIT: DAVID GARTEN

"El Tata Cimarrón" (1983) — Also from the 1983 *Calzada Del Cerro* album, "El Tata" opens with a sacred batá rhythm to Babalú Ayé,[19] the Yoruban *orisha* (deity) of smallpox (syncretized with Saint Lazarus), and a spoken word invocation written by Chucho and recited by Oscar Valdés about Tata Cimarrón, an elder runaway slave who escapes into the mountains and defies captivity. This piece represents a cross-pollination between sacred *lucumí* (Yoruba) chants and the quasi-religious *palo* traditions of *bantú* (Congolese) origin in Cuba, a frequent occurrence in Afro-Cuban culture in general. The first few choruses are in Spanish, and the last call-and-response section features a hybrid *bantú-lucumí* praise song to Yoruba deity Changó, "Zarabanda Changó." There is also a well-known song called "Changó Ta Vení" composed in 1947 by Justi Barreto, and this brief chorus is likely a reference to that piece.[20] What makes this piece so compelling (and equally daunting) is the extraordinary mixture of cultural and rhythmical elements, including patterns, references and lyrics. The primary groove can best described as a mixture of *son, rumba, timba* and *songo* combined with *lucumí* batá rhythms. Irakere's signature approach has always been the amalgam of musical languages spoken all at once, as if to say, "it all works together because it comes from the same place."

---

[19] The specific *toque* (batá drum rhythm) used in the song is called Yeguá (or Yewá), and the particular "road" or segment featured here is typically played for the *arará* deity Asojano, who is equated with the *lucumí* deity of Bablú Ayé. This is an example of a cross-pollination between Yoruban and Dahomean sacred traditions in Cuba.

[20] "Changó Ta Vení" was composed in 1947 by percussionist Justi Barreto and covered by many artists including Machito and Celia Cruz. The lyrics are derived from a *bantú* (Congolese) legend in the *palo mayombe* tradition surrounding Zarabanda (or Sarabanda), a mythical king who encounters several obstacles during his voyages through the mountains, which seems a suitable metaphor for the lyrics of "El Tata," a runaway slave who eludes his captors. Changó is the Yoruban orisha in the Regla de Ocha or Santería tradition, and historically is identified as the third king of the Oyo Kingdom in Nigeria. The cross-pollination of *bantú* and *lucumí* mythologies is very common in Afro-Cuban folklore. In the bantú language spoken in Cuba, "tata" means "father," and *cimarrón* is the Spanish word for runaway slave (or maroon). Cabrera, Ortiz, León, etc.

The main head alternates between *son* and *rumba clave* at the A section, and the song changes *clave* direction multiple times (often, jumping the *clave*) at each subsequent *coro* (chorus), with *coro* #1 in 3-2 clave, *coro* #2 in 2-3, and *coro* #3 in 3-2. "El Tata" is also an example of Chucho's increasing use of synthesizers, with the Roland Jupiter-8 taking center stage. After several iterations of the refrain and repeat of the introduction, there is a dramatic shift with the introduction of a "bridge" with a serious horn soli that modulates away from the original key (C-minor) to an ascending series of suspended chords. It seems to appear out of nowhere, but segües perfectly into a reprise of the introduction before the next refrain, leading to a high-energy trumpet solo. Chucho notes that this piece was another example of how Irakere could pull off such a seemingly overwhelming amount of content and still achieve a convincing level of cohesion. When you are playing for dancers, you need to know how to keep them moving no matter how many bebop riffs or breaks you throw their way!

"Around the time I composed this piece, I had been listening to a **lot** of McCoy (Tyner). That unison line for piano and bass toward the beginning is difficult to play (see fragment below in fig. 6.1), but I thought it would be interesting to start off the tune with an instrumental intro instead of a vocal line or a verse, just like we did with 'Bacalao Con Pan.' So I wrote a melody line for the horns to play, followed by the piano/bass soli between the verses, that way we instrumentalists could enjoy ourselves before the main vocal part came in. The dancers love when the singing starts, and that first chorus was a kicker! 'Saca la(s) mano(s), saca los pies, y saca la cabeza si no te quieres perder' (free your hands, free your feet, and free your head if you don't want to get lost!). Sure, people danced during the instrumental opening, but they really cut loose once the chorus came in after the verses. And boy, the energy would go through the roof! The powerful blending of the African praise songs, the vocal and instrumental solos, the jazz harmony and chord changes...it was about breaking the cycle of the popular dance music, going beyond those limits of call-and-response vocals that we typically hear in Cuban dance music, inserting jazz phrasing, more contemporary chord changes, a sudden instrumental riff or solo, and African chants into this ebb and flow. It was about changing the paradigm for the Cuban public as to what dance music was and could be."

THE SONGS   CHAPTER 6

6.1 - Fragment from 'El Tata Cimarrón'

Basic Analysis:
- Form: Spoken word intro, instrumental intro, piano/bass soli, verse/horn moña, intro repeats, refrain (call-and-response)+horn moña, intro, refrain, bridge, refrain, coda.
- Key: C-minor
- Solos: synth, lead vocals, trumpet
- Rhythmical styles: The opening batá rhythm is a *toque* for Babalú Ayé called *Yewá* (or *Yeguá*), and is played using all three drums. The piano-bass soli features a conga pattern often referred to as "a caballo" (on horseback), a derivative style that became known as *pachanga*, and the main groove is Irakere's signature *songo-timba-rumba-guaguancó* mix (listed as "son-batá" on most recordings). At 6 minutes in, the groove changes to include a different batá rhythm, *chachálokpafúñ*, with only the largest of the drums used (the Iyá) combined with the congas. At around minute 7:20, a 6/8 bell is added on top of the percussion and the drums lay out, hinting at a Bantú *palo* fell, before the drums come back in at 8 min with the signature groove.
- Clave directions: multiple, alternating between *son clave* and *rumba clave* during the verses and main refrain, and **jumping** the clave between the vocal section and the horn *moña* (horn shout); 6/8 *clave* is also used during the "Zarabanda Changó" chorus.
- Tempo (bpm): 130
- Notes: Given the multiple *clave* changes and jumps, this tune is recommended for advanced rhythm section players!
- Cited recordings: Irakere. *Calzada del Cerro* (Areito, 1983)

CHAPTER 6 — THE SONGS

"Lo Que Va a Pasar" (1985) — An example of the danceable half of Irakere's bifurcated repertoire, "Lo Que Va a Pasar" is another crowd-pleaser, composed during the band's second iteration in the 1980s. Like most of their dance-centric tunes, "Lo Que Va a Pasar" blends torrid, bop-infused horn lines and rapid-fire percussion breaks with a simple, catchy chorus. As with "Bacalao Con Pan" back in the 70s, this song began as an instrumental piece and was later modified with a vocal refrain. It was José Luis Cortés, aka "El Tosco" (flute and baritone sax), who came up with the infectious chorus, "Tú verás lo que va a pasar," after Chucho was stuck trying to come up with a lyric. El Tosco would foment his own leadership skills a few years later when he went on to form N.G. La Banda with several other Irakere horn players who followed his exodus. "Lo Que Va a Pasar" is the perfect example of the types of tunes NG would become known for in the 90s, clearly marking the importance of Tosco's tenure with Irakere, as well as his prior years with super-group Los Van Van during the 1970s. A key element introduced in this tune became a baseline in virtually all of *timba*: the insertion (once again) of a breakdown. It is during this section that the lead vocalist engages with the crowd and gets everyone clapping the *clave* (or in this case, a more intricate rhythm). A direct influence from American funk and the legacy of James Brown and others, the inclusion of the breakdown is an opportunity to get the audience involved, and also serves to "reset" the groove for an even more powerful refrain. It can be argued, therefore, that this song was another predecessor of the infectious *timba* genre that would be the cornerstone of 90s dance music in Cuba.[21]

The challenge for students of Afro-Cuban music lies in the multiple shifts in *clave* direction, including a jump between the introduction and the A section (as noted in the preceding song). Although no *clave* pattern is actually played during the *cumbia*-inspired intro, the melody clearly feels 3-2, but instead, the rhythmical emphasis is on the backbeat, as drummer Enrique Plá hits the high-hat emphatically on beats 2 and 4, creating a sort of "*clave* limbo." Following the break to set up the horn pick-up into letter A, the *clave* direction shifts to 2-3, which signals a literal jump in direction. As discussed previously (in Chapter II), it is a common trend in contemporary Cuban dance music to shift or jump *clave* direction midway through, but only when there is a break or a stop in the groove, which is exactly what happens here. And quite a fierce break it is, with a chromatic 8th-note triplet unison scale by the horns and piano, leading to a dramatic stop on beats 2+ and 3. Upon the return to the intro, the *clave* direction switches back to 3-2, which perfectly sets up the first *coro* (refrain), and now creates an even funkier groove by utilizing *rumba clave*. Another interesting tidbit is the insertion of a quote from the Bill Withers tune, "Just The Two of Us" (recorded in 1980 by Withers and Grover Washington Jr.), but rhythmically altered to line up with the 3-2 *clave* direction to make it feel Cuban. No doubt that Chucho was having fun with this tune, no matter how crazy the *clave* issues became!

"My lyric writing is pretty limited, so for this tune I really focused on the intro and the melody. Plus, I wanted to do something a little different rhythmically and decided to give it this South American flavor, sort of like a *cumbia*.[22] At first we couldn't find a chorus part, so El Tosco was the one who came up with it, just like what happened with 'Bacalao Con Pan.' The crowd would always go crazy when the vocals come in anyway, which is typical for dance music in Cuba, so once the refrain started, the energy would go ballistic. Now, the issue with the *clave* direction at the beginning is this: I **feel** the *clave* and know intuitively how the rhythm should line up, but I don't necessarily manage it well. So in

---

[21] See Chapter V.
[22] The *cumbia* is a folkloric genre originating in the Atlantic Coast of Colombia, and is one of the most popular styles heard throughout South and Central America.

THE SONGS CHAPTER 6

this tune, the intro feels 3-2, even though the *clave* pattern is not literally played. Once the A section comes in, we needed to switch (or jump) the *clave* to 2-3 to align correctly with the instrumental melody, so the only way to do that is to flip the direction. Doing it during a break is the best way of course, and that's what happened in this song, but there are several times where the *clave* would be *montado* (crossed), so we needed to adjust again, and play the chorus in 3-2 direction. Oh, and by the way, the song ended up being used in the early 90s by a Brazilian *telenovela* (soap opera)![23] I can't remember exactly the first time we played the song, but I do know it was at a theater in Havana. However, the first recording was done live at Ronnie Scott's (released in 1988)."

Basic Analysis:
- Form: Intro, ABAC, intro, refrain (call-and-response), D section (perc solos), E (moña) plus flute solo, breakdown (with quote from "Just The Two of Us"), F (chorus + moña), Intro and break
- Key: A-minor
- Solos: timbales, flute
- Rhythmical style: *timba*
- Clave direction: implied 3-2 clave during intro, 2-3 for A section, 3-2 for refrain
- Tempo (bpm): 218
- Notes: The intro has a subtle hint of a Colombian *cumbia* feel, and the *clave* direction is only implied, not literally played
- Cited recordings: Irakere. *The Legendary Irakere in London* (Jazz House, 1988).

"Anabis" (1988) - First recorded live at Ronnie Scott's in 1989 (and released in 1991 on *Felicidad*), "Anabis" originally debuted in Havana in 1988. There are two other live versions, one with Irakere in Canada in 1994 (on the album *¡Afrocubanismo Live!* released by Bembé Records), and the other in 2000 with Chucho's Quartet at the Village Vanguard in New York (on the Blue Note label). The fiery tempo and premeditated use of mixed meter during the percussion break was something Chucho was intent on doing with this piece, in particular to showcase the amazing talent of one of the newest additions to the band, percussionist Miguel "Angá" Diaz. The opening piano introduction on the live recording is classic Chucho, leading to a meditative modal section in a slow 6/8, with McCoy Tyner-inspired quartal harmonic sensibility. (The simplified version presented here foregos the 6/8 intro.) What follows is a dramatic shift in tempo to the A section, which Chucho sets up with an up-tempo chordal melody. The tune is a welcome feature for his blazing piano work, and with the exception of the live recording at Banff in 1994 (where the horns respond antiphonally to his melodic calls), "Anabis" typically showcases only the rhythm section (with Carlos del Puerto, Oscar Valdés, Miguel "Angá" Diaz and Enrique Plá).

"One of my objectives with this piece was to fully notate the figures and breaks played by the rhythm section, to create a deliberate mix of meters, and provide the percussionists (Plá, Oscar and Angá) with detailed and complex figures to play together, like a type of horn soli, played in unison. (Chucho uses the term *bloque* here to refer to the rhythmically dense figures.) Then for the bridge, we used a fast samba, to create a nice alternative groove to the fast *son* feel of the head. But the main idea of the tune was to orchestrate the percussion breaks as an ensemble, to distinguish this approach from the fills

---

[23] Several of Chucho's songs have been used in Cuban television broadcasts as well.

and ad-libbed things drummers and percussionists normally do. It was also an opportunity to feature Angá, so there is some call-and-response between the piano and the congas before we let him go. After this recording, we basically made this Angá's feature in the set whenever we'd play it live, giving him an extended solo so he could interact with the public and have fun."

Basic Analysis:
- Form: piano fast intro, AABCA, solos over AAB, then C on cue, AAB
- Key: D-minor
- Solos: piano, congas
- Rhythmical styles: slow 6/8 (optional), very fast *guaracha*, *samba*, mixed meter breaks
- Clave direction: 2-3
- Tempo (bpm): 340
- Notes: Lightning fast, breakneck speed, killer mixed meter breaks…not for the faint of heart!
- Cited recordings: Irakere. *Felicidad* (Jazz House, 1991); Irakere. ¡Afrocubanismo Live! (Bembe, 1996); Chucho Valdés. *Live at the Village Vanguard* (Blue Note, 2000).

"San Francisco" (1995) - Released on the Blue Note/Capitol album *Yemayá*, "San Francisco" captures the West Coast Latin jazz spirit, with echoes of the blues, and it was written by Chucho in November of 1995, which was a turning point in many respects, primarily given the fact that Irakere was now transitioning into its fourth iteration. A fortuitous moment emerged that year, when several of us in San Francisco decided to produce a concert of Irakere's music after learning that Chucho was being invited to New York, so we proceeded to coordinate the invitation of several members of the band in order to recreate some of Irakere's classic repertoire. In addition to Chucho, we were thrilled to learn that joining him on the trip would be bassist Carlos del Puerto, guitarist Carlos Emilio Morales, and percussionist Miguel "Angá" Díaz. However, since we knew it would be nearly impossible to perform any of that music without an amazing drummer such as Enrique Plá, we located Horacio "El Negro" Hernández, who had been a part of Gonzalo Rubalcaba's stunning *Grupo Proyecto,* and had left Cuba in 1990. Reserving the classic Great American Music Hall (one of the City's oldest venues) for two nights in November, we set out on an adventure, marketing what would be a historic concert as "Irakere West." The result was not only memorable for the music played on stage those two nights, but also for the combination of personnel assembled together for the first time, taking on the material penned by one of Cuba's most important musicians and composers. In addition, our hope was to surprise Chucho with two very special guests who would join him on stage: guitarist Carlos Santana, and Chucho's dear father, Bebo Valdés, the latter who had been living in Sweden.

Upon Chucho's arrival (along with the other three Irakere members), we began preparing the necessary repertoire and finding the remaining musicians needed to play the tunes. We transcribed as many of the horn arrangements as we could in the days before the concerts, and had about 4 or 5 tunes ready to go when Chucho had the idea of writing a new piece. Inspired by the guitar solos of Carlos Santana and the boogaloo grooves of Mongo Santamaría, he composed the bluesy cha-cha-chá "San Francisco," a day or two before the first concert. The rest, as they say, is history.

"I remember writing that song while we were all at Susan Sillins' house (our dear friend and the co-producer of the event). I was thinking about the way Santana solos, and actually called the song 'A Santana' before deciding to change the title. I wanted it to be funky, bluesy and fun. We ended up recording it in Havana, and later on it was used as the theme for a nightly television show at 7pm in Havana! Even though Angá was with us in San Francisco, he had actually already left Irakere (in 1994), since he wanted to be with his wife and family in Paris.[24] That time in San Francisco was magical for so many reasons. First of all, to be reunited with Bebo after so many years...this was the beginning of an entirely new relationship between us, with several recordings that we went on to do, as well as the appearance in *Calle 54* (the documentary by Academy-award winning director Fernando Trueba), where we played Lecuona's "La Comparsa" together. It was also a wonderful moment to resurrect Bebo's solo career, since Paquito (D'Rivera) came out to California while we were all there, and we ended up recording together at Fantasy Studios."[25]

Basic Analysis:
- Form: Intro, ABAB
- Key: G-Major
- Solos: over AB, or often extended A with B on cue
- Rhythmical style: *cha-cha-chá*
- Clave direction: (*cha-cha-chás* are generally in 2-3 *clave*, but the pattern is implied)
- Tempo (bpm): 130
- Notes: A fun and accessible tune with the perfect blend of blues, funk and Cuban soul
- Cited recordings: Irakere. *Yemayá* (Blue Note, 1999).

Not included in this collection, but certainly worth mentioning, are two other important works in the Irakere repertoire that have endured as dramatic examples of the band's far-reaching depth and range: "Juana 1600" (composed in 1976), and "Estela Va a Estallar" (composed in 1985). The former became the signature opener for the band for virtually every live concert, featuring the percussion "arsenal" as well as the blazing horn section in a prime example of Chucho's suite-like compositional approach. "Juana 1600" has symbolic references in the title, referring to the name Columbus gave to Cuba when he "christened" it in 1492 as "Isla Juana," as well as the century (the 16th) when the first enslaved Africans were brought to the island.[26] The piece opens with a medley of *toques de batá* (batá rhythms) that invoke several *orishas* (deities),[27] followed by a jazz-funk swirl of Fender Rhodes and electric bass/guitar grooves, Yoruba chants to the goddess Oshún and another to Changó, and a horn soli that is truly death-defying. The definitive version of this tune is the live recording at the Capitol Theater in New Jersey (in March of 1979), where the audience seems to literally go berzerk (perhaps in disbelief of the musical onslaught they had just experienced).[28] As Irakere has continued to play it over the years in various iterations, the selection of Yoruban chants and *toques* may vary, but the impressive nature of the horn arrangement has remained unmatched.

---

[24] Angá and his wife were parents of twins, who have since gone on to establish a career as the critically acclaimed duo Ibeyi. Angá died suddenly in 2006, but left a remarkable legacy as one of Cuba's greatest *congueros*.
[25] "San Francisco" appears on the recording *Paquito D'Rivera Presents Cuba Jazz,* later reissued by Verve in 2005.
[26] Many historical accounts indicate that there were Africans in Cuba as early as the 1520s, some of them free blacks who arrived from Spain. Childs, etc.
[27] Fragments of these *toques* appear in Chapter V and in Appendix A.
[28] The live recording from New Jersey is included on a compilation entitled *Grandes Éxitos de Irakere* reissued in 1990. There are also a handful of live international performances available on YouTube, with a particularly excellent version filmed in 1985 at Ronnie Scott's in London.

CHAPTER 6 — THE SONGS

"Estela Va a Estallar" is the perfect example of Chucho's inspiration by and immersion into the jazz standard canon as both interpreter and composer, in that he follows the longstanding tradition used for decades: that of composing new material on a preexisting harmonic sequence, known as a "contrafact." Based on the Victor Young classic "Stella By Starlight," Chucho completely transforms the conceptual idea of the song, not only with the rhythmical structure (applying a *guaracha* style at a moderate and danceable tempo), but writing a bebop-infused horn melody that challenges even his top-notch ensemble. "Estela" was recorded in 1985 on the album *Tierra en Trance* by the second iteration of Irakere, featuring Germán Velasco and Carlos Averhoff on saxes, Juan Munguía and José Crego on trumpets, and José Luis Cortés on bari sax and flute, and features a masterful guitar solo by Carlos Emilio Morales on the debut recording. The soli writing is, as they say, ridiculously difficult, with lengthy and detailed passages not only for the horn section, but for the electric guitar and bass as well.[29] After an antiphonal section with a slightly swung feel, the band cuts into a *descarga*-like atmosphere to feature the brilliant flute work of Cortés (aka "El Tosco"). Years later, it feels as fresh as it did back in the 80s. Another example of Chucho's adoption of the contrafact can be heard on his tune "Stella, Pete, Ronnie," which is based on "I'll Remember April," highlighting Irakere's use of the jazz canon to express this "bilingual" fluency.[30]

For a comprehensive list of Chucho's works, we have compiled an alphabetical listing in Appendix B, indicating the year the work was composed, rhythmical style(s) used, and album(s) in which the song appears. We realize the original recordings of some songs may be difficult to locate, primarily due to the many compilations created well after the original release dates, and the redundancy of many older songs being included in recent reissues. However, consider this listing as a valuable source from a historical perspective, as the maestro himself has verified this collection as accurate. Some of the works pre-date the formation of Irakere and were first recorded by Chucho's Trio or Combo (in the 1960s), while others were composed for his later ensembles, including the Afro-Cuban Messengers. It is our hope that this information has, in some way, not only helped to decode the nuances of Irakere's extremely diverse repertoire, it has also served you as the interpreter as well as appreciator of Afro-Cuban jazz. Any musical tradition, no matter how seemingly complex, can be demystified with a decent amount of analysis. However, what is abundantly clear is that Irakere's music embodies an inordinate amount of historical, cultural, musicological as well as philosophical references that require much more understanding, and this could not be possible without the generosity of the architect behind it all, Chucho Valdés. It is not often that one has the opportunity to sit down with a creative person of any discipline and literally uncover the many layers (not to mention the behind-the-scenes anecdotes) that are involved in the compositional process. While there are certainly stories and details that may not be revealed here, our intention is to provide as much context as possible to allow you, the reader, into this magnificent world, Chucho's world, and marvel at the depth not only of Afro-Cuban music, but of his own deeply personal journey in leading one of the world's most unusual ensembles in modern music.

• • •

---

[29] Several rare videos demonstrate Chucho's doubling of the soli lines on the piano!

[30] The progression from Gene de Paul's "I'll Remember April" is the harmonic structure for Chucho's "Stella, Pete, Ronnie," composed in 1991 and recorded live at Ronnie Scott's in London (featured on the album *Felicidad* on JazzHouse records). Although Chucho's piece begins with a laid back bluesy shuffle, the principal melody is a torrid explosion of bebop riffs for the entire horn section. Another example of Chucho's use of the contrafact is on the lovely ballad penned for his mother, "Pilar," which features a section utilizing the same ten-measure sequence from Bill Evans' "Blue in Green."

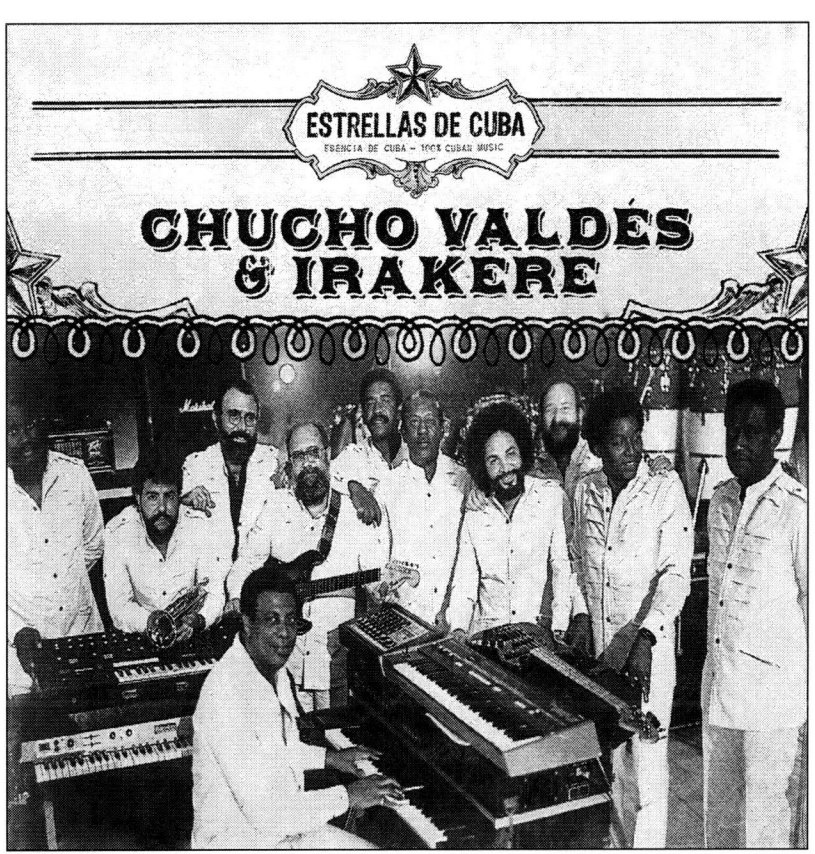

Estrellas de Cuba album cover, one of many compilations and reissues, ca 1985. AUTHOR'S COLLECTION

Mambo Influenciado

Guaracha 2-3

© 1963 Chucho Valdés

THE SONGS CHAPTER 6

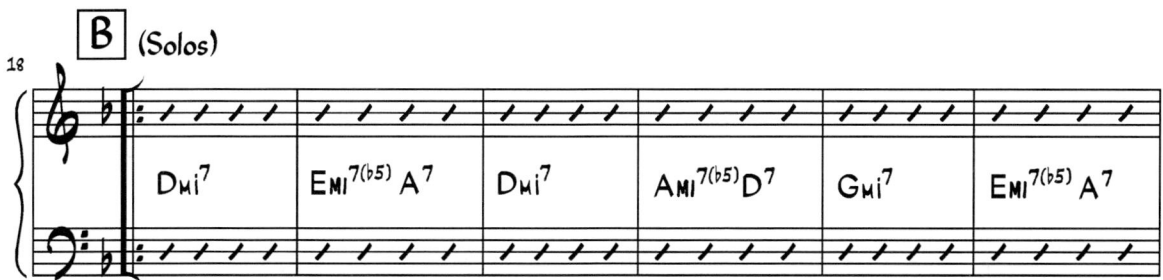

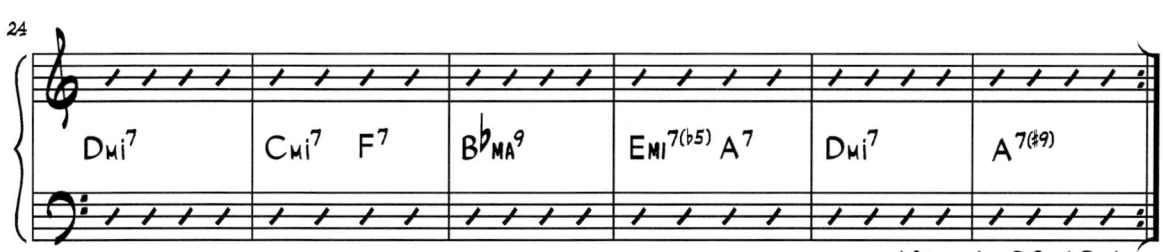

After solos, D.S. al Coda
(with repeat)

Mambo Influenciado

Misa Negra

Suite

© 1969 Chucho Valdés

THE SONGS CHAPTER 6

Misa Negra

109

Misa Negra

The Songs

Chapter 6

Misa Negra

Chapter 6 — The Songs

Misa Negra

The Songs — Chapter 6

Misa Negra

113

Misa Negra

The Songs CHAPTER 6

Misa Negra

Neurosis

The Songs

Chapter 6

Neurosis

117

CHAPTER 6 — THE SONGS

Neurosis

118

The Songs — Chapter 6

Neurosis

Bacalao Con Pan

Son-Batá (2-3)

© 1973 Chucho Valdés

The Songs

Chapter 6

Bacalao Con Pan

CHAPTER 6 — THE SONGS

Bacalao Con Pan

Bacalao Con Pan

Aguanile Bonkó

The Songs
Chapter 6

Aguanile Bonkó

Aguanile Bonkó

Aguanile Bonkó

CHAPTER 6
THE SONGS

Aguanile Bonkó

The Songs — Chapter 6

Claudia

Bolero

© 1978 Chucho Valdés

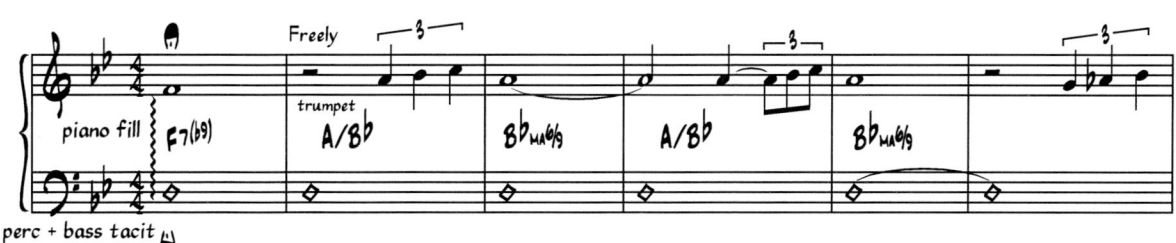

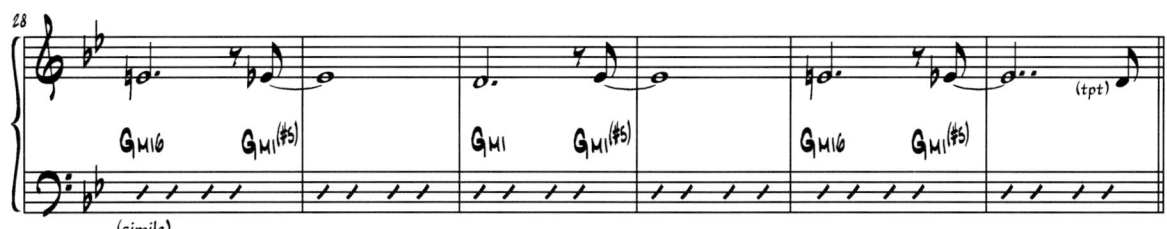

Claudia

The Songs CHAPTER 6

Claudia

131

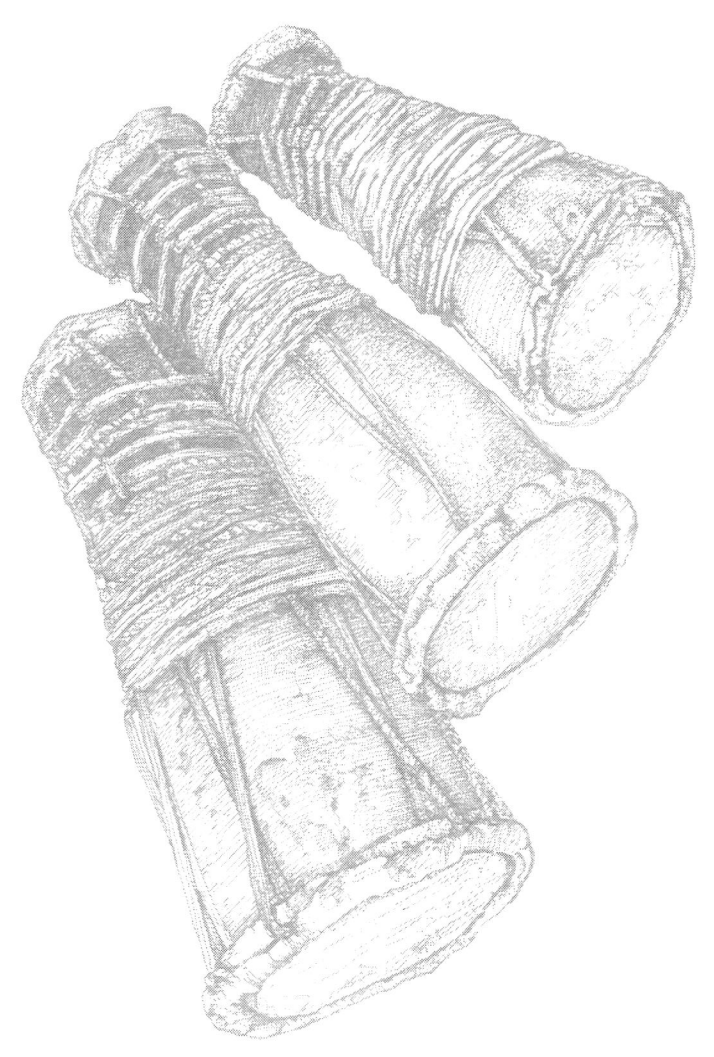

The Songs

Chapter 6

Calzada del Cerro

Cha-cha-chá

© 1983 Chucho Valdés

CHAPTER 6 — THE SONGS

Calzada del Cerro

The Songs

Chapter 6

Calzada del Cerro

CHAPTER 6 — THE SONGS

Calzada del Cerro

136

The Songs

CHAPTER 6

El Tata Cimarrón

Son-Batá (clave direction varies)

© 1983 Chucho Valdés

CHAPTER 6 — THE SONGS

El Tata Cimarrón

El Tata Cimarrón

El Tata Cimarrón

The Songs CHAPTER 6

El Tata Cimarrón

El Tata Cimarrón

The Songs

Chapter 6

El Tata Cimarrón

CHAPTER 6

THE SONGS

El Tata Cimarrón

The Songs   Chapter 6

El Tata Cimarrón

El Tata Cimarrón

The Songs

Chapter 6

El Tata Cimarrón

147

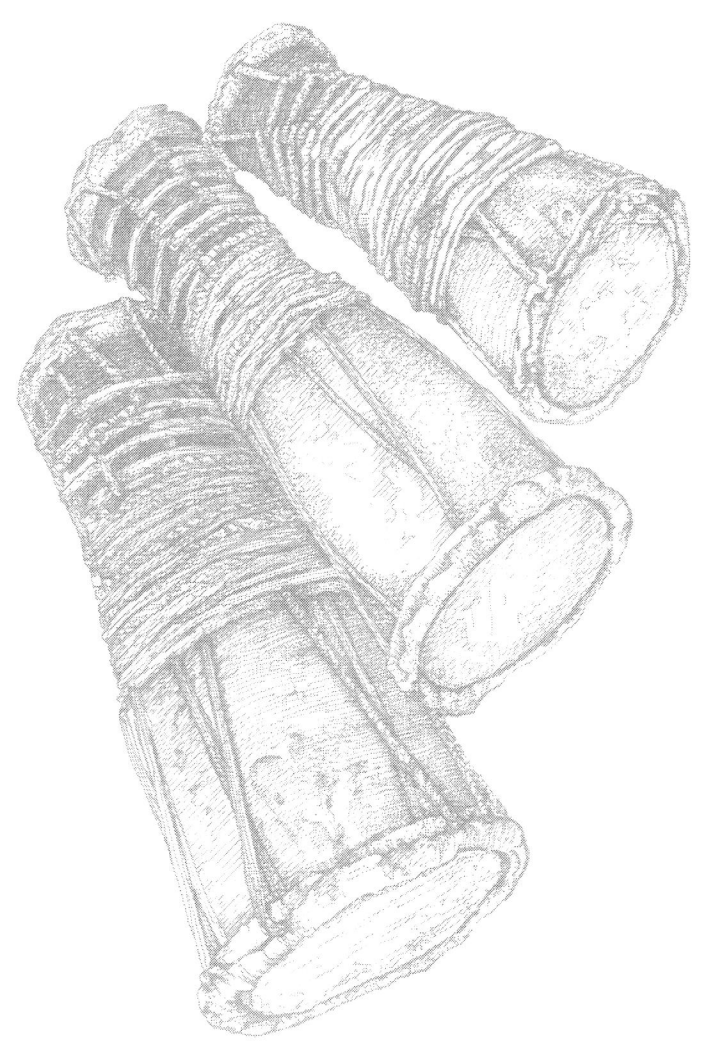

The Songs

Chapter 6

Lo Que Va a Pasar

Guaracha 2-3*
*(song begins 3-2 clave, then 'jumps')

© 1985 Chucho Valdés

Lo Que Va a Pasar

The Songs CHAPTER 6

Lo Que Va a Pasar

151

CHAPTER 6 — THE SONGS

Lo Que Va a Pasar

The Songs

CHAPTER 6

Lo Que Va a Pasar

153

CHAPTER 6 — THE SONGS

Lo Que Va a Pasar

154

The Songs

Chapter 6

Anabis

Fast Guaracha/Samba 2-3

© 1988 Chucho Valdés

CHAPTER 6 THE SONGS

Anabis

156

The Songs

Chapter 6

Anabis

157

CHAPTER 6 — THE SONGS

Anabis

The Songs

Chapter 6

Anabis

CHAPTER 6 — THE SONGS

Anabis

160

The Songs

Anabis

Chapter 6 — The Songs

San Francisco

© 1995 Chucho Valdés

162

The Songs

Chapter 6

San Francisco

163

CHAPTER 6 THE SONGS

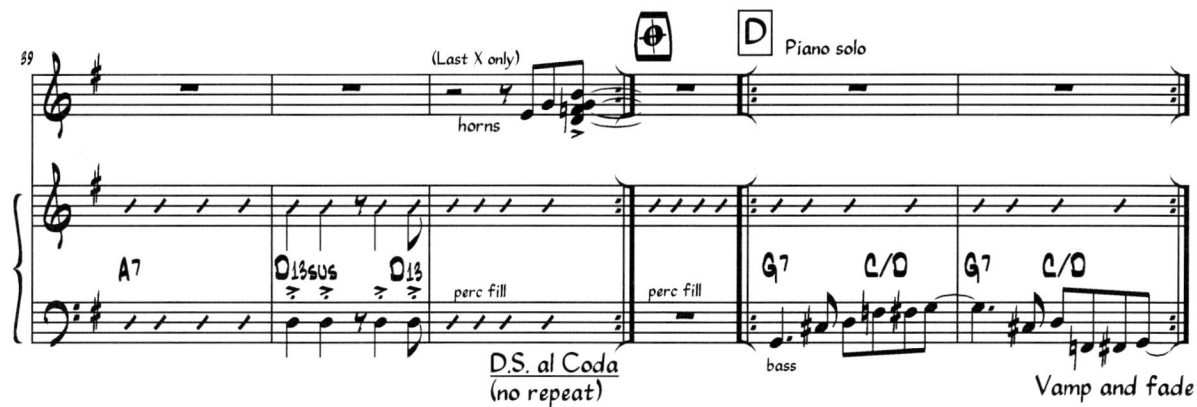

San Francisco

Chucho Valdés and Rebeca Mauleón conducting a masterclass at the SFJAZZ Center, August, 2014.
PHOTO CREDIT: MANOLO SANTANA

QUESTIONS FOR THE MAESTRO — CHAPTER 7

We polled several hundred young music students and jazz musicians, many of them working professionals, on the challenges of delving into Afro-Cuban jazz from a pedagogical perspective. Those surveyed were asked some general questions, and also given the opportunity to ask Maestro Valdés anything they wanted. The following will hopefully serve both students and educators in further informing the narrative on how this music can be both shared, and taught, using real world examples of technical, historical and philosophical questions that often arise in a learning environment.

The following questions were asked of the students:

- *What would you like to know about Afro-Cuban jazz that is relevant or important for you as a musician?*
- *As a student of Afro-Cuban music, what is the most challenging aspect you have encountered?*
- *Would you like to ask Maestro Chucho Valdés a question about his music or Cuban music in general?*

We received a range of insightful questions ranging in scope from the seemingly "ordinary," including "how many hours a day do you practice," (the answer of course, is "as many as possible!"), to many inquiries about the role of the *clave*, many of which are addressed throughout this book, along with a number of musicological as well as philosophical questions. What follows are several of these questions, followed by Chucho's answers to each of them.

• • •

Q: How best can you incorporate or work with the *clave* while soloing?
A: This is hard to explain, mainly because it is something that you need to carry inside you in a more organic way. It's not as if I think about the *clave* in a "mechanical" way and plan my improvisation based on some technical methodology with the *clave*. When I'm working within a style or rhythm that is already *clave*-based, especially something very polyrhythmic, then I do pay attention so that whatever counterpoint I create compliments (or accentuates) the *clave* rhythmically. I do this as a way to "play around" with the *clave*, creating phrases that highlight the *clave* direction or feeling. But again, this is difficult to explain technically!

Q: What inspires you these days in this second half of your career, and how do you stay relevant?
A: I listen to many pianists of varying styles of music, although I certainly have my favorites. For example, I am very inspired by classical pianists, and by the way they interpret the repertoire, both technically as well as stylistically, and this gives me plenty of ideas. Some of the gifted young pianists such as Lang Lang and Yuja Wang are doing amazing things, and I enjoy hearing their approach to works by composers such as Prokofiev and Rachmaninoff, the way they explore the themes, the variations they come up with, especially the overall structure of the pieces; I use this as inspiration for my own improvisation. It's not about copying or imitating what others are doing; I use this inspiration as a foundation to create my own music, especially when I play solo. It's the same for me when I listen to jazz pianists, especially renowned musicians such as Herbie (Hancock), the lyrical playing of (Keith) Jarrett, also Cecil Taylor, and a young pianist on the scene now, Craig Taborn—he is really interesting—as well as Jason Moran. I am always interested in what other musicians are doing, and use this as inspiration to evolve my own playing.

CHAPTER 7 — QUESTIONS FOR THE MAESTRO

Q: How would you describe the interaction between European classical repertoire and African diasporic forms and genres in Afro-Cuban music?

A: When I was studying Baroque music with (my teacher) Zenaida Romeu, such as Bach fugues and such, for me it always came out more rhythmical. Sometime when she would leave the room for a moment, I would take those same fugues and play them as *tumbaos*! She would run back in the room and ask me, "What the heck are you doing?!" After a while of hearing me do this, she paused and said, "I like it! You know it's not proper, of course, but I like it." It takes me back to the 1960s with groups like the Swingle Singers,[1] who added bass and drums to Bach fugues in their vocal arrangements. There was also a French pianist who recorded many classical works in a trio setting...Jacques Loussier, (b. 1934), including all of Bach's chromatic pieces. In other words, you could do the same thing by adapting classical repertoire "in clave," playing Mozart's Sonata in C Major as a conga style, for example (Chucho then sings Mozart's melody while clapping *rumba clave*). These days, when I'm taking a solo, I often insert a classical theme or motif, beginning with it in its original context, then manipulating it in an Afro-Cuban context or some other way.

Q: What effect does technique have on creativity?

A: In my opinion, technique is the tool you need to realize and bring forth your musical ideas, no matter how simple or how complex they may be. Technique is really the tool that is necessary to achieve creativity; technique in and of itself is not creative, but you need to have certain skills in order to fully express your ideas.

Q: How many hours a day do you practice?

A: (Laughs) As many as I can, but it is totally inconsistent. For example, when I'm home, I start in the morning and go for a few hours, take a break, then get back into it until I get tired. That's my routine in general when I'm not touring. Being on the road is harder of course; sometimes you only have the sound check to warm up, and work things out as best you can.

Q: What role do Lucumí and other Afro-Cuban folkloric traditions play within Cuban music?

A: I'd say it's all relative. Those of us (in Cuba) who grew up within a particular folk tradition, whether Lucumí or Bantú, etc, found ways to incorporate these expressions into the more Creole popular music. It can be very profound, very deep, and in order to appreciate it, you need to go way back. Much of our popular music also has a great degree of Spanish influence, but what resulted was a mixture of Africa and Spain. In other words, the music itself may have elements from these foundational traditions, but it certainly evolved over time. Now, those of us who are practitioners of the Lucumí religion, for example, who sing the sacred melodies and play the batá drums, are able to further enrich the Creole music by having a more direct link to this folklore. And this might have been different with, say, the 19th century danzas and contradanzas by Manuel Saumell and Ignacio Cervantes, who were certainly "informed" or "inspired" by folkloric idioms, but created a music that was more of a hybrid, leaning on the classical side or the more Creole sound. There are musicians who play those pieces, for example, who do not possess the same stylistic approach as someone who might be more involved or immersed in the afrocentric traditions. These wind up sounding more "creolized" than "folkloric," you see.

---

[1] The Swingle Singers were a French vocal group founded in 1962, known for their performance and recordings of Bach's *Well Tempered Klavier* and other works using an 8-voice choir with drums and acoustic bass.

Questions for the Maestro — Chapter 7

Q: When you compose, do you begin first with the melody or the rhythm?
A: Great question! Generally, I begin with the melody; not always, but maybe 95% of the time I hear a melody first. There are times when I deliberately choose to create a melody based on the harmonic progression of a standard (such as "Stella by Starlight" or "I'll Remember April"), or to focus on a particular rhythmical style or genre, but it's usually melody first for me.

Q: How has Cuban music influenced North American music?
A: I think the influence has primarily been a rhythmical one. Take for example the work of Chano Pozo with Dizzy Gillespie, with Chano bringing Afro-Cuban rhythms into the jazz big band, which created a new and different sound in jazz. I think this is the most significant influence, more so than say melodic or harmonic elements, and because of the many varieties of rhythms and genres that we have—from the *son, mambo, cha-cha-chá, rumba, danzón, bolero,* etc.

Q: Is the *clave* rhythm that we hear in American popular music, say from the 1950s and 60s, a direct influence from Cuba?
A: I believe it is!

Q: And how about the *clave* rhythms heard in say Uruguay or Brazil; were those also influenced by Cuban music?
A: I'm not certain about that. Imagine, all of these musical traditions share the same African lineage, so this might be more of a "chicken-and-egg" question! It's hard to say which came first. I remember one time I was visiting Johannesburg South Africa, and I heard a school band playing some of their music, and they were using the *son clave* rhythm. Now South Africa doesn't have this particular pattern incorporated into its folk or popular music as far as I know, but there it was, exactly the same! Who knows? Perhaps it's universal!

Q: Do Cuban musicians approach the groove or the feel differently than North American musicians?
A: Perhaps what we Cubans feel is a concept of the beat or pulse itself in a different way. Most Cubans, even non-musicians, will mark the pulse on the downbeat, for example, interpreting a binary phrase such as the *clave* and marking it by clapping on the 1 and 3, whereas most North American musicians tend to "feel" the pulse on the backbeat or upbeats (on 2 and 4), like the hi-hat played by the jazz drummer. So yes, I think we do perceive the groove differently, at least from a rhythmical perspective. Even in terms of melodic phrasing, we Cubans tend to push ahead just a bit, where a jazz musician might lay back more. It can be subtle, but it's definitely perceptible from a musical point of view.

Q: Why do **you** make music, and what are your goals and dreams for your music?
A: I can't even imagine what my life would be without music. Since my earliest memories, music has always been who I am! My dreams? I live as I dream, every day, trying new projects, dreaming up new ideas, sometimes getting into challenging or musically demanding situations that require so much effort and imagination. This year alone (in 2017) I collaborated with eight different pianists on a range of projects, and this work can be difficult but so rewarding. If I am dreaming this life, I don't want to wake up!

CHAPTER 7   QUESTIONS FOR THE MAESTRO

Q: What makes Cuban music so special, and what does it give to the world that is important and unique?
A: First of all, I think the richness of Cuba's music lies in its great **rhythmical** variety, not only in the more recognized popular music styles, but our traditional genres as well, including the *danza*, *contradanza, danzón* and a ton of other rhythms. It is an enormous and very broad range of musical traditions that we draw from; you could do a set of Cuban music with ten songs, and each tune could be based on a completely different rhythm! It is, of course, also extremely rich from a melodic and harmonic standpoint as well, and I think this has a lot to do with the African influences, especially the Lucumí elements, that we have only just begun to explore in our popular music. Just looking at the sacred music of one of these traditions, and you have an extraordinary wealth of material to discover!

Q: Why should people around the world learn more about Cuban music?
A: I think it's important to study Cuban music as well as other musical traditions. Our music has many deep roots, both African and European, and is generally a "happy" as well as danceable music, even if it isn't intended for dancing per se.

Q: Which artists should I listen to in order to learn more about Afro-Cuban jazz?
A: You must listen to Mario Bauzá, Machito, Pérez Prado, Arsenio Rodríguez, Antonio Arcaño's orchestra (Arcaño y sus Maravillas), Los Muñequitos de Matanzas...there are so many! We should also recognize Antonio María Romeu, who took the very first piano solo in a *danzón*. The improvised solo he did on the song "Tres Lindas Cubanas" became such a standard, that it's almost like you're not playing the tune if you don't play his solo! And of course there is Bebo!

Q: When did you compose your first jazz tune?
A: I must have been around 15 years old and I wrote a blues head.

Q: How would you describe the Cuban musician's approach to the time or the feel in the music?
A: I'd say it has to do with both **where we feel the pulse** (on the downbeat vs the backbeat, for example), and also **how we internalize the *clave*** as we play. For most of us, I'm sure it's not always a deliberate thing, but more of an extension of how our music needs to **feel** in order to motivate the dancing public, for example.

Q: How do Cubans come up with so much great original music?!
A: That's hard to answer. But let me say this: everything we do in life, or art, comes from something and starts somewhere. We need to have a point of reference, not necessarily to copy what came before, but certainly to draw from it, such as a specific style or rhythm that moves us, so we continue to push it forward. I was greatly inspired early on by the pianist Peruchín;[2] Bebo would always encourage me to go to Peruchín's house and take some lessons, but he would also tell me, "Don't imitate him! Just go there and tell him I sent you to take some lessons, and see if you can find a way to express your own ideas using what you've learned." Bebo would remind me that no one starts from square one with a complete package or defined musical style; you need to follow in the footsteps of those who came before, and only then can you begin to define who you are as an artist. I would say that I discovered my own creative self when I composed "Mambo Influenciado" (in 1963). It was as if I found my individuality as an artist when that song came to me; it clearly was a composite of everything in my

---

[2] Pedro Justiz Peruchín (1913-1977) was a pianist, composer, arranger and bandleader known for his remarkable jam session recordings, big band arrangements, and jazz-influenced playing. He was also a close friend of Chucho's father Bebo.

musical life that had transpired until that moment, everything I had heard, studied, applied, imitated, etc. And there it was: all of those influences were now a part of me and came out through this piece. That was a defining moment in my journey as a composer.

• • •

There is no doubt that what Afro-Cuban music has contributed to the world is enormous in scope; it is also highly questionable that one could surmise all of the nuance, language and creativity developed by one of the most groundbreaking ensembles in music without leaving out a significant amount of information. This work is a mere glimpse, a conversation on a topic literally without end. Given that we are attempting to synthesize a compositional process and, at the same time, showcase the breadth of information that has gone into Irakere's amalgamation of sound, we can only hint at how truly massive the source material is. The decoding of musicological processes is tedious, but greatly rewarding for anyone seeking to broaden their knowledge, or to expand their musical vocabulary and performance practice techniques. This book is the result of Chucho Valdés' decades of musical explorations, contributions and experiences, and as with any creative endeavor of this nature, it is the ultimate hope that the material contained here will serve to inspire, motivate, and stimulate new sonic possibilities for you, the reader. It was Chucho's vision that shaped the evolution of Irakere's genre-defying sound, and his wish that we shed some light onto the story of how that sound came to be, if only to provide guidance to those who may feel compelled to take the torch and push the music further. With gratitude to all of those who came before and "set the stage" for Afro-Cuban jazz—from the generations of ancestors, pioneers and innovators, to the next generation of its fiercest advocates—we thank you for embarking on this journey, and hope you will treasure its many possibilities.

Many thanks to the students who participated in this survey, and who continue to explore the many riches of Afro-Cuban jazz. We truly hope this book will serve as inspiration, and that it will motivate you to find your own creative selves, and also honor the many musicians who came before.

• • •

DISCOGRAPHY

The following comprehensive discography includes all recordings referenced throughout this book, as well as a complete listing of albums (and reissue information where pertinent) of all works by Chucho Valdés (as soloist, leader and co-leader), and those of Irakere.

• • •

Andre's All-Stars. *Cubano*. Mercury, 1952.
Blood, Sweat & Tears. *Blood, Sweat & Tears*. Columbia, 1969.
Borcelá, Amado con Chucho Valdés y su Combo. *Guapachá en La Habana*. Areito, 1964.
Brouwer, Leo & Irakere. *Leo Brouwer & Irakere*. Areito, 1978.
Buika, Concha & Chucho Valdés. *El Último Trago*. Casa Limón, 2009.
Cruz, Celia. *Canta Celia Cruz*. Seeco, 1956.
D'Rivera, Paquito & Arturo Sandoval. *Reunion*. Messidor, 1992.
D'Rivera, Paquito. *Paquito D'Rivera Presents Cuba Jazz*. RMM, 1996.
Durán, Hilario. *From the Heart*. Alma Records, 2006.
Earth, Wind & Fire. *That's The Way Of the World*. Columbia, 1975.
Fischer, Clare. *Manteca*. Pacific Jazz, 1965.
Grupo Afrocuba. *Dile Que Vuelvo*. Areito, 1981.
Hancock, Herbie. *Head Hunters*. Columbia, 1973.
Hargrove, Roy. *Habana*. Verve, 1997.**
Irakere. *2*. Columbia, 1980.
_____ *¡Afrocubanismo Live!* Bembe, 1996.
_____ *Babalú Ayé*. Bembe, 1999.
_____ *Bailando Así*. Areito, 1985. (Reissue: *Irakere Colección Vol. IX*, Egrem, 1995)
_____ *Calzada del Cerro*. Areito, 1983.
_____ *Catalina*. Messidor, 1986. (Reissue: *Homenaje a Benny Moré*, Egrem, 1991)
_____ *Chekeré Son*. Integra, 1979.
_____ *Cuba Libre*. JVC, 1980. (Reissued on Far Out Recordings, 2010)
_____ *El Coco*. JVC, 1982.
_____ *Exuberancia*, Jazz House, 1989.
_____ *Felicidad*. Jazz House, 1991.
_____ *From Havana With Love*. West Wind, 1994.
_____ *Great Moments*. Milan Latino, 1996.
_____ *Grupo Irakere*. Areito, 1974. (Reissue: *Chekeré*, Love Records, 1976)
_____ *Indestructible*. Sony Music, 1999. (Reissued under several labels)
_____ *Irakere*. Areito, 1982. (Reissue: *Irakere Colección Vol. VI*, Egrem, 1995)
_____ *Irakere*. Columbia, 1979.** (Reissue: *The Best of Irakere*, CBS Records, 1994)
_____ *Live in Sweden*. A Disc, 1981.
_____ *Misa Negra*. Messidor, 1987.
_____ *Música Cubana Contemporánea*. Areito, 1980. (Reissue: *Colección Irakere Vol. IV*, Egrem, 1995)
_____ *No Quiero Confusión*. Areito, 1981. (Reissue: *Para Bailar Son*, Egrem, 1995)
_____ *Orquesta Sinfónica Nacional*. Areito, 1983. (Reissued in 1995 on Egrem)
_____ *Quince Minutos*. Areito, 1986. (Reissued in 1995 on Egrem)
_____ *Recital - Teatro Amadeo Roldán*. Areito, 1974.
_____ *Selección de Éxitos 73-80 Vol. I*. Areito, 1981.
_____ *The Best of Irakere*. Columbia Records, 1994.

DISCOGRAPHY

_____ *The Legendary Irakere in London*. Jazz House Records, 1988.
_____ *Tierra en Trance*. Areito, 1985.
_____ *Yemayá*. Blue Note, 1999.
_____ *Live at Ronnie Scott's*. World Pacific, 1993.
Lecuona, Ernesto. *Lecuona Toca Lecuona*. Egrem, 1992.
Lins, Ivan, Chucho Valdés & Irakere. *Ao Vivo*. Velas / Egrem, 1996.
Lloyd, Charles. *Forest Flower*. Atlantic, 1967.
López, Israel "Cachao." *Cuban Jam Sessions in Miniature*. Panart, 1957.
Milanés, Pablo & Chucho Valdés. *Más Allá de Todo*. Wrasse, 2009.
Portuondo, Omara & Chucho Valdés. *Desafíos*. Intuition, 1997.
Portuondo, Omara & Chucho Valdés. *Omara & Chucho*. World Village, 2011.
Rodríguez, Arsenio. *Montuneando*. Tumbao Cuban Classics, 1993.
Rodríguez, Silvio. *Causas y Azares*. Fonomusic, 1986.
Rodríguez, Silvio. *En Chile (Vols 1, 2 & 3)*. Areito, 1991.
Sandoval, Arturo. *Turi*. Areito, 1981.
Sandoval, Arturo & Chucho Valdés Quartet. *Straight Ahead*. Jazz House, 1988.
Silver, Horace. *The Stylings of Silver*. Blue Note, 1957.
Sosa, Patricia & Chucho Valdés. *Once - Concierto Para Dos*. Media Music, 2017.
Tyner, McCoy. *Today and Tomorrow*. Impulse!, 1964.
Tyner, McCoy (Trio). *Inception*. Impulse!, 1962.
Valdés, Bebo. *Bebo de Cuba*. Calle 54 Records, 2005.**
_____ *Bebo Rides Again*. Messidor, 1995.
_____ *El Arte del Sabor*. Blue Note, 2001.**/***
Valdés, Bebo & Chucho. *Juntos Para Siempre*. Calle 54 Records, 2008.**
Valdés, Bebo & Diego El Cigala. *Lágrimas Negras*. Calle 54 Records, 2003.**
Valdés, Bebo & His Orchestra. *Cuban Dance Party*. Everest, 1959.
Valdés, Chucho. *Bele Bele en La Habana*. Blue Note, 1998.
_____ *Border Free*. Comanche, 2013.
_____ *Briyumba Palo Congo*. Blue Note, 1999.
_____ *Cancionero Cubano*. Egrem, 2005.
_____ *Canciones Inéditas*. Egrem, 2002.***
_____ *Chucho Valdés*. Areito, 1970.
_____ *Fantasía Cubana: Variations on Classical Themes*. Blue Note, 2002.
_____ *Invitación*. Areito, 1986.
_____ *Live at the Village Vanguard*. Blue Note, 2000.**
_____ *Lo Mejor de Chucho Valdés*. Apple Music, 2017.
_____ *Lucumí Piano Solo*. Messidor, 1988.
_____ *New Conceptions*. Blue Note, 2003.***
_____ *Piano 1*. Areito, 1976.
_____ *Solo: Live in New York*. Blue Note, 2001.
_____ *Solo Piano*. Blue Note, 1991.
_____ *Tema de Chaka*. Areito, 1981.
Valdés, Chucho & Rubén González. *Tumi Sessions*. Tumi Music, 2008.
Valdés, Chucho & Special Guests. *Live*. RMM, 1999.
Valdés, Chucho & the Afro-Cuban Messengers. *Border Free*. Comanche Music, 2013.
_____ *Chucho's Steps*. Four Quarters, 2010.**

DISCOGRAPHY

_____ *Tribute to Irakere: Live in Marciac.* Comanche Music, 2015.**

Valdés, Chucho, Gonzalo Rubalcaba & Michel Camilo. *Playing Lecuona.* Insularia Creadores/Sony Music, 2015.

Valdés, Chucho (Trio). *Jazz Batá.* Areito, 1973.

Valdés, Chucho y la Orquesta Sinfónica Nacional de Cuba. *Canto a Dios.* Mondopolitan, 2015.

Valdés, Chucho y Su Combo. *Cuban Jazz Revolution.* Soul Vibes 2014.

_____ *Jazz Nocturno.* Areito, 1964.

Various Artists. *¡Con Mucho Ritmo! The Very Best of TropiJazz.* Verve, 2005.

Various Artists. *Havana Jam.* Columbia, 1979.

Williams, Anthony. *Life Time.* Blue Note, 1964.

**GRAMMY award
***Latin GRAMMY award

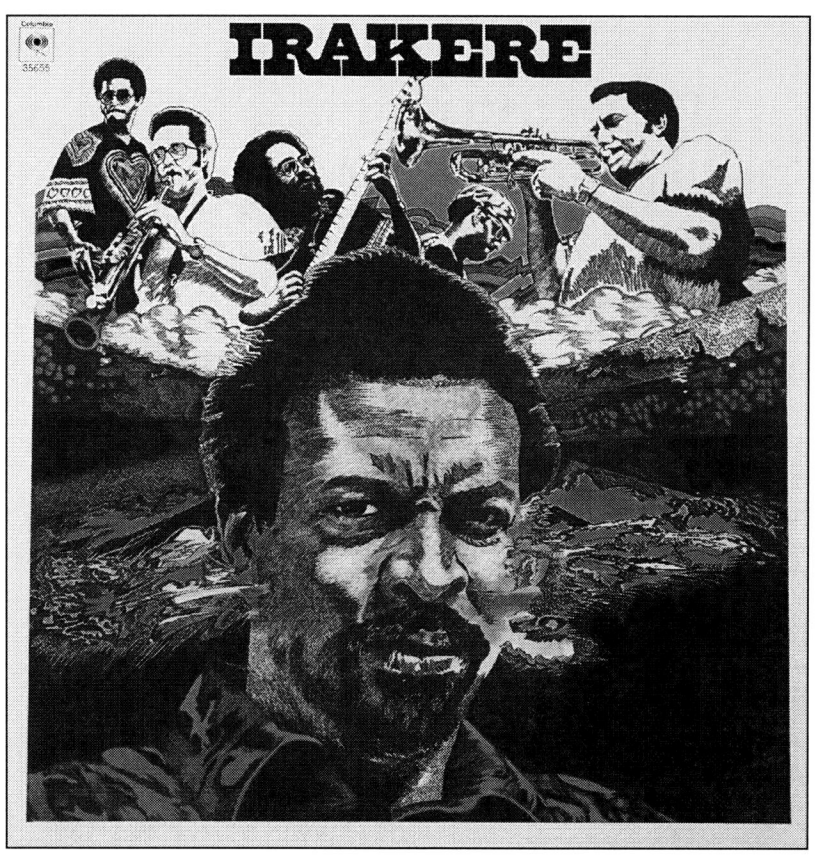

Irakere Columbia Records album cover, 1979. AUTHOR'S COLLECTION

BIBLIOGRAPHY

"11 Irakere & Chucho Valdés Songs You Must Hear." *SFJAZZ*. Web. 19 June 2017.
Acosta, Leonardo. *Cubano Be, Cubano Bop: One Hundred Years of Jazz in Cuba*. Washington: Smithsonian, 2003. Print.
Acosta, Leonardo. *Del Tambor al Sintetizador*. La Habana, Cuba: Editorial Letras Cubanas, 2014. Print.
"Adiós Al Gran Justi Barreto." *Sinfonía.com*. 19 Jan 2015. Web.
Agencias. "Legendaria Banda Del Latin Jazz Cubano, Irakere, Vuelve Sin Paquito Ni Arturo Sandoval." *Radio Y Televisión Martí | Martinoticias.com*. Radio Y Televisión Martí | Martinoticias.com, 04 Nov. 2015. Web.
Alén, Olavo. *De Lo Afrocubano a La Salsa: Géneros Musicales De Cuba*. Habana, Cuba: Ediciones ARTEX, 1994. Print.
Alonso, Guillermo Andreu. *LosArarás En Cuba: Florentina, La Princesa Dahomeyana*. La Habana: Editorial De Ciencias Sociales, 1995. Print.
"American Historical Association 131st Annual Meeting (January 5-8, 2017) January 05 - 08, 2017." *Paper: The Footsteps of Nieves Fresneda: Folkloric Dance and Racial Politics in Revolutionary Cuba (131st Annual Meeting (January 5-8, 2017))*. Web. 13 July 2017.
Amira, John, and Steven Cornelius. *The Music of Santería: Traditional Rhythms of the Batá Drums*. Reno, NV: White Cliffs Media, 1999. Print.
"Antonio Carlos Jobim." BrainyQuote.com. Xplore Inc, 2017. 29 June 2017.
"Antonio María Romeu." *Wikipedia*. Wikimedia Foundation, 09 Apr. 2017. Web.
AllMusic.com.
Aquique, Dariela. "La rumba también es Cuba." *HavanaTimes.com*. 6 Oct 2013. Web.
Arcos, Betto. "A Jazz Pianist Considers Fidel Castro's Music Education Legacy." *NPR*. NPR, 30 Nov. 2016. Web.
"Arturo Sandoval - Turi." *Discogs*. Web. 20 June 2017.
Ayala, Cristobal Diaz. *Música Cubana: Del Areyto Al Rap Cubano*. Miami: Ed. Universal, 2003. Print.
Barnet, Miguel. *Afro-Cuban Religions*. Princeton: Markus Wiener, 2001. Print.
Barnet, Dr. Miguel, et al.. "La Ruta Del Esclavo." *Fundación Fernando Ortiz - Inicio*. 2004. Web. 18 July 2017.
"Batanga Con Nieve." *Diario De Cuba*. Web. 19 June 2017.
"Bebo Valdés." *Wikipedia*. Wikimedia Foundation, 04 June 2017. Web.
"Benny Moré." *Benny Moré - EcuRed*. Web. 08 July 2017.
Berlin, Ira. "The Discovery of the Americas and the Transatlantic Slave Trade." *The Gilder Lehrman Institute of American History*. 17 Oct. 2012. Web.
Blais, Martin. Index of Toques. *Furius.ca*. 2004. Web.
"Brikamo Mañongo Usagaré." *Without Masks*. Web. 19 July 2017.
"Bomb." *BOMB Magazine — Orlando "Maraca" Valle by Ned Sublette*. Web. 22 June 2017.
Brown, David H. *Santería Enthroned: Art, Ritual, and Innovation in an Afro-Cuban Religion*. Chicago (Ill.): U of Chicago, 2003. Print.
"Bruce Lundvall." *Wikipedia*. Wikimedia Foundation, 18 June 2017. Web.
Burnett, Victoria. "In Havana, Jam Sessions With a Master Trumpeter." *The New York Times*. The New York Times, 10 Oct. 2010. Web.
Burns, James. "Rhythmic Archetypes in Instrumental Music from Africa and the Diaspora." *Music Theory Online*, 1 Dec. 2010. Web.
"Cabaret Sans Souci: Según Algunos, El Cabaret Y Casino Más Exclusivo De La Habana." *CUBA En La Memoria*. 17 Mar. 2013. Web.
Cabrera, Lydia. *Anagó: Vocabulario Lucumí (el Yoruba Que Se Habla En Cuba)*. Miami, FL: Ediciones

BIBLIOGRAPHY

Universal, 1986. Print.

Cabrera, Lydia. *El Monte: Igbo, Finda, Ewe Orisha, Vititi Nfinda: Notas Sobre Las Religiones, La Magia, Las Supersticiones Y El Folklore De Los Negros Criollos Y El Pueblo De Cuba*. Miami, FL: Ediciones Universal, 2006. Print.

"Calzada Del Cerro." *World Monuments Fund*. Web. 21 June 2017.

"Carnaval De La Habana, Fiesta De Tradiciones." *Granma.cu*. 5 Aug 2015. Web.

Carpentier, Alejo, Timothy Brennan, and Alan West-Durán. *Music in Cuba*. Minneapolis: U of Minnesota, 2001. Print.

Carpentier, Alejo. *Obras Completas De Alejo Carpentier*. Mexico: Siglo Veintiuno Ed., 1987. Print.

Cartaya, Rolando. "En Noche De Jazz En La Casa Blanca, Obama Elogia El Que Escuchó En La Habana." *Radio Y Televisión Martí | Martinoticias.com*. Radio Y Televisión Martí | Martinoticias.com, 02 May 2016. Web.

Cartwright, Garth. "Obituary: Israel 'Cachao' López." *The Guardian*. Guardian News and Media, 23 Mar. 2008. Web.

"Category: Grammy Award Winners." *Wikipedia*. Wikimedia Foundation, 09 Jan. 2016. Web.

Cerra, Steven A. "Jazz Profiles." *The Evolution of the Piano in Jazz*. 01 Jan. 1970. Web.

Chase, Gilbert. *The Music of Spain*. New York, NY: Dover Publications, 1976. Print

"Chico O'Farrill to Be Laid to Rest in Cuba." *Billboard*. 11 Nov 2016. Web. 0

Childs, Matt D. *The 1812 Aponte Rebellion in Cuba and the Struggle against Atlantic Slavery*, University of North Carolina Press, 2006. Print.

Chinen, Nate. "Bruce Lundvall, Who Revived Blue Note Jazz Label, Dies at 79." *The New York Times*. The New York Times, 20 May 2015. Web.

Chinen, Nate. "Chucho Valdés, the Pianist, Reflects on Irakere and His Career." *The New York Times*. The New York Times, 01 Nov. 2015. Web.

Chiu, Lisa. "A Historical Overview of the Chinese in Cuba." *ThoughtCo*, 28 Feb. 2017. Web.

"Chucho Valdés a Dazzling Display." *Stuff*. 10 June 2013. Web.

"Chucho Valdés Holds Court at Copley." *San Diego Story*. 25 May 2017. Web.

"Chucho Valdés Wins His Sixth Grammy." *Oncubamagazine*. 14 Feb. 2017. Web.

"Ciboney." *Wikipedia*. Wikimedia Foundation, 04 May 2017. Web.

Cirules, Enrique. *El Imperio De La Habana: Testimonio*. La Habana: Casa De Las Américas, 1993. Print.

Cohen, Hannah Berkeley. "A Steinway From New York Meets Virtuosos in Havana." *The New York Times*. The New York Times, 10 Oct. 2015. Web.

Coles, T.J., Robert Jensen, Earl Bousquet, and Enrique Montesinos. "Cuban Musician Chucho Valdes Wins Grammy Award." *News | TeleSUR English*. Web. 21 June 2017. "Clare Fischer." *Wikipedia*. Wikimedia Foundation, 20 June 2017. Web.

Concha-Holmes, Amanda D. "Cuban Cabildos, Cultural Politics, And Cultivating A Transnational Yoruba Citizenry." *Cultural Anthropology*. 26 July 2013. Web.

CongaMasterClass.com.

"Congolese Rumba." *Wikipedia*. Wikimedia Foundation, 23 June 2017. Web.

Cornish, Audie, and Monika Evstatieva. "Radical Grooves And Hometown Heroes: Cuba's Lasting Jazz Legacy." *NPR*. NPR, 28 Apr. 2017. Web.

"Cuban Jam Sessions in Miniature." *Wikipedia*. Wikimedia Foundation, 01 July 2017. Web.

"Cuba Today (Winter 2000)." *ReVista*. Web. 20 June 2017.

Daniel, Yvonne. *Rumba: Dance and Social Change in Contemporary Cuba*. Bloomington: Indiana University, 1996. Print.

"Danzonete." *Danzonete - EcuRed*. Web. 08 July 2017.

BIBLIOGRAPHY

Davenport, Gabrielle. "Cuba 'Auténtica:' Discusiones Sobre La Rumba Como Folklore Cubano." *Journal of Undergraduate Research*, Volume 1.1, Columbia University | LAIC, Department of Latin American and Iberian Cultures. 24 Feb 2015. Web.

DeFore, John. "'Playing Lecuona': Montreal Review." *The Hollywood Reporter*. 06 Sept. 2015. Web.

De La Torre, Miguel A. *Santería: The Beliefs and Rituals of a Growing Religion in America*. Grand Rapids, MI: William B. Eerdmans Pub., 2004. Print.

"Descarga." *Wikipedia*. Wikimedia Foundation, 18 June 2017. Web.

Dianteill, Erwan. "Kongo in Cuba: The Transformations of an African Religion." *Archives De Sciences Sociales Des Religions*. Editions De L'E.H.E.S.S., 30 Nov. 2002. Web.

Discogs.com.

Doerschuk, Robert L. *88: The Giants of Jazz Piano*. San Francisco, Calif: Backbeat, 2002. Print.

D'Rivera, Paquito. *My Sax Life: A Memoir*. Northwestern Univ Pr, 2008. Print.

"El Espacio Audiovisual Iberoamericano." *Programa Ibermedia*. 10 Sept. 2015. Web.

El Fenómeno De Chucho Valdés; El Verdadero Legado De Los Genios - Diario Dominicano. 15 Mar 2015. Web.

"Encomienda." *Wikipedia*. Wikimedia Foundation, 28 June 2017. Web.

"Enrique Bonne: Creador Del Ritmo Pilón." *Caribbean News Digital*. 25 Sept 2014. Web.

"Enrique Jorrín." *Enrique Jorrín - EcuRed*. Web. 08 July 2017.

Fernandes, Sujatha. *Cuba Represent!: Cuban Arts, State Power, and the Making of New Revolutionary Cultures*. Durham: Duke UP, 2006. Print.

Fordham, John. "Valdés/Lovano Review – Intricate Contemporary Jazz Meets Sensual Cuban Dance Music." *The Guardian*. Guardian News and Media, 25 Oct. 2016. Web.

Fowler, Victor. "Chucho Valdés." *Havana Music School*. 09 June 2017. Web.

Fraginals, Manuel Moreno. *Africa in Latin America: Essays on History, Culture and Socialization*. New York: Holmes & Meier, 1984. Print.

Fuerte, Cafe. "Chucho Valdes Wins Grammy for His Tribute to Irakere," *HavanaTimes.org*. 14 Feb 2017. Web.

Garelick, Jon. Album Review: Chucho Valdés & the Afro-Cuban Messengers, 'Border-Free' - The Boston Globe. *BostonGlobe.com*. 08 July 2013. Web.

Ginori, Yin Pedraza. "Salón Mambí De Tropicana." *El Blog De Pedraza Ginori*. 01 Jan. 2017. Web.

Gioia, Ted. *The Jazz Standards: A Guide to the Repertoire*. Oxford University Press, 2012. Print.

Giró, Radamés. *Diccionario Enciclopédico De La Música En Cuba*. La Habana, Cuba: Letras Cubanas, 2009. Print.

Giró, Radamés. *Panorama de la Música Popular Cubana*. Editorial Letras Cubanas, 1998. Print.

"Grammy Award for Best Latin Jazz Album." *Wikipedia*. Wikimedia Foundation, 10 June 2017. Web.

Grammy.com.

Granberry, Julian. "Lenguas indígenas del Caribe." *Cuba Arqueológica,* Año V, No. 1, 2012.

Griswold, Daniel. "Four Decades of Failure: The U.S. Embargo against Cuba." Cato Institute. 12 Oct. 2005. Web.

"Guanahatabey." *Wikipedia*. Wikimedia Foundation, 22 June 2017. Web.

"Havana Jam." *Wikipedia*. Wikimedia Foundation, 15 June 2017. Web.

Haven, Paul. "Wynton Marsalis Brings Music, Message to Cuba." *The Seattle Times*. The Seattle Times Company, 08 Oct. 2010. Web.

Helzer, Richard A. "Cultivating the Art of Jazz Composition," *Jazz Education Journal*. May 2004. Web.

Hernández Busto, Ernesto. "Oyendo a Irakere." *Penúltimos Días*. 29 July, 2007. Web.

"Historia De Zarabanda." *Palo Mayombe, InsikiMalongo Blog*. 4 Mar 2008. Web.

BIBLIOGRAPHY

"History and Discography of Irakere." *Timba*. 2007. Web. 23 July 2017.

Ho, Fred Wei-han., and Bill Mullen. *Afro Asia: Revolutionary Political and Cultural Connections between African Americans and Asian Americans*. Durham: Duke UP, 2008. Print.

Hu-Dehart, Evelyn. "Chinese Coolie Labour in Cuba in the Nineteenth Century: Free Labour or Neo-slavery?" *Slavery & Abolition* 14.1 (1993): 67-86. Print.

"Iberian Roots of the Transatlantic Slave Trade, 1440–1640." *The Gilder Lehrman Institute of American History*. 17 Oct. 2012. Web.

IFE-ILE Afro-Cuban Dance Traditions - Congo Abakuá Arará. Web. 19 July 2017.

"Index of Cantos." *Santeria DB: Index of Cantos*. Web. 19 June 2017.

"Index of Toques." *Santeria DB: Index of Toques*. Web. 19 June 2017.

"International Jazz Day 2017 to Take Place April 30th Worldwide and in 2017 Global Host City Havana, Cuba." *UNESCO*. 03 May 2017. Web.

"Irakere." *Wikipedia*. Wikimedia Foundation, 17 June 2017. Web.

"Irakere 40: The Re-imagining of an Iconic Cuban Ensemble." *SFJAZZ*. Web. 20 June 2017.

Jarenwattananon, Patrick. "Jazz At Lincoln Center Opening Night: WBGO and Jazz At Lincoln Center." *NPR*. NPR. Web. 7 Oct 2014.

"Jazzday." *International Jazz Day*, April 30, 2017.Web.

"José Antonio Méndez." *José Antonio Méndez - EcuRed*. Web. 19 June 2017.

"José Manuel Aniceto Díaz." *José Manuel Aniceto Díaz - EcuRed*. Web. 08 July 2017.

Kernis, Mark. "Irakere: Fusing Conga and Cuba in Jazz." *The Washington Post*. WP Company, 16 Mar. 1979. Web.

Knight, Franklin W., ed. *General History of the Caribbean: Volume III: The Slave Societies of the Caribbean*. London: UNESCO, 1997. Print.

Kozak, Roman. "Irakere Band Records Fusion LP," *Billboard Magazine*, July 22, 1978. "Billboard." *Google Books*. Web. 19 June 2017.

Kuss, Malena. *Music in Latin America and the Caribbean: An Encyclopedic History*. Austin: U of Texas, 2004. Print.

"La Historia Del Bolero Latinoamericano." *Analítica.com*. 07 Jan. 2000. Web.

Lam, Rafael. "Aclaraciones sobre el ritmo pilón." *Nostalgia Musical, UNEAC*. 12 Mar 2017. Web.

LatinGrammy.com.

"Latin Music USA." *PBS*. Public Broadcasting Service. Web. 01 July 2017.

Lau, Stuart. "Lost in Cuba: China's Forgotten Diaspora." *South China Morning Post*. 24 Sept. 2016. Web.

Leifeste, Luke. "Jazz Great Wynton Marsalis Releases Historic 'Live in Cuba' Album." *NBCNews.com*. NBCUniversal News Group, 20 Aug. 2015. Web.

León, Argeliers. *Música Folklórica Cubana*. La Habana: Ediciones Del Dept. De Música De La Biblioteca Nacional José Martí, 1964. Print.

Leymarie, Isabelle, and Joan Sardáa. *Jazz Latino*. Barcelona, España: Ediciones Robinbook, 2005. Print.

Linares, María Teresa. *La Música Y El Pueblo*. Ciudad De La Habana: Ed. Pueblo Y Educación, 1989. Print.

Linares, María Teresa. "La Más Pura Expresión de Cubanía." *LaJiribilla.com*. 26 Nov 2001. Web.

Linares, María Teresa. "SALA FERNANDO ORTIZ Del Museo Nacional De La Música." *Recursos Sobre Música Cubana*. Rodrigo Ronda León. Web. 14 July 2017.

"Living Tradition." *OJUNDEGARA: Tradición Viva Africana*. Web. 18 July 2017.

López Valdés, Rafael L. *Africanos De Cuba*. San Juan, P.R.: Centro De Estudios Avanzados De Puerto Rico Y El Caribe, 2004. Print.

"Palo (religion)." *Wikipedia*. Wikimedia Foundation, 03 July 2017. Web.

Perez de la Riva, Juan. "Demografía de los culíes chinos en Cuba (1953-1874)," *El barracón y otros*

BIBLIOGRAPHY

ensayos (La Habana: Editorial de Ciencias Sociales). 1971. Print.
Preston, George. "Arará and Afro-Cuban Music: The Heartbeat of Black Atlantic History." *Stanfordjazz.com*. 29 July 2010. Web.
"Makuta." *Makuta - CongaMasterClass.com*. Web. 13 July 2017.
Martínez, Chema García, and Consuelo Bautista. "Un Cubano En La Casa Blanca." *EL PAÍS*. 30 Apr. 2016. Web.
Martínez Rodríguez, Raúl. "La Rumba." *LaJiribilla*. 27 May 2005. Web.
Mason, John. *Orin Òrìsà: Songs for Selected Heads*. Brooklyn, NY: Yorùbá Theological Archministry, 2013. Print.
Mauleón, Rebeca. *Salsa Guidebook: For Piano and Ensemble*. Petaluma, CA: Sher Music, 1993. Print.
Mauleón, Rebeca. "Chucho Valdés: A True Messenger of the Afro-Cuban Tradition." *SFJAZZ.blogspot.com*. 4 Aug 2014. Web.
Mauleón-Santana, Rebeca. *101 Montunos*. Petaluma, CA: Sher Music, 1999. Print.
Mauleón-Santana, Rebeca. *The Cuban Clave: Its Origins and Development in World Musics*. 1997. Unpublished.
McG. Thomas Jr, Robert. 19 May 1996. *Willis Conover, 75, Voice of America Disc Jockey*. New York Times Obituary. Web. 06 July 2017.
Miller, Ivor L. "A Secret Society Goes Public: The Relationship Between *Abakuá* and Cuban Popular Culture." *African Studies Review,* 43.1 (2000), 164.
Miller, Ivor L. "From Creole to Carabalí." *Voice of the Leopard* (2009): 103-18. Print.
Moore, Kevin. "Havana D' Primera." *Timba*. 10 Dec 2012. Web.
Moore, Robin Dale. *Nationalizing Blackness Afrocubanismo and Artistic Revolution in Havana, 1920-1940*. Erscheinungsort Nicht Ermittelbar: U of Pittsburgh, 1998. Print.
Moreno, Dennis. *Un Tambor Arara*. La Habana: Editorial De Ciencias Sociales, 1994. Print.
"Music of Cuba." *Wikipedia*. Wikimedia Foundation, 18 June 2017. Web.
Murray, D. R. "Statistics of the Slave Trade to Cuba, 1790–1867." *Journal of Latin American Studies* 3.02 (1971): 131. Print.
Núñez, Luis M. "Drumming the Gods: Selections for Traditional Santería Drumming." *Furius.ca*. 1995-1997. Web.
Obit. "Falleció El Saxofonista Cubano Carlos Averhoff." *Radio Y Televisión Martí | Martinoticias.com*. Radio Y Televisión Martí | Martinoticias.com, 25 Dec. 2016. Web.
"Orestes López Valdés." *Orestes López Valdés - EcuRed*. Web. 07 July 2017.
Orovio, Helio. *Cuban Music from A to Z*. London: Tumi Music, 2004. Print.
Orovio, Helio. *El Bolero Latino*. Montréal: Les Éditions Du CIDIHCA, 2001. Print.
Orovio, Helio. *El Carnaval Habanero: Su Música Y Sus Comparsas*. La Habana: Extramuros, 2005. Print.
"Orquesta América." *Orquesta América - EcuRed*. Web. 08 July 2017.
"Orquesta Cubana De Música Moderna." *Orquesta Cubana De Música Moderna - EcuRed*. Web. 24 June 2017.
Ortiz, Fernando. *La Africanía De La Música Folklórica De Cuba. 2 Ed. Revisada*. Habana: Editora Universitaria, 1965. Print.
Ortiz, Fernando. *La Música Afrocubana*. Habana: Dirección De Cultura Del Ministerio De Educación, 1975. Print.
Ortiz, Fernando. *Los Instrumentos De La Música Afrocubana*. Habana: Dirección De Cultura Del Ministerio De Educación, 1952. Print.
"Oye Como Va." *Wikipedia*. Wikimedia Foundation, 06 July 2017. Web.
Padrón, Juan Alexander. "Jorge Varona: Legend of the Trumpet of Cuba." *Havana Music School*. 30 Mar.

BIBLIOGRAPHY

2017. Web. 20 June 2017.

"Palo (religion)." *Wikipedia*. Wikimedia Foundation, 03 July 2017. Web.

"Pello El Afrokán." *CiberCuba*. Web. 08 July 2017.

Perez, Rafa. "Cuando El Café Y La Música Se Unen: El Pilón De Pacho Alonso Y Enrique Bonne." *CiberCuba*. 07 July 2016. Web.

Picart, Gina. "Pello El Afrokán, Un Fantasma De La Música Cubana." *Hija Del Aire*. 12 Nov 2013. Web.

Profiles, Jazz. "Jazz Profiles." *IRAKERE*. 01 Jan. 1970. Web.

Ramos, Miguel. "Lucumí (Yoruba) Culture in Cuba: A Reevaluation (1830s-1940s)." (2013) *FIU Electronic Theses and Dissertations*. 1 Nov 2013. Web.

Ratliff, Ben. "Bebo Valdés, a Force in World of Cuban Music, Dies at 94." *The New York Times*. The New York Times, 24 Mar. 2013. Web.

Ratliff, Ben. "Chico O'Farrill, 79, Musician And Leader in Afro-Cuban Jazz." *The New York Times*. The New York Times, 28 June 2001. Web.

Reich, Howard. "U.S.-Cuban Love Affair Continues, via Jazz." *Chicagotribune.com*. 14 Nov. 2015. Web.

Reich, Howard. "U.S.-Cuban Normalization Could Shake up Jazz." *Chicagotribune.com*. 20 Jan. 2015. Web.

Retrofuzz. "Chucho Valdés | Artists." *Blue Note Records*. Web. 23 June 2017.

Romero, Angel. "Chucho Valdés Wins Best Latin Jazz Album Grammy Award." *World Music Central.org*. February 13, 2017. Web.

Romeu, Zenaida. "Mi Vida Cambió Cuando Aprendí el Lenguaje de las Manos." *Cubadebate*. 03 Nov. 2013. Web.

Ruidiaz, A. Rodriguez. "El Origen De La Música Cubana. Mitos Y Realidades." *Academia.edu - Share Research*. Web. 04 July 2017.

"Santería Music Database." *Santeria Music Database*. Web. 03 July 2017.

Saunders, Nicholas J. *The Peoples of the Caribbean an Encyclopedia of Archeology and Traditional Culture*. Santa Barbara (Calif.): ABC-CLIO, 2006. Print.

Sayre, Elizabeth. "Women and the Cuban Batá Drums: An Open Question." *Music and Culture, Blogspot*. 30 Mar 2008. Web.

Schweitzer, Kenneth. "Santería Music in Cuba." *Lameca.org*. Web. 17 July 2017.

Schweitzer, Kenneth. *The Artistry of Afro-Cuban Batá Drumming: Aesthetics, Transmission, Bonding, and Creativity*. Jackson: U of Mississippi, 2013. Print.

Scott, Rebecca J. *Slave Emancipation in Cuba: The Transition to Free Labor*. N.J., 1985. Print.

Shahadah, Alik. "Religion in Africa and the Diaspora." *AfricanBelief.com*. 23 Mar 2017. Web.

Silot Bravo, Eva, "Reimagining Cubanidad: Transnational and Alternative Spaces in Contemporary Cuban Cultural Production," *Scholarly Repository, University of Miami*, Open Access Dissertation, June 1, 2016. Web.

"Silvio Rodríguez En Chile." *Wikipedia*. Wikimedia Foundation, 20 June 2017. Web.

Simpson, George Eaton. *Black Religions in the New World Columbia University Press*. New York, 1978. Print.

Sinclair, Pat. "The Roots and Rhythms of the Congo." *The Washington Times*. The Washington Times, 23 June 2016. Web.

Slavery and Atlantic Slave Trade Facts and Figures. Web. 15 July 2017.

"Slavery in Cuba." *Wikipedia*. Wikimedia Foundation, 20 June 2017. Web.

"Smithsonian Jazz Oral History Program." *National Museum of American History*. 03 Apr. 2017. Web.

Sosa, Enrique. *Los Ñáñigos*. La Habana: Ediciones Casa de las Américas, 1982. Print.

Sturman, Janet Lynn. *Zarzuela: Spanish Operetta, American Stage*. Urbana: U of Illinois, 2000. Print.

BIBLIOGRAPHY

Sublette, Ned. *Cuba and Its Music: From the First Drums to the Mambo*. Chicago: Chicago Review, 2007. Print.

Sublette, Ned. "Rumba of Cuba: Chano Pozo and Beyond." *LaMeca.org*. Feb 2013. Web.

"Taíno." *Wikipedia*. Wikimedia Foundation, 16 June 2017. Web.

"The Music Of Congo." *World Music Network*, 03 Nov 2010. Web.

"The Stylings of Silver." *Wikipedia*. Wikimedia Foundation, 17 June 2017. Web.

Thomas, Hugh. *The Slave Trade: The Story of the Atlantic Slave Trade, 1440-1870*. New York, NY: Simon & Schuster, 1999. Print.

Triana, Mauro García, Pedro Eng Herrera, and Gregor Benton. *The Chinese in Cuba: 1847- Now*. Lanham: Lexington, 2009. Print.

"Trova." *Wikipedia*. Wikimedia Foundation, 03 Mar. 2017. Web.

"U.S.-Cuba Musical Relations: A Timeline of Milestones." *Billboard*. 19 Dec. 2014. Web.

Vaughan, Umi, and Carlos Aldama. *Carlos Aldama's Life in Batá: Cuba, Diaspora, and the Drum*. Bloomington: Indiana UP, 2012. Print.

Villepastour, Amanda, and John David Yeadon Peel. *The Yorubá God of Drumming: Transatlantic Perspectives on the Wood That Talks*. Jackson: U of Mississippi, 2015. Print.

Vinueza, María Elena. *Presencia Arará En La Música Folclórica De Matanzas*. Ciudad De La Habana: Casa De Las Américas, 1989. Print.

"Voice of America Jazz Hour." *Wikipedia*. Wikimedia Foundation, 20 Feb. 2017. Web. 06 July 2017.

Yanow, Scott. "Jazz Bata - Chucho Valdés | Songs, Reviews, Credits." *AllMusic*. Web. 19 June 2017.

YorubaCuba.org.

"Yoruba Religion." *Wikipedia*. Wikimedia Foundation, 30 June 2017. Web.

YouTube.com.

"Yuka (music)." *Wikipedia*. Wikimedia Foundation, 02 July 2017. Web.

Yun, Lisa. "Chinese Freedom Fighters in Cuba." *Afro Asia* (2008): 30-54. Print.

"Zarzuela." *Wikipedia*. Wikimedia Foundation, 01 July 2017. Web.

• • •

GLOSSARY

Abakuá: 1. A secret fraternal society formed in Cuba be descendants of the Calabar region of Nigeria, referred to as the *carabalí*. 2. The ritual music and dance of the Abakuá society, which has greatly influenced Cuban music and cultural, notably, the genre of *rumba*.

Abanico: The rimshot and roll of the timbales.

Afro: A hybrid form of Cuban popular music developed during the early 1940s derived from various rhythms played by the sacred batá rhythms.

Agbe (also Aggüe or Agwe): The Yoruba term for the beaded gourd instrument known as the *chékere* or *shékere*.

Arará: The denomination (in Cuba) for Africans of Dahomean origin, as well as the sacred music, language, and cultural practices of their descendants in Cuba. The *arará* are considered the fourth largest African cultural group brought to Cuba.

Areito: 1. A term derived from the indigenous tribes living in Cuba before the arrival of European colonizers, referring to elaborate religious celebrations of music, dance and theater. 2. A style of post-revolutionary hybrid Cuban music pioneered by groups such as the Orquesta Ritmo Oriental, featuring a highly syncopated texture, and played primarily by *charanga* orchestras.

Atcheré: A rattle or shaker, made either of wood, gourd, metal or other materials, used to accompany sacred instruments such as the batá drums in liturgical *lucumí* music.

Bantú: The denomination for Africans of Congolese or Bantú origin in Cuba, considered the largest and most influential cultural group on the island and perhaps throughout the Caribbean.

Baqueteo: The rhythmical ostinato pattern played by the timbales in the *danzón*.

Batá: The hourglass-shaped drums of Yoruba origin used in liturgical ceremony, consisting of a set of three drums in Cuba: the Iyá (largest), Itótele (middle) and Okónkolo (smallest). There are literally hundreds of sacred rhythms played for various *orishas* (deities) during *lucumí* religious ceremonies, using the consecrated drums known as *fundamento*. In the 1930s, ethnographer Fernando Ortiz commissioned the creation of a non-consecrated set of drums, known as *aberikulá*, which are the drums used in popular ensembles such as that of Irakere.

Batanga: A predecessor style to the Cuban *mambo* pioneered by Bebo Valdés (father of Chucho Valdés), combining the influences of American big band jazz with *son* and other popular styles, along with the addition of the batá drums in the rhythm section.

Bembé: One of the most commonly used forms in *lucumí* liturgical music, with several interpretations used throughout Cuba. This 6/8 style is traditionally played on three drums and accompanied with a cowbell and a shaker.

Bloque: A term literally meaning "block" and referring to breaks as well as soli passages by the horn section or the entire ensemble.

Bolero: A slow, lyrical ballad form developed in the late 19th century in Eastern Cuba, pioneered by *trovador* (troubadour) José Pepe Sánchez. The *bolero* became the embodiment of romantic ballad singing throughout Latin America, with a long-standing tradition of shared compositions throughout the decades.

GLOSSARY

Bomba: An Afro-Puerto Rican music and dance genre comprising several sub-styles, dating back to the late 19th century. Consisting of a highly interactive atmosphere, *bomba* is one of the strongest expressions of the African diaspora in Puerto Rico, resembling Cuban *rumba* in structure and context, but containing a broader range of styles. Played on barrel-shaped drums known as *barriles* or *bombas*, as well as several hand percussion instruments, *bomba* is highly syncopated and improvisational, and features call and response singing. As with *plena* (see below), *bomba* was adopted into popular dance music such as salsa.

Bombo: 1. The Spanish term for bass drum. 2. The syncopated note highlighted in many Cuban rhythms, placed on the "and" of the third beat (in an 8th-note subdivision) in 4/4 time, or the fourth 16th note in a 2/4 measure.

Bongos (or Bongó): A percussion instruments consisting of a pair of small Cuban drums held together with a thick piece of wood, developed in the 19th century in Eastern Cuba. The bongos are sometimes referred to in singular form (as *bongó*), and emerged as a principal instrument in the Cuban *son*, eventually becoming part of the instrumentation for salsa music. The bongos are played while held between the knees; the larger of the two drums is called the *hembra* (female), and the smaller is the *macho* (male). They remain as one of the most important percussion instruments in all of Latin music.

Botija (or Botijuela): A ceramic jug originally used to import Spanish olive oil, used to provide a bass accompaniment in the early *son* style.

Caballo (or A caballo): Literally meaning "horse" or "on horseback" in Spanish, respectively, the name of a conga drum pattern used in mid 20th century styles such as the *pachanga*, emphasizing the slap tone on the downbeat of each measure.

Cajón(es): Wooden boxes used in early interpretations of *rumba*, and still commonly played today. The Cuban *cajón* consists of varying sizes, and was developed during a time when Afro-Cuban musicians were discouraged from playing their drums, becoming a substitute for carved or slatted wood drums with skins during the colonial era.

Canción: A simple yet fundamental form of vocal and guitar music developed in Cuba's *trova* genre.

Carnaval: Carnival in Cuba.

Cáscara: 1. The shell or sides of the timbales. 2. The pattern typically played on the shell of the timbales, primarily used in the popular dance styles such as the *guaracha*.

Catá: A thick piece of bamboo laid (or mounted) horizontally on a stand that serves as a key anchor in *rumba* ensembles, and is used to play the *palitos* pattern.

Cierre: A term literally meaning "closing," but specifically referring to written, sometimes ornate breaks played by the percussion or rhythm section.

Cencerro: A hand-held cowbell, struck with a stick, often used by the bongo player in a *son* group (*sexteto* or *septeto*) as well as a *conjunto*.

Cha-cha-chá: A style developed within the *danzón* in its evolution through the early to mid 20th century, eventually evolving into its own separate musical and dance tradition. The *cha-cha-chá* was created in 1951 by violinist Enrique Jorrín, who observed the movements of the dancers' feet as they scraped the floor, and pioneered the style within the *charanga* instrumentation. Eventually, the *cha-cha-chá* would break away from the *danzón* and spread around the world, becoming one of the most popular Cuban forms ever.

GLOSSARY

Changüí: An early style of Cuban *son* originating in the Guantánamo province, featuring an instrumentation including the *tres, bongos, guayo, maracas* and Congolese derived *marímbula* (bass lamellophone). The texture of the *changüí* is highly syncopated, and provides many of the foundational elements heard in more contemporary *son* as well as salsa.

Charanga: An instrumentation developed during the early 20th century in Cuba, consisting of a flute, two or three violins, piano, double bass, timbales (or pailas), güiro, and 1 conga drum which was added in the late 1930s. This ensemble became primarily associated with the interpretation of the *danzón* and, later, the *cha-cha-chá*. (The origins of this instrumentation feature Afro-Haitian influences; it was first known as the *charanga francesa*).

Charanguita: A popular instrumentation in peasant or country music parties known as *guateques*, consisting of accordion, timbales and a güiro.

Chékere (or Shékere): A beaded gourd instrument of African origin used in Cuban sacred music, the *chékere* (or *shékere*) is also sometimes referred to as *güiro* for the style of music in which it is used, called *toque the güiro*.

Cierre: A term used to refer to a percussion break, as well as one played by the entire ensemble.

Cinquillo: A five-note pattern or cell derived from the *contradanza*, which features Afro-Haitian influences that came into Eastern Cuba after Haiti's revolution in 1791. The pattern is highlighted in the *baqueteo* pattern played in the *danzón* by the timbales.

Clave: 1. In Spanish, a term referring to the given key of a song. 2. A rhythmical pattern (comprising several varieties) that is considered a foundational guide to virtually all of Cuban music. The binary structure of the *clave* consists of an antecedent and consequent phrase in a relationship of tension-release, which is a reflection of the melodic phrase in a given song, and has its roots in West African rhythmical timelines. There are several *clave* patterns associated with folkloric and popular styles of Cuban music, and each of these acts as an anchor in stabilizing the rhythm as well as identifying the relationship between all of the interlocking percussion parts in the ensemble. The two most commonly used *clave* patterns in popular music are *son clave* and *rumba clave*. The African-derived 6/8 bell rhythm used primarily in liturgical music in Cuba can also be thought of as a *clave* pattern.

Claves: The Cuban idiophone instrument consisting of two rounded, polished sticks.

Columbia: One of three styles of the Cuban *rumba* genre, structured in a polymetric cross of 4/4 and 6/8 time, and containing many African (mostly Bantú) elements in its highly improvisational interpretation of song, drumming and dance. The *columbia* is typically the fastest of the three styles of *rumba*, and features a blending of Spanish and Bantú words and expressions, as well as the influence of Abakuá elements.

Combo: An adaptation of the North American jazz combo instrumentation developed in Cuba during the 1950s.

Comparsa: The name of the ensemble or contingent for Cuba's Carnaval celebration, the typical *comparsa* is primarily a percussion ensemble featuring bass drums, conga drums, brake drums or frying pans, cowbells and other instruments, along with brass or double-reeded horns. The *comparsas* primarily play the styles associated with Carnaval, including the *conga, mozambique* and others.

Conga (drum): A Cuban drum derived from several African predecessors, known as the *tumbadora*, originally carved from a solid hollow log and topped with a nailed-on rawhide skin. Eventually transformed using slats of wood glued together and tuneable metal hardware, the *conga* drum (consisting of three general widths) became one of the most important percussion instruments in the world. In addition to hardwood, the conga can also be made from fiberglass.

GLOSSARY

Conga (style): 1. A style of Cuban percussion ensemble music and dance used for Carnaval. There are two principal styles, one from Havana (known as *conga habanera*) and the other from Santiago (called *conga santiaguera*). 2. The dance step performed to either *conga* style. As a processional music and dance genre, the *conga* inspired the commonly known style of dancing known as the "conga line."

Conjunto: A specific style of instrumentation developed by *tres* player and bandleader Arsenio Rodríguez around 1940, consisting of guitar, *tres*, double bass, bongos, piano, conga drum, two to four trumpets, and two to three vocalists (who often play hand percussion such as claves and maracas). Eventually, the guitar and tres would be omitted, leaving the piano to provide the harmonic as well as rhythmic foundation along with the bass.

Contradanza: (Also called *contradanza criolla*), an 18th century style derived from European court and country dances, and a predecessor to the Cuban *danzón*, containing many Creole and Afro-Haitian elements in its instrumentation and interpretation.

Corneta china (also see **Trompeta china**): A double-reeded instrument of Chinese origin (known as the *suona*) used in Cuban *conga de comparsa* music for Carnaval, specifically, the style from Eastern Cuba called the *conga santiaguera*.

Coro: Chorus.

Coro de clave: A vocal ensemble originating in the 19th century featuring a vocal soloist and large chorus, often accompanied by guitars, claves, and other small percussion.

Danza: A mid to late 19th century musical and dance form developed from the *contradanza*, serving as an important ancestor to the Cuban *danzón*. Played using varying instrumentations, *danzas* were also composed for solo piano, notably the compositions of Manuel Saumel and Ignacio Cervantes, who ushered in an important nationalist sensibility by exploring the African rhythmical influences in an otherwise European-derived style.

Danzón: Cuba's national dance, developed from earlier Western European court and country forms including the French *contredanse*, the Creole *contradanza*, *danza* and *habanera*. Composed in 1879 by Miguel Faílde in the city of Matanzas, the first *danzón* was "Las Alturas de Simpson." Early *danzones* were played using an instrumentation called the *orquesta típica*, evolving later to the *charanga* orchestra, with flute, strings and Cuban rhythm section. The form is structured in a *ritornello* or *rondo* form (ABACAD), with the "A" section of the form, called the *paseo* (promenade), highlighting a 5-note rhythmic cell known as the *cinquillo*, which serves as a cue to the dancers to change partners. Around 1910, elements of the *son* began to penetrate the style, such as in the piece "El Bombín de Barreto" (composed by José Urfé). In the late 1930s, influences from the Cuban *son* led to the addition of a rhythmical ostinato over which several instruments would improvise (largely spearheaded by the López brothers, Orestes and Israel, who were intrigued by the increasingly syncopated environment); this new "E" section became known first as *nuevo ritmo* (new rhythm), and later, *mambo*, before breaking off as its own style, the *cha-cha-chá*.

Danzonete: A hybrid of the Cuban *danzón* and *son* styles developed by Aniceto Díaz, with an added vocal part to what was previously an instrumental style. The first danzonete was "Rompiendo La Rutina," composed by Díaz in 1929.

Décima: A traditional form of Spanish poetry developed in the 16th century (by writer and musician Vicente Espinel), consisting of a 10-line stanza, with each line containing seven to eight syllables, as well as a highly complex rhyming structure. *Décimas* are widely used throughout the Spanish speaking world, and are a major component of Cuban *trova* music, where they are commonly improvised in spontaneous poetic duels known as *controversias*.

GLOSSARY

Descarga: 1. The Cuban colloquial term for jam session. 2. A genre of Cuban music popularized during the 1950s, encompassing the gamut of the island's rhythms and styles, and featuring a high degree of spontaneity. Among the pioneers of this tradition were Israel "Cachao" López, Bebo Valdés, Tata Güines, Frank Emilio Flynn, Pedro Justiz "Peruchín," El Niño Rivera, Guillermo Barreto, El Negro Vivar, Julio Gutiérrez, José Fajardo, Walfredo de los Reyes Sr., and "Nuyorican" bandleader and *timbalero*, Tito Puente.

Diana: The vocal scat introduction in the Afro-Cuban folkloric genre of *rumba*, which effectively "tunes up" the ensemble and introduces the melody.

Estribillo: Refrain or chorus.

Filin: A blending of American jazz and Cuban music during the 1940s through 60s, with a concentration on ballad singing and highly stylized repertoire. *Filin* became widespread in Cuba's cabaret scene, and was fueled by the highly dramatic interpretations of singer-songwriters such as José Antonio Méndez, César Portillo de la Luz and others.

Guajeo: A term used to refer to the repeated ostinato figure of the string instruments in a given ensemble, and sometimes used to refer to the horns or piano patterns as well. (In some circles, the terms *montuno, guajeo* and *tumbao* may be interchangeable.)

Guajira: An arpeggiated and floral song form derived from the *son*, and one of the most widely-known forms of Cuban *trova*.

Guaracha: 1. A form of popular street music, similar to light opera or musical theater, popular in Cuba during the 18th and 19th centuries. 2. A stylized form of Cuban dance music derived from the *son* and developed during the 1940s and 50s, eventually becoming the blueprint for salsa music interpretation.

Guarapachangueo: A contemporary interpretation of the *guaguancó* style of *rumba*, wherein one player adapts several parts normally played by multiple players. The *guarapachangueo* tends to feature a highly syncopated environment and more musical fluidity (as opposed to more repetitive playing).

Guayo: A metal scraper played with a metal rod or forked brush, commonly used in older styles of Cuban music such as the *changüí*.

Güiro: 1. A serrated gourd scraper played with a stick, with indigenous roots, and widely used throughout Latin America in popular dance music. 2. Term used to refer to *lucumí* sacred music played by chékeres (or shékeres), known as *toque de güiro*.

Habanera: A precursor to the Cuban danzón developed in the late 1880s, and one of the most popular genres to influence varying genres around the globe, including the Argentine tango.

Itótele: The middle-sized drum in the set of three batá drums.

Iyá: The largest drum in the set of three batá drums. The word "Iyá" means "mother" in Yoruba.

Iyesá: Iyesá music is a component of the *lucumí* tradition of liturgical music, and is exclusively from the province of Matanzas, stemming from the various *cabildos* founded in the region by direct descendants of the Iyesá people from Nigeria. This tradition has its own distinct instruments (a set of four cylindrical drums plus two iron bells), but the rhythms can also be played using other instruments, such as the batá.

Kachimbo (or **Cachimbo**): The pulse pattern played by one of the chékeres in the *toque de güiro*.

Lucumí (or **Lukumí**): The term in Cuba for descendants of the Yoruba people.

GLOSSARY

Mambo: A term with multiple meanings, the origins of the word are Bantú, referring to the act of storytelling or singing. Its use in Cuban popular music emerged in 1938 with the composition entitled "Mambo" by Orestes López (brother of Israel "Cachao" López), which was an abbreviated *danzón* consisting only of the introductory *paseo* followed by the *nuevo ritmo* (new rhythm) section. The term would eventually be used to refer to the contrasting instrumental sections of many popular dance tunes, and would spawn several new styles in the 1940s and 50s in the United States and México. In New York City, Cuban bandleader Frank Grillo "Machito" and his brother-in-law Mario Bauzá introduced jazz arrangements into Cuban music, recording many dance hits and spawning an a new musical hybrid, eventually branded as "Afro-Cuban jazz." Mambos were among the many Cuban dance styles recorded by Machito and his Afro-Cubans. Among the most celebrated of Cuba's "mambo kings" was pianist and bandleader Dámaso Pérez Prado, known for his stylized big band interpretations of *mambos*, and for successfully capturing a wide audience with his onstage antics and catchy compositions.

Makuta: A form of Bantú religious music and dance in Cuba, with its own distinct barrel-shaped drums that are considered important predecessors to the conga drums.

Maracas: Hand-held rattles or shakers of indigenous origin found throughout the Americas, which can be made from gourds, wood, coconuts or rawhide.

Marímbula: A large bass box or lamellophone of Bantú origin used primarily in Eastern Cuban music such as the *changüí*.

Martillo: The repeated pattern of the bongos, which is frequently ad-libbed (played improvisationally).

Maruga: A metal shaker or rattle, often used in folkloric ensembles interpreting *rumba*.

Merengue: The national dance of the Dominican Republic, developed during the late 19th century, which is a fast, two-step dance.

Montuno: 1. The repeated ostinato pattern played by the piano in a salsa or Cuban dance band. 2. The main groove section of a song (such as a *son* or *guaracha*) containing the call and response vocal improvisation or *estribillo* (refrain) as well as instrumental solos.

Moña: A term used to refer to the horn lines played during a bridge or other contrasting section other than the main *montuno*, serving as a dynamic transition before the return to the refrain.

Mozambique: A rhythmical style derived from the Cuban *conga* style (used for Carnaval) developed by Pedro Izquierdo (aka Pello el Afrokán) during the 1960s. The *mozambique* was adopted and adapted in the United States by several Puerto Rican and Nuyorican musicians, including Eddie Palmieri and Manny Oquendo.

Música campesina: A term referring to a broad range of country or peasant music derived from the Spanish troubadour tradition, generally consisting of poetic verses accompanied by guitars.

Nueva trova: A post-revolutionary interpretation of Cuba's troubadour movement following the political and social changes on the island during the 1960s, highlighting ideological lyrics that concentrated on issues such as colonialism, racism, oppression and injustice.

Nuevo ritmo: Meaning "new rhythm" in Spanish, this term refers to the added section of the *danzón* form in the early 1940s (by Orestes and Israel López), which would later be known as the *mambo*.

Okónkolo: The smallest in the set of batá drums.

GLOSSARY

Orquesta típica: Instrumentation developed in Cuba during the mid 19th century and used in the interpretation of the *contradanza, danza* and *early danzón*, consisting of woodwinds, brass, strings, güiro and tympani. The tympani would eventually be replaced by the Cuban timbales, and the horn section would gradually diminish, paving the way for the development of the *charanga* instrumentation.

Pachanga: A popular and rigorous dance style developed within the *charanga* orchestras during the 1950s.

Paila (also Paila criolla or Pailas criollas): A term for a set of smaller Cuban timbales.

Palitos: Literally meaning "little sticks," this term refers to the two sticks and the respective patterns they play in Cuban *rumba*. The sticks strike a piece of bamboo mounted horizontally on a stand (known as the *catá*); the bamboo can be substituted by a woodblock (or modern-day fiberglass jam block).

Palo: 1. Literally meaning "stick" in Spanish, the term refers to liturgical traditions of Bantú origin in Cuba known as *Reglas de Palo*. 2. The sacred music associated with the *palo* ritual tradition in Cuba, and one of three primary styles associated within Bantú religious practice. The rhythm is a fast 6/8 style played by drums and cowbell, often combining Spanish and Bantú words within the songs. Known as *ciclo congo*, the three rhythms associated with this cycle are *palo, makuta* and *yuka*.

Paseo: The introduction or promenade section of the *danzón* form, wherein the dancers walk (instead of dancing) to select their partner. This is the section of the music that highlights the five-note *cinquillo* rhythm, signalling the dancers to change partners.

Pilón: A style of dance music developed in the mid-1960s by composer and bandleader Enrique Bonne, and later popularized by singer Pacho Alonso, inspired by the mechanical sounds of the órgano oriental and the movements of agricultural workers as they pounded coffee beans. The word "pilón" in Cuba refers to the large mortar and pestle used to grind coffee beans by hand; Pilón is also a town and a municipality in Southeastern Cuba.

Plena: A Puerto Rican style of folk music, often containing sociopolitical commentary and lyrics that speak to the daily lives of the people. Like *bomba*, the *plena* has also been adopted into popular dance music such as salsa.

Ponche: The fourth beat of a measure (in 4/4 time), and a commonly accented beat in Cuban music as well as salsa.

Pregón: 1. An old Spanish tradition of the sales pitch sung by street vendors, adopted throughout Latin America. 2. The lead vocal improvisation in popular Cuban songs, which alternates with a fixed, repetitive chorus during the *estribillo* (refrain).

Quijada: A dried jawbone of a mule or donkey used in many forms of Latin American country music, and the predecessor to the modern day vibra-slap.

Quinto: The lead and highest pitched conga drum in a folkloric ensemble, primarily played in the performance of *rumba*.

Rebajador: One of the *tumba* (bass drum) parts in the *conga habanera* rhythm.

GLOSSARY

Rumba: One of Cuba's most important secular forms of folk music and dance, dating back to the late 19th century and created in the city of Matanzas. *Rumba* consists of three primary styles: *yambú* (the oldest), *guaguancó* (moderate to fast tempo), and *columbia* (the fastest in tempo and consisting of both 4/4 and 6/8 meters). The instrumentation includes *cajones* (box drums), *tumbadoras* (conga drums), the claves, a piece of bamboo known as the *catá*, and a metal shaker known as the *maruga*. A blend of Bantú and Spanish flamenco influences, *rumba* is a highly improvisational and interactive genre. The structure of almost all *rumba* songs is fairly consistent, beginning with the claves to establish the tempo, followed by the lead singer's *diana* (scat-sung melody) to define the key, later leading to the *estribillo* (refrain), wherein the dancers begin to dance. The *quinto* player (lead drummer) attempts to mimic the dancers' feet with the drum, creating a constant and fluid improvisation throughout the songs. In 2016, *rumba* was officially declared "Intangible Cultural Heritage of Humanity" by UNESCO, and continues to evolve to this day.

Rumba flamenca: The style of *rumba* from Southern Spain, sometimes called *rumba gitana* (gypsy rumba), which influenced Cuban *rumba*.

Rumbero/a: An expert player, singer or dancer of Cuban *rumba*.

Salidor: One of the *tumbadora* (bass drum) parts in the *conga habanera* rhythm.

Sartenes: Frying pans used as instruments in the Cuban *conga de comparsa*.

Segundo (or **Tres Dos**): The middle or second drum in the set of *tumbadoras* (conga drums) used in Cuban *rumba*.

Septeto: A Cuban instrumentation developed in 1927 by bassist, composer and bandleader Ignacio Piñeiro and his band, the Septeto Nacional, consisting of a trumpet added to the previous *sexteto* (sextet) group.

Sexteto: A style of instrumentation founded in 1920 by the Sexteto Habanero, consisting of the Cuban *tres*, guitar, double bass, bongos, claves and maracas, the latter two of which are played by vocalists.

Son: Cuba's most important primordial music and dance tradition, developed in the late 19th century in the province of Guantánamo and later spreading throughout the island. The *son* blends African and Spanish rhythms and melodies, and was some of the first Caribbean music to be recorded in the early 20th century. Early *son* styles or predecessors included the *nengón* and the *changüí*, which emerged in the Cuban countryside (specifically, the mountains). The instruments used in these early styles included the newly created *tres* guitar (consisting of three double courses of strings) and the *bongos*, along with a Congolese-derived *marimbula* (bass lamellophone), a metal *guayo* scraper, and maracas. By the 1920s, the *son* genre developed a "formal" instrumentation known as the *sexteto*, consisting of the signature *tres* and *bongos*, and adding on a regular 6-string Spanish guitar and the European double bass. The *guayo* would disappear and the claves would enter, marking a significant evolution and stylistic trend. This more "accessible" and mainstream combination became marketable, as *son* recordings began to circle the globe.

Son-Montuno: A hybrid of the *son* developed by musicians including Ignacio Piñeiro and, later on, Arsenio Rodríguez, wherein the most essential aspects of the music were highlighted, reducing a given song to a simple refrain and cutting to the chase, so to speak. *Son-montunos* are still one of the preferred styles used in playing for dancers in an impromptu setting, such as the Cuban *descarga* (jam session).

GLOSSARY

Songo: A contemporary (post-revolutionary) style of Cuban dance music developed by bassist and bandleader Juan Formell (founder of Los Van Van), taking elements from the *son* and adding varying ingredients inspired by American pop and rock music. *Songo* evolved as a direct result of the specific songs composed for Los Van Van, creating unique rhythmical patterns and phrases to emphasize the individual characteristics of each song. Not limited to one particular pattern, *songo* is more of a conceptual way of playing Cuban dance music that responds to the inherent nature or sentiment of a tune, and the most notable characteristics are the percussion and drum patterns developed by José Luis Quintana, aka "Changuito," who helped create the genre.

Tambor de conga: Specific name for the conical hand drum used in Cuban Carnaval music.

Timba: A term referring to the interpretation of contemporary Cuban dance music during the 1990s, wherein elements of funk and hip-hop were fused with a more aggressive approach to the *son*. As with *songo*, *timba* is a conceptual style that draws from various modern influences, providing more freedom to the rhythm section in contrast to the generally repetitive or redundant techniques of earlier styles. Many of these stylistic elements can be heard going back to Irakere's repertoire during the 1970s, as the players found ways to combine elements of folkloric and popular styles in a more fluid way, blending them with jazz, funk and rock. Among the characteristics of *timba* are the density of the texture, the accenting of unusual or atypical beats in a given phrase, a general rhythmical intensity, frequent breaks by the percussion section, and the funk-inspired techniques of the electric bass (including slapping and pulling the strings).

Timbales: A set of Cuban drums derived from the European tympani, mounted on a stand and played with sticks, and including varying accessories such as cowbells and woodblocks, ride cymbal, etc. The *timbalero/a* is similar in many ways to the jazz drummer, defining each dynamic section of a given song by creating a range of patterns and textures, and also cueing the band during important transitions. In many contemporary groups, the timbales may be integrated into a drummer's set-up, but can also be a stand-alone instrument. Along with the congas and the bongos, the timbales are an essential component of the percussion triumvirate found in salsa music.

Toque: A term referring to the playing of a given percussion instrument or battery of instruments, as well as the specific patterns played in liturgical music.

Tres: A Cuban stringed instrument derived from the Spanish guitar, consisting of three sets of double strings, played with a pick. The tres is one of the signature instruments of the *son*, and is responsible for the repetitive ostinato lines (referred to as the *montuno*) that eventually led to the piano's role in popular dance music by the 1930s. Traditional *son* music emphasizes the role of the *tres* as both harmonic and melodic, with a highly improvisational approach.

Tresillo: A ubiquitous rhythmic cell of African origin found in musics throughout the Caribbean and Latin America, and highlighted in Cuban folkloric as well as popular music. The *tresillo* is the subdivision of an 8-beat count using a **1**-2-3-**4**-5-6-**7**-8 structure (or **1**+2+3+**4**+), as in the three-side of the clave pattern. Notated in 4/4, the pattern consists of dotted quarter-note + dotted quarter-note + quarter-note, and is one of the most foundational of all African-derived rhythms in the Americas.

Trompeta china (also see **Corneta china**): A double-reeded instrument of Chinese origin (known as the *suona*) used in Cuban *conga de comparsa* music for Carnaval, specifically, the style from Eastern Cuba called the *conga santiaguera*.

GLOSSARY

Trova: One of the principal foundations of Cuba's popular music, rooted in Spanish poetry along with the use of the guitar and its descendants. Representative of the tradition of European troubadours, *trova* emerged in the 19th century among a group of itinerant musicians, and contains both extemporaneous as well as through-composed repertoire, comprising several well known styles, including the *cancíon, guajira, bolero, punto guajiro* and others. The founder and acknowledged "father" of the *trova* tradition was José Pepe Sánchez, and the genre remains as one of the most important and lyrical art forms throughout the island.

Trovador/Trovadora: Spanish word meaning "troubadour."

Tumbadora: The formal name for the Cuban conga drum, which is derived from African instruments and originally consisted of a hollowed out log with a tacked-on skin made of rawhide. Over time, and with the adaptation of several sacred as well as secular drumming traditions in Afro-Cuban folklore, the *tumbadoras* emerged as a composite of varying Bantú drums, notably the *makuta* and *yuka* drums. There are three main sizes (widths) of *tumbadoras*: the *quinto* (highest pitched drum), the *segundo* or *tres-dos* (middle drum), and the *tumba* (lowest pitched drum).

Tumba francesa: A folkloric genre of Afro-Haitian origins developed in Cuba's Oriente province, created by Africans of Dahomean descent, particularly those arriving in Cuba during and after Haiti's revolution in 1791. *Tumba francesa* is reminiscent of many Creole forms, combining European and African influences, and became an important influence in the "Africanization" of European styles on the island, including the *contradanza* and the *danza*, eventually playing a role in the rhythmical structure of Cuba's national dance, the *danzón*.

Tumbao: Term used to refer to the repeated ostinato pattern of the bass as well as the conga drums in popular dance music. The *tumbao* can also be used to describe the overarching groove of a given song, and in some circles, the repetitive patterns played by the piano.

Yambú: The oldest of the three styles of the Cuban *rumba* genre, developed during the colonial era, and originally interpreted on box drums known as *cajones*. The *yambú* is slow in tempo, and danced gracefully by male-female dancers.

Yoruba: The people (and language) from Nigeria, and one of the most influential cultures throughout the Caribbean and South America.

Yuka: An influential secular music and dance style of Bantú origin, containing its own cylindrical drums, and representative (in the dance) of the pelvic movements used in the *guaguancó* style of *rumba*.

• • •

APPENDIX A: AFRO-CUBAN RHYTHM GLOSSARY

This listing comprises the various rhythmical genres and styles referenced throughout the book, with notated fragments of both folkloric and popular rhythms as interpreted by Irakere. While there may be some redundancy with some of the information provided throughout this book, the purpose of this appendix is to provide the reader with a comprehensive listing in a practical manner that can serve as a handy reference guide, especially to those interested in understanding and adopting Afro-Cuban rhythms into your performance practice regimen. To facilitate ease of use and ability to identify and locate a given style, the rhythms are presented alphabetically.

Abakuá

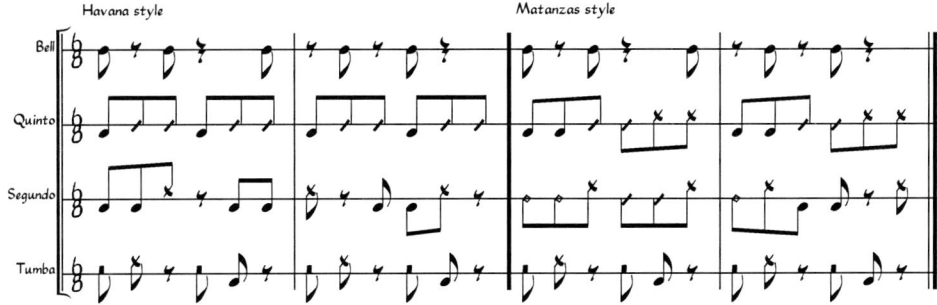

Afro

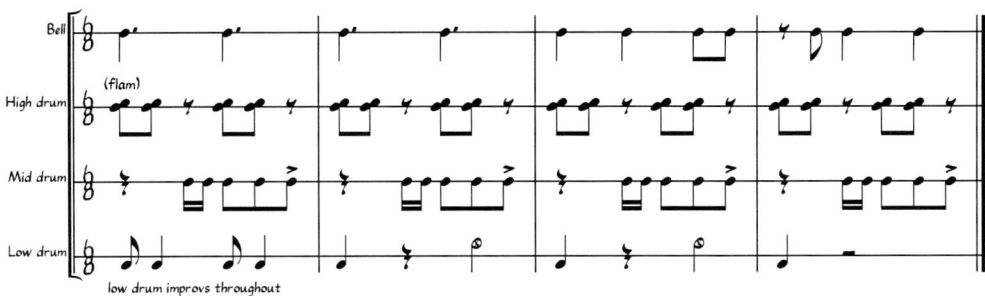

Arará

Appendix A: Afro-Cuban Rhythm Glossary

BATÁ RHYTHMS (toques de batá)

Alaró (or Aro) ~ toque for Yemayá

The Iyá part is generally fluid and varied

Bariba ogé de ma ~ toque for Babalú Ayé (clave 3-2)

This toque follows an AAB, 12-bar form   (1st X only)

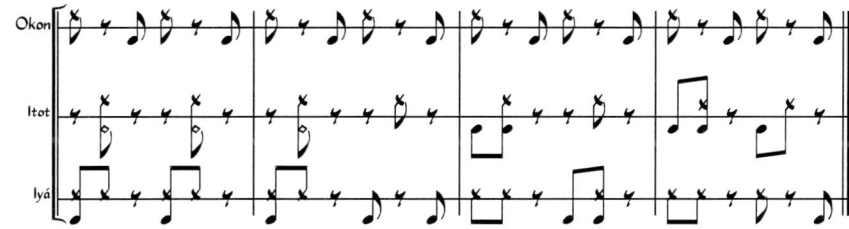

Chachálokpafúñ ~ played for multiple orishas (clave 3-2)

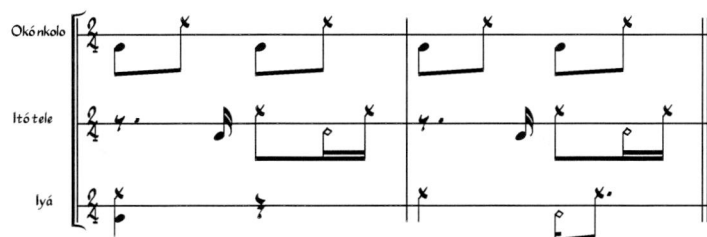

Iyesá ~ played for multiple orishas (clave 3-2)

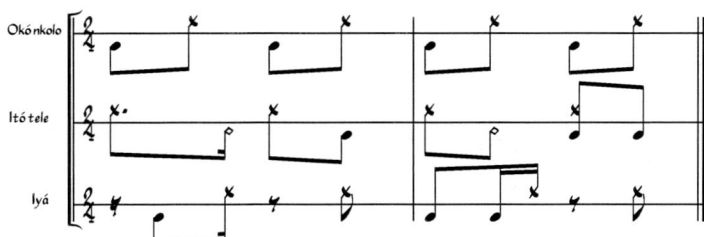

Appendix A: Afro-Cuban Rhythm Glossary

Latokpa ~ toque for Eleguá (clave 3-2)

Rumba Obatalá ~ toque for Obatalá (clave 3-2)

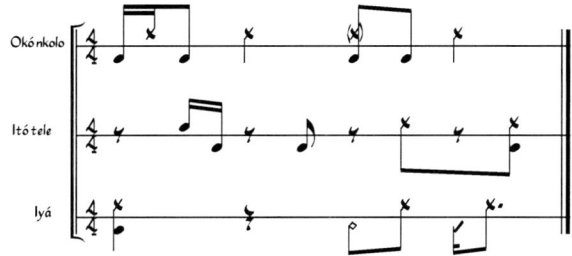

Yakotá ~ played for multiple orishas

Yeguá ~ toque for Babalú Ayé

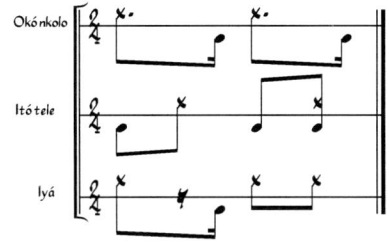

• •

Bembé

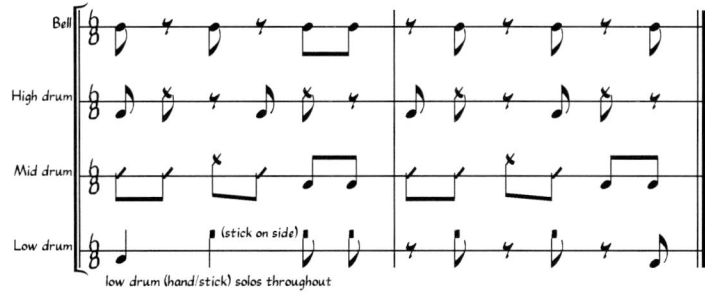

Appendix A: Afro-Cuban Rhythm Glossary

Bolero

Cha-cha-chá

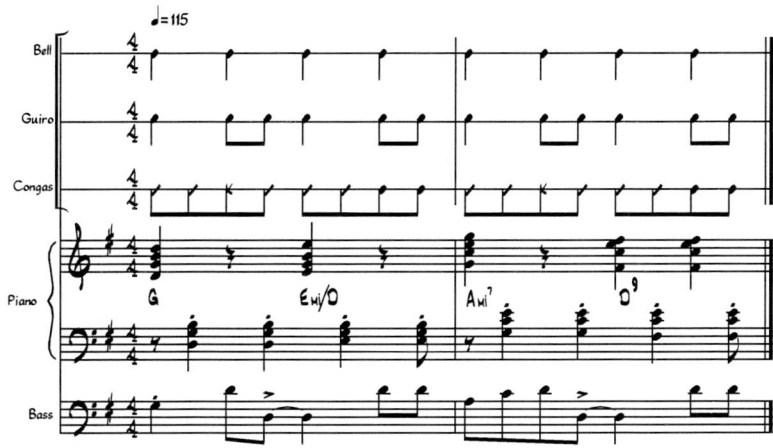

Conga Habanera

bombo ad libs freely

Appendix A: Afro-Cuban Rhythm Glossary

Conga Santiaguera

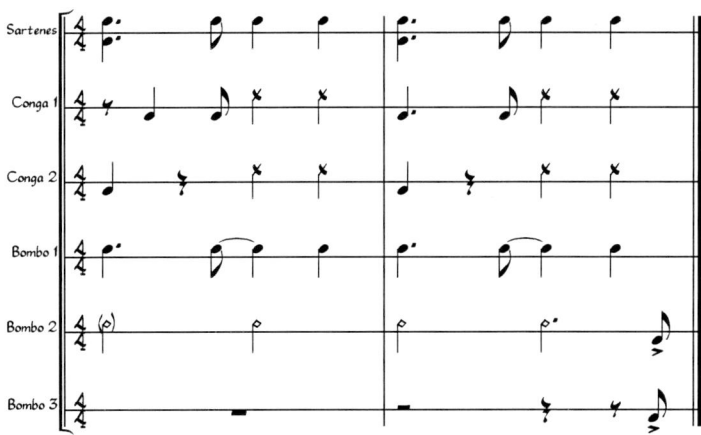

Danzón

Guajira

Appendix A: Afro-Cuban Rhythm Glossary

Guaracha (clave 2-3)

Güiro (toque de)

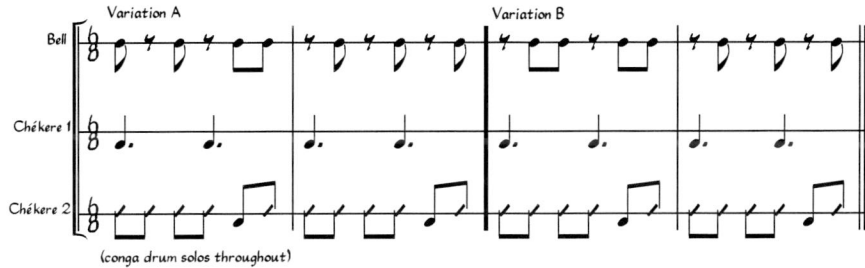

Iyesá

Appendix A: Afro-Cuban Rhythm Glossary

Mozambique

Palo

Pilón

Appendix A: Afro-Cuban Rhythm Glossary

Rumba-Columbia

Rumba-Guaguancó (Havana & Matanzas styles)

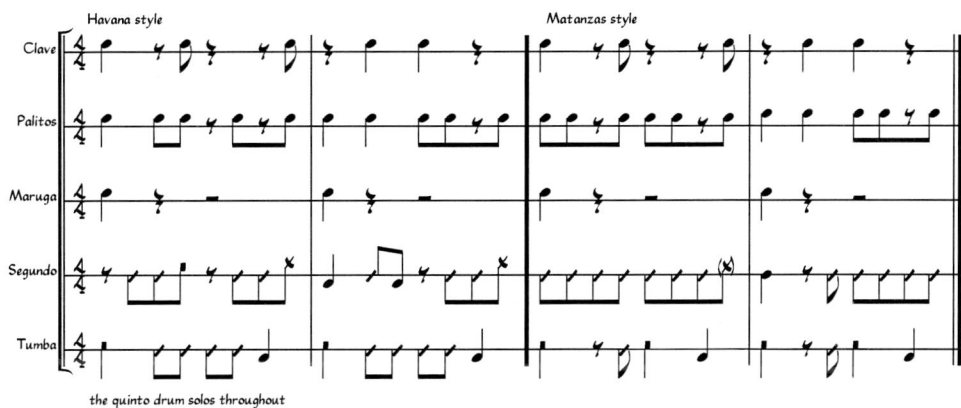

Rumba-Yambú

Appendix A: Afro-Cuban Rhythm Glossary

Son (clave 3-2)

Songo ca 1970s (clave 2-3)

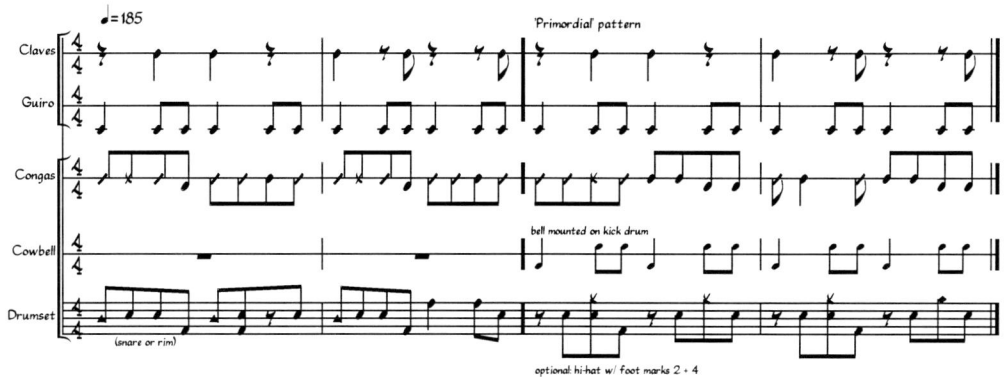

Songo ca 1990s (Rumba clave 2-3)

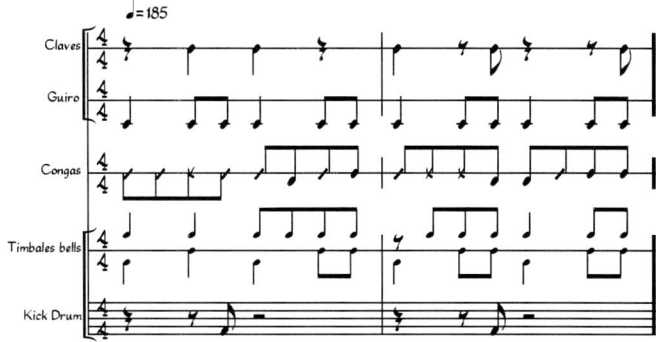

Appendix A: Afro-Cuban Rhythm Glossary

Son-Montuno (Clave 2-3)

Timba (Rumba clave 2-3)

This example features the timbales integrated into the drumset, with the non-dominant hand playing the bell mounted to the timbales.

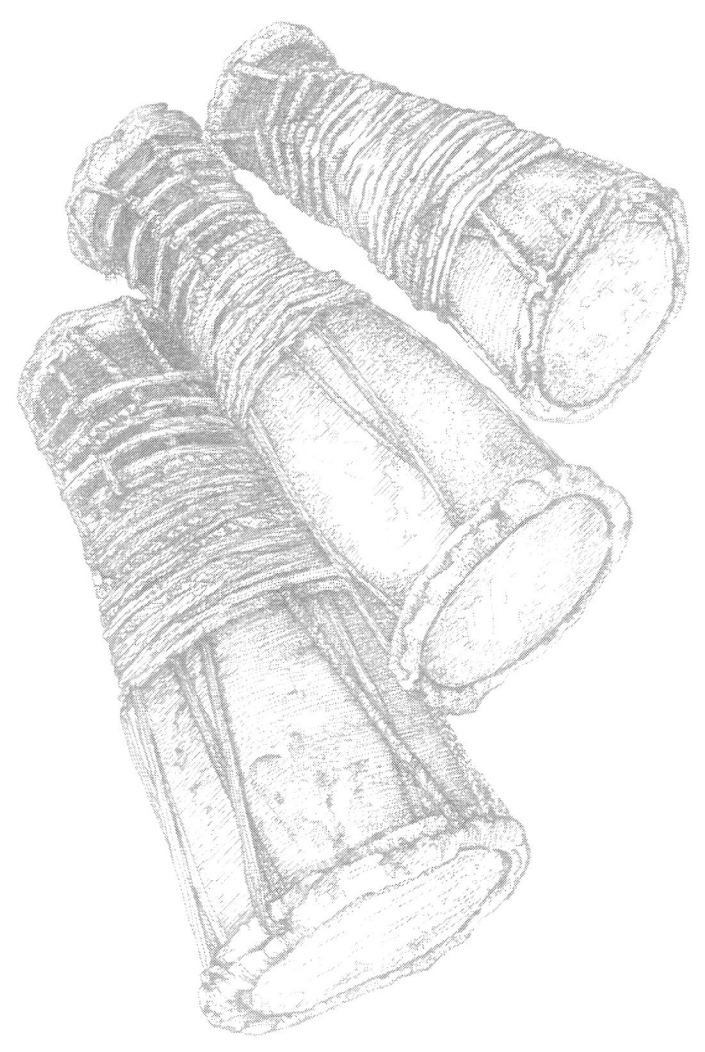

Appendix B: Annotated List of Works

The compositional process is complex, and there are likely almost as many works in an artist's life that don't make the final cut as there are those worthy of performance or recording. That said, what follows here is Maestro Valdés's personal recollection of his works, some dating back to his teen years, resulting in as comprehensive a collection as possible anywhere in print. The date in column two refers to the year of creation, which may or may not coincide with the album release date (in the fifth column). Furthermore, the subsequent releases or album reissue dates are given not only for context, but to provide a reference to more accessible versions, given the original albums may no longer be commercially available. The specific genre in column three is a reference to the rhythmic style(s) used in the original work, which may not necessarily reflect the entire scope of genres played in a given performance. Column four is intended to clarify the ensemble for which the composition was originally intended, as well as the various instrumentations or formats used over the years since the creation of the work.

• • •

Title	Date	Genre	Format/Artist	Album
38 1/2	1976	Cha-cha-chá/rock	Irakere	*Grupo Irakere*, Areito, 1976.
A				
Abdel	2012	Afro-flamenco	Afro-Cuban Messengers	*Border-Free*, Jazz Village, 2013.
Adiva	1988	Solo piano	Chucho Valdés Solo piano	*Lucumí Piano Solo*, Messidor, 1988.
Afro-Comanche	2012	Funky cha-cha-chá	Afro-Cuban Messengers	*Border-Free*, Jazz Village, 2013; *Tribute to Irakere: Live in Marciac*, Jazz Village, 2016.
Aguanile Bonkó	1978	Son-batá	Irakere	*Irakere*, Columbia, 1979; *The Best of Irakere*, Columbia, 1994; *Recital en Teatro 12 y 23*, Egrem, 2011.
A Jessica	1988	Solo piano	Chucho Valdés Solo piano	*Lucumí Piano Solo*, Messidor, 1988.
Amanecer	1988	Solo piano	Chucho Valdés Solo piano	*Lucumí Piano Solo*, Messidor, 1988; *Canciones Inéditas*, Egrem, 2002.
Anabis	1988	Guaracha-samba	Irakere	*Felicidad*, Jazz House, 1991.
B				
Babalú Ayé	1997	Praise songs to Babalú Ayé	Irakere with Lázaro Ros	*Babalú Ayé*, Bembe, 1999.
Bacalao Con Pan	1973	Son-batá	Irakere	*Grupo Irakere*, Areito, 1974.
Baila mi ritmo	1993	Disco	Irakere	*En Vivo*, Artex, 1993.
Bebada	1964	Descarga	Chucho Valdés y su Combo	*Cuban Jazz Revolution*, Soul Vibes, 2014.
Bebo	2012	Guajira-son	Afro-Cuban Messengers	*Border-Free*, Jazz Village, 2013.
Begin To Be Good	2010	Cha-cha-chá	Afro-Cuban Messengers	*Chucho's Steps*, Four Quarters, 2010.

Appendix B: Annotated List of Works

Berceuse a Jessie	1986	Improvisation	Solo piano	*Invitación*, Areito, 1986.
Balada a Caridad y Emilio	2002	Balada	Solo piano	*Canciones Inéditas*, Egrem, 2002.
Bill (Evans)	1993	Improvisation	Solo piano	*Solo Piano*, Blue Note, 1993
Bolero	1999	Improvisation	Solo piano	*Briyumba Palo Congo*, Blue Note, 1999.
Boliviana	1985	Bolero-son	Irakere	*Bailando Así*, Egrem, 1985.
Both Sides	2010	Jazz-funk	Afro-Cuban Messengers	*Chucho's Steps*, Four Quarters, 2010.
Bown Music	1988	Funk-guaracha	Irakere	*Exuberancia*, Jazz House, 1989.
Blue Yes	1993	Improv/swing	Chucho Valdés Solo piano	*Solo Piano*, Blue Note, 1993
Briyumba Palo Congo	1999	Palo	Irakere	*Briyumba Palo Congo*, Blue Note, 1999.
C				
Calle 7ma	2002	Guajira	Solo piano	*Canciones Inéditas*, Egrem, 2002.
Calzada del Cerro	1983	Cha-cha-chá	Irakere	*Calzada del Cerro,* Areito, 1983.
Camagüey	1979	Cha-cha-chá/rock/son-montuno	Irakere	*Chekeré-Son*, JVC, 1979.
Camino de Vuelta Abajo	1964	Huapango	Symphony	*(Bulgarian orchestra live recording, out of print)*
Canción de Cuna	1976	Canción	Solo Piano	*Piano 1*, Areito, 1976.
Canción de Palia	1967	Son-rock/bolero	Orquesta Egrem/Paquito D'Rivera	Paquito D'Rivera, *Instrumental*, Areito, 1964.
Canción Para Yousy	1976	Son	Solo Piano	*Piano 1*, Areito, 1976; *Love Jazz 30 Vuotta*, Love Records, 1996.
Canto a Dios	2014	Suite	Sinfónica Nacional de Cuba	*Canto a Dios*, Mondopolitan, 2015.
Caridad Amaro	2012	Canción	Afro-Cuban Messengers	*Border-Free*, Jazz Village, 2013.
Cha-cha-chá	1970	Cha-cha-chá	Irakere	*Chekeré-Son*, JVC, 1979; *¡Afrocubanismo Live!*, Bembe, 1996.
Cha Cha Niña	1964	Cha-cha-chá	Chucho Valdés y su Combo	*Cuban Jazz Revolution*, Soul Vibes, 2014.
Changó	1988	Suite	Irakere	*Live at Ronnie Scott's Vol. 2*, Jazz House, 1989; *Exuberancia*, Jazz House 1994; *30 Años*, Egrem, 2004.
Chorriño	1999	Chorinho	Irakere	*Yemayá*, Blue Note, 1999.
Chucho's Steps	2010	Guaracha	Afro-Cuban Messengers	*Chucho's Steps*, Four Quarters, 2010.
Claudia	1978	Bolero	Irakere	*Irakere 2*, Columbia, 1980; *Live at Ronnie Scott's*, World Pacific, 1993.
Concierto	2002	Concerto	Solo piano	*Canciones Inéditas*, Egrem, 2002.
Concerto Andino	1990	Concerto	Irakere with Silvio Rodríguez	*Silvio Rodríguez en Chile*, Areito, 1991.
Concierto Para Metales	1987	Suite	Irakere	*Misa Negra*, Messidor, 1987.
Conga Carnaval	2005	Conga-pop	Miguel Angá Diaz	*Echú Mingúa*, World Circuit, 2005.

Appendix B: Annotated List of Works

Congadanza	2012	Conga-danza	Afro-Cuban Messengers	*Border Free*, Jazz Village, 2013; *Tribute to Irakere: Live in Marciac*, Jazz Village, 2016.
Contradanza No. 1	1976	Contradanza	Solo Piano	*Piano 1*, Areito, 1976.
D				
Danzón	2002	Danzón (played as a jazz ballad on *Chucho's Steps*)	Solo piano	*Canciones Inéditas*, Egrem, 2002; *Chucho's Steps*, Four Quarters, 2010.
Danzón Para Sylvia	1996	Danzón	Chucho Valdés & Special Guests (combo)	*Live*, RMM, 1999.
Dembo	1988	Improvisation	Solo piano	*Lucumí Piano Solo*, Messidor, 1988.
E				
El Bolero	2002	Bolero	Solo piano	*Canciones Inéditas*, Egrem, 2002.
El Rumbón	1999	Guaguancó	Irakere	*Briyumba Palo Congo*, Blue Note, 1999.
El Tata Cimarrón	1983	Rumba-guaguancó, bon-batá	Irakere	*Calzada del Cerro*, Areito, 1983.
Estela Va a Estallar	1985	Guaracha	Irakere	*Tierra en Trance*, Areito, 1985; *The Legendary Irakere in London*, JazzHouse, 1988
Evocación a Ignacio Cervantes	1986	Improvisation	Solo piano	*Invitación*, Areito, 1986.
Evocación a Manuel Saumell	1986	Improvisation	Solo piano	*Invitación*, Areito, 1986.
Evocación a Lico Jiménez	1986	Improvisation	Solo piano	*Invitación*, Areito, 1986.
Evocación a José White	1986	Improvisation	Solo piano	*Invitación*, Areito, 1986.
F				
Fantasía Cubana	2002	Improvisation	Solo piano	*Fantasía Cubana: Variations on Classical Themes*, EMI, 2002.
Felia	1993	Improvisation	Solo piano	*Solo Piano*, Blue Note, 1993
Feliz Cumpleaños	1996	Guaracha	Irakere	*Lo Que Está Pegao'*, Areito, 1996
Flute Notes	1991	6/8, fast guaracha	Irakere	*Live at Ronnie Scott's*, World Pacific, 1993
G				
Guajison	1968	Guajira-son-blues	Combo	*Cuban Jazz Revolution*, Soul Vibes 2014. (reissue)
H, I				
Hay Mucho Que Contar	1987	Bolero-cha	Irakere	*Hay Mucho Que Contar*, Egrem, 1987.
Homenaje al Beny	1987	Son-montuno	Irakere	*Bailando Así*, Areito, 1985. *Hay Mucho Que Contar*, Areito, 1987.
Ileana	2002	Bolero	Solo piano	*Canciones Inéditas*, Egrem, 2002.
Impromptu	2002	Improvisation	Solo piano	*Fantasía Cubana: Variations on Classical Themes*, EMI, 2002.
Improvisación	2002	Improv/conga	Solo piano	*Canciones Inéditas*, Egrem, 2002.
Indestructible	1964	Bossa Nova	Combo	*Guapachá en La Habana*, Areito, 1964; *Desafíos*, Nube Negra, 1997; *Indestructible*, Sarabandas, 1998.

Appendix B: Annotated List of Works

Invento No. 4	1970	Blues-rock	Chucho Valdés Trio	*Chucho Valdés*, Areito, 1970.
Irakere	1973	Jazz waltz	Chucho Valdés Trio	*Jazz Batá*, Areito, 1973.
Isanusi	1993	Improvisation	Solo piano	*Solo Piano*, Blue Note, 1993
J, K				
Jessie y Leyanis	2002	Improvisation	Solo piano	*Canciones Inéditas*, Egrem, 2002.
Jica	1988	Ballad	Solo piano	*Lucumí Piano Solo*, Messidor, 1988.
Juana 1600	1976	Suite (various)	Irakere	*Grupo Irakere*, Areito, 1976; *Selección de Éxitos 1973-1978*, 1981; *Grandes Éxitos de Irakere*, CDA Music Group, 1990
Julián	2010	Canción	Afro-Cuban Messengers	*Chucho's Steps*, Four Quarters, 2010.
Keisy	1998	Canción	Irakere	*Indestructible*, Sarabandas, 1998; *Canciones Inéditas*, Egrem, 2002.
L				
La Campesina	2002	Improvisation	Solo piano	*Fantasía Cubana: Variations on Classical Themes*, EMI, 2002.
La Explosión	1996	Guaracha-swing	Irakere	Ivan Lins, *Ao Vivo, Egrem, 1996.* Irakere, *Yemayá*, Blue Note, 1998.
La Pastora	1991	Merengue-conga	Irakere	*Felicidad*, Jazz House, 1991.
La Sombra	1970	6/8	Chucho Valdés Trio	*Chucho Valdés*, Areito, 1970.
Las Hijas de Anajo	1982	Haitian Mereng	Irakere	*El Coco*, Milestone, 1982.
Las Margaritas	1985	Joropo/jazz waltz	Irakere	*Tierra en Trance*, Areito, 1985.
La Tormenta y la Calma	2015	Jazz	Solo piano	*Canto a Dios*, Mondopolitan, 2015.
Laureen	1973	Balada	Chucho Valdés Trio	*Jazz Batá*, Areito, 1973.
Lo Que Va a Pasar	1985	Guaracha, timba	Irakere	*The Legendary Irakere in London*, Jazz House, 1988.
Lorena's Tango	2015	Tango congo/son/blues	Afro-Cuban Messengers	*Tribute to Irakere: Live in Marciac*, Jazz Village, 2016.
Lorraine	1998	Balada-cha	Chucho Valdés Quartet	*Bele Bele en La Habana*, Blue Note, 1998.
Lorraine's Habanera	1999	Habanera	Chucho Valdés Quartet	*Live at the Village Vanguard*, 2000.
Los Güiros	2002	Guaguancó-jazz	Afro-Cuban Messengers	*New Conceptions*, Blue Note, 2003.
M				
Mambo en Re Menor	2002	Mambo	Solo piano	*Canciones Inéditas*, Egrem, 2002.
Mambo for Roy	1997	Guaracha, mambo	Roy Hargrove's Crisol	Roy Hargrove's Crisol, *Habana*, Verve, 1997.
Mambo Influenciado	1963	Guaracha, mambo	Combo, Solo	*Jazz Nocturno,* Areito, 1964; *Piano 1*, Areito, 1979; *Lucumí Piano Solo*, Messidor, 1988.
Marcia	2002	Bolero	Solo piano	*Canciones Inéditas*, Egrem, 2002.
Misa Negra	1969	Suite	Combo, Irakere	*Irakere*, Columbia, 1979; *Misa Negra*, Messidor, 1987.
Mister Bruce	1997	Guaracha, mambo	Roy Hargrove's Crisol	Roy Hargrove's Crisol, *Habana*, Verve, 1997; *Yemayá*, Blue Note, 1999.
Moane	1988	Solo piano	Solo piano	*Lucumí Piano Solo*, Messidor, 1988.
N				
Nandy	1993	Improvisation/son	Solo piano	*Solo Piano*, Blue Note, 1993

Appendix B: Annotated List of Works

Nanu	2002	Waltz	Solo piano/Afro-Cuban Messengers	*New Conceptions*, Blue Note, 2003
Neurosis	1972	Guaracha-swing	Combo, Irakere	*Jazz Batá*, Areito, 1972; *Live at Ronnie Scott's*, World Pacific, 1993; *¡Afrocubanismo Live!*, Bembe, 1996.
New Orleans	2010	Various	Afro-Cuban Messengers	*Chucho's Steps*, Four Quarters, 2010.
Niebla	2002	Improvisation	Solo piano	*Canciones Inéditas*, Egrem, 2002.
Noliu	1993	Improvisation/guaracha	Solo piano	*Solo Piano*, Blue Note, 1993
O, P				
Ofelita	2002	Improvisation	Solo piano	*Canciones Inéditas*, Egrem, 2002.
Osun	1988	Improvisation	Solo piano	*Lucumí Piano Solo*, Messidor, 1988.
Oyambo	1988	Improvisation	Solo piano	*Lucumí Piano Solo*, Messidor, 1988.
Palia	1973	Improvisation	Chucho Valdés Trio/Solo piano	*Jazz Batá*, Areito, 1973; *Piano 1*, Areito, 1976.
Para Pilar	2002	Canción	Solo piano	*Canciones Inéditas*, Egrem, 2002.
Pilar	2012	Ballad	Afro-Cuban Messengers	*Border Free*, Jazz Village, 2013.
Pónle la Clave	1999	Guaracha	Quartet	*Briyumba Palo Congo*, Blue Note, 1999.
Por Culpa del Guao	1985	Merengue	Irakere	*Bailando Así*, Egrem, 1985.
Preludio	1976	Son	Solo piano	*Piano 1*, Areito, 1976.
Preludio No. 1 en D	1970	Rock	Chucho Valdés Trio	*Chucho Valdés*, Areito, 1970.
Preludio Para Bebo	2007	Improvisation	Solo piano	*Juntos Para Siempre*, Sony, 2008.
Punto Cubano	1999	Punto Cubano	Chucho Valdés Quartet	*Live at the Vilage Vanguard*, 2000.
Q, R				
Que Puedo Hacer	2002	Bolero	Solo piano	*Canciones Inéditas*, Egrem, 2002.
Quince Minutos	1979	Canción	Irakere	*Chekeré-Son*, JVC, 1979.
Realidad	2002	Improvisation	Solo piano	*Canciones Inéditas*, Egrem, 2002.
Ruta 43	1986	"Rucu Rucu" (conga)	Irakere	*Hay Mucho Que Contar*, Areito, 1987; *Colección Irakere Vol. XI*, Egrem, 1995.
S				
Samba Para Enrique	1986	Samba	Irakere	*Misa Negra*, Messidor, 1986.
San Francisco	1995	Cha-cha-chá	Irakere	*Yemayá*, Blue Note, 1999.
Santa Amalia	1998	Guaracha	Irakere	*Yemayá*, Blue Note, 1999.
Santa Cruz	2012	Baião-son	Afro-Cuban Messengers	*Border-Free*, Jazz Village, 2013.
Sentimental	2002	Bolero	Solo piano	*Canciones Inéditas*, Egrem, 2002.
Siete Tazas de Café	1981	Disco-conga	Irakere	*Irakere*, Areito, 1982.
Sin Clave Pero Con Swing	2002	Guaracha, swing	Afro-Cuban Messengers	*New Conceptions*, Blue Note, 2003
Sonidos Siderales	1967	Son-rock	Combo	*Cuban Jazz Revolution*, Soul Vibes, 2014. (reissue)
Son Montuno	1998	Son-montuno/guaracha	Chucho Valdés Quartet	*Bele Bele en La Habana*, Blue Note, 1998.

Appendix B: Annotated List of Works

Son No. 2	1970	Son	Chucho Valdés Trio	*Jazz Batá*, Areito, 1973.
Son No. 3	1976	Son	Solo piano	*Piano 1*, Areito, 1976.
Son No. 4	1976	Son	Solo piano	*Piano 1*, Areito, 1976.
Son No. 5	1976	Son	Solo piano	*Piano 1*, Areito, 1976.
Son No. 6	1976	Son	Solo piano	*Piano 1*, Areito, 1976.
Son Para Leyanis	1981	Son	Solo piano	*Tema de Chaka*, Areito, 1981.
Stella, Pete, Ronnie	1989	Guaracha	Irakere	*Felicidad*, Jazz House, 1991.
Sunrise	2002	Improvisation	Solo piano	*Fantasía Cubana: Variations on Classical Themes*, EMI, 2002.
T				
Tema de Chaka*	1981	6/8 (bembé)	Irakere	*Tema de Chaka*, Areito, 1981. *Orquesta Sinfónica Nacional*, Areito, 1983. *This is the basis for "Tributo a Africa" (2005)
Te Tocó Perder	1985	Bossa-son	Irakere	*Bailando Así*, Egrem, 1985.
Tierra en Trance	1985	Suite	Irakere	*Tierra en Trance*, Areito, 1995.
To Bud Powell	1999	Son/Calypso/swing	Chucho Valdés Quartet	*Live at the Village Vanguard*, 2000.
Toga	1993	Improvisation/son	Solo piano	*Solo Piano*, Blue Note, 1993
Tres Días	1980	Guaracha	Irakere	*En Vivo: Poliedro de Caracas, Mayo 14, '81*, Integra, 1982.
Tributo a África	2015	Suite	Symphony	*Canto a Dios*, Mondopolitan, 2015. *Based on original theme from "Tema de Chaka"
Tritón	1981	Guaracha	Irakere	*Tema de Chaka*, Areito, 1981.
Tumbao	1996	Descarga	Chucho Valdés & Special Guests (combo)	*Live*, RMM, 1999.
Tumbao	2002	Son-montuno	Solo piano	*Fantasía Cubana: Variations on Classical Themes*, EMI, 2002.
Tunes a Coy	1996	Guaracha	Chucho Valdés & Special Guests (combo)	*Live*, RMM, 1999.
U, V, W				
Una Tarde en Alamar	1993	Danzón	Paquito D'Rivera	*Paquito D'Rivera Presents: 40 Years of Cuban Jam Session*, Messidor, 1993
Valle Picadura	1974	Balada, danzón-mambo	Irakere	*Grupo Irakere*, Areito, 1974; *Great Moments*, Egrem, 1991.
Wakamba	2002	Improvisation/afro	Solo piano	*Fantasía Cubana: Variations on Classical Themes*, EMI, 2002.
X, Y, Z				
Yansá	2010	Cha-cha in 7/4	Afro-Cuban Messengers	*Chucho's Steps*, Four Quarters, 2010.
Yemayá	1997	6/8 bembé	Irakere	*Yemayá*, Egrem, 1997.
Zanaith	1981	Balada/bolero	Irakere	*Tema de Chaka*, Areito, 1981; *Canciones Inéditas*, Egrem, 2002.
Zawinul's Mambo	2010	Mambo	Afro-Cuban Messengers	*Chucho's Steps*, Four Quarters, 2010.

• • •

Irakere 40 performing at the SFJAZZ Center, October, 2015. PHOTO CREDIT: RICK SWIG

APPENDIX C: REFERENCED AUDIO RECORDINGS

The following listing cites the discographical reference for the definitive version of each work highlighted in this book (in bold), followed by any subsequent or notable versions, and the specific link(s) of the file(s) on the iTunes digital music service. Note the songs are listed here in alphabetical order by title. **To access these links, please visit the Sher Music website at *shermusic.com/decoding*.** Please refer to the Discography for a complete listing of recordings by Chucho Valdés (as solo artist and in small group formats as a leader), Chucho with the Afro-Cuban Messengers, and by Irakere. Appendix B contains a comprehensive alphabetical list of Maestro Valdés' works, and includes discographical citings.

Song Title: **"Aguanile Bonkó"**
Album(s): ***Irakere*, Columbia (1979)** (reissued as *The Best of Irakere,* Columbia Records, 1994)
https://itunes.apple.com/us/album/aguanile-bonko-en-vivo/1100956892?i=1100957502

Live debut recording on *Recital en Teatro 12 y 23*, Areito (1978)
https://itunes.apple.com/us/album/aguanile-bonko/id457709326?i=457709435

Song Title: **"Anabis"**
Album(s): ***Felicidad*, Jazz House (1991)**
https://itunes.apple.com/us/album/anabis-live/id585556909?i=585556925

¡Afrocubanismo Live! Bembe (1996)
https://itunes.apple.com/us/album/anabis/id200333371?i=200333573

Chucho Valdés (Quartet), *Live at the Village Vanguard*, Blue Note (2000)
https://itunes.apple.com/us/album/anabis/id724342730?i=724342891

Song Title: **"Bacalao con pan"**
Album: ***Grupo Irakere*, Areito (1974)**
https://itunes.apple.com/us/album/bacalao-con-pan/id152509840?i=152509997

Song Title: **"Calzada del Cerro"**
Album(s): ***Calzada del Cerro*, Areito (1983)**
https://itunes.apple.com/us/album/calzada-del-cerro/id1184756507?i=1184756590

Paquito D'Rivera Presents Cuba Jazz (RMM, 1996) with Bebo & Chucho Valdés and members of Irakere, recorded at Fantasy Studios in 1995.
https://itunes.apple.com/us/album/calzada-del-cerro/id61316856?i=61316878

Song Title: **"Claudia"**
Album(s): **Irakere, *Live at Ronnie Scott's*, World Pacific (1993)**
https://itunes.apple.com/us/album/claudia-live/id724452690?i=724453403

Arturo Sandoval & Chucho Valdés Quartet, *Straight Ahead* (1988)
https://itunes.apple.com/us/album/claudia/id448453944?i=448453985
Paquito D'Rivera & Arturo Sandoval, *Reunion*, Messidor (1992)
https://itunes.apple.com/us/album/claudia/id83946811?i=83946777

APPENDIX C: REFERENCED AUDIO RECORDINGS

Irakere 2, Columbia (1980) - Out of print and unavailable on iTunes.
Arturo Sandoval, *Turi*, Areito (1981) - Out of print and unavailable on iTunes.

Song Title: **"El Tata Cimarrón"**
Album: ***Calzada del Cerro*, Areito (1983)**
https://itunes.apple.com/us/album/el-tata/id1184756507?i=1184756692

Song Title: **"Lo Que Va a Pasar"**
Album: ***The Legendary Irakere in London*, Jazz House Records (1988)**
https://itunes.apple.com/us/album/lo-que-va-a-pasar-live/id585556909?i=585557072

Song Title: **"Mambo Influenciado"**
Album(s): ***Lo Mejor de Chucho Valdés* (Apple Music compilation)**
https://itunes.apple.com/us/album/mambo-influenciado/id1213352792?i=1213352912

Debut recording by Chucho Valdés & Su Combo, *Jazz Nocturno*, Areito (1964)
https://itunes.apple.com/us/album/mambo-influenciado/id1166929705?i=1166929826

Piano 1, Areito (1976) (solo piano version)
https://itun.es/us/HHaseb?i=1145572056

Lucumí Piano Solo, Messidor (1988) (solo piano version)
https://itunes.apple.com/us/album/mambo-influenciado/id84634288?i=84633982

Song Title: **"Misa Negra"**
Album(s): ***Irakere*, Columbia (1979)** (reissued as *The Best of Irakere,* Columbia Records, 1994)
https://itunes.apple.com/us/album/misa-negra/id1002890642?i=1002890961

Studio recording on the album *Misa Negra*, Messidor (1987)
https://itunes.apple.com/us/album/misa-negra-rezo-acercamiento-llegada-y-desarrollo-despadid/
id83919084?i=83918959

Song Title: **"Neurosis"**
Albums: ***Irakere - Live at Ronnie Scott's*, World Pacific (1993)**
https://itunes.apple.com/us/album/neurosis-live/id724452690?i=724453233
Chucho Valdés Trio, *Jazz Batá*, Areito (1973) (Apple Music compilation *Lo Mejor de Chucho Valdés*
https://itunes.apple.com/us/album/lo-mejor-de-chucho-vald%C3%A9s/id1213352792

Irakere, ¡Afrocubanismo Live! Bembe (1996)
https://itunes.apple.com/us/album/neurosis/id200333371?i=200333763

Song Title: **"San Francisco"**
Album: ***Yemayá,* Egrem (1997)** (reissued in 1999 on Blue Note)
https://itunes.apple.com/us/album/san-francisco/id1002890642?i=1002890970

INDEX

A

Abreu, Yaroldy, 62, 63
Acao, Irving Michel, 61
Acosta, Leonardo, 41, 56, 88
Águila, Rafael, 63
Alfonso, Jorge "El Niño," 55, 56, 60, 62, 88,
Alfonso, Lázaro "El Tato," 56
Alonso, Alicia, 49
Alonso, Pacho, 17, 81, 186
Alsop, Marin, 50
Álvarez, Carlos, 61
Álvarez, Reynaldo Melián, 63
Amadeo Roldán Theater, 54
Amram, David, 53, 57
Aragón, Orquesta, 16, 58
Arango, Feliciano, 18
Arcaño, Antonio (y Sus Maravillas), 16, 168, 170
Armenteros, Zenaida, 43, 166
ARTEX, 173, 201
Aspiazú, Don (Havana Casino Orchestra), 13
Averhoff, Carlos, 55, 56, 60, 62, 93, 94, 104

B

Bach, J.S., 37, 47, 166
Bamboleo, 19
Barbón, Carlos, 55
Barreto, Guillermo, 53, 56, 184
Barreto, Justi, 173
Barreto, Rodney, 63
Bauzá, Mario, 2, 13, 15, 168
Bayán, Rodulfo, 91
Berklee College of Music, 51
Betancourt, Joaquín, 45
Billboard Magazine, 176
Blakey, Art (& the Jazz Messengers), vi, 43, 63
Blanco, Juan Carlos de Castro
Blood, Sweat & Tears, 92
Blue Note Records, 59, 61
Bola de Nieve, 39
Bonne, Enrique, 17, 81
Borcelá, Amado "Guapachá," 41
Bouffartique, Óscar Muñoz, 38
Boulanger, Nadia, 47
Brackeen, Joanne, 57
Brecker, Michael, 94
Bringuez, Ariel, 63
Brouwer, Leo, 41, 43, 49, 170
Brown, James, 100
Brubeck, Dave, 43, 44, 47, 54

Buena Vista Social Club, 11
Buika, Concha, 48
Burke, Elena, 11, 58

C

"Cachao" (Israel López), vii, 10, 15, 16, 17, 171
Camilo, Michel, 50, 172
Carnegie Hall, 50, 58, 93
Carpentier, Alejo, 22, 174
Casa de las Américas, 174, 179
Cervantes, Ignacio, 9, 37, 166, 183
"Changuito" (José Luis Quintana), 18, 81, 92, 190
Chappotín, Félix, 14, 62
Chattaway, Jay, 58
Chicago (band), 56, 57
Chicoy, Jorge Luís Valdés, 61
Club, Ronnie Scott's, 59, 85, 90, 95, 101, 103, 104, 202, 204
Coltrane, John, 40, 45
Columbia Records, 44, 57, 58, 88, 170, 208
"Compay Segundo" (Francisco Repilado), 10
Conjunto Casino, 14
Conover, Willis, 47, 177
Consejo Nacional de Cultura (CNC), 41, 44, 54
Conservatorio Amadeo Roldán, 38, 41
Conservatorio Municipal de la Habana, 38
Coolidge, Rita, 58
Corona, Manuel, 10
Cortés, José Luis "El Tosco," 44, 59, 60, 100, 104,
Crego, José Miguel, 60, 104
Cruz, Celia, 14, 38, 42, 97, 172
Cuervo, Armando, 56, 89
Cueva, Julio, 13, 37
Cuní, Miguelito, 14

D

De Castro Blanco, Juan Carlos "El Peje," 62
Degara, Ojún, 73
Delgado, Issac, 19
Del Puerto, Carlos, 18, 53, 55, 60, 61, 90, 91, 101, 102
Desmond, Paul, 43
Diákara, 61
Díaz, Aniceto, 10, 183
Díaz, Miguel Angá, 60, 61, 86, 97
Diddley, Bo, 23
D'Rivera, Paquito, 41, 42, 46, 47, 53, 54, 55, 57, 59, 87, 94, 95, 96, 103, 170
Durán, Hilario, 87, 88
Durruthy Bombalé, Dreiser, 62, 63

INDEX

E

Earth, Wind & Fire, 56, 57
EGREM Label/Studios, 58, 87, 91, 93, 94, 172, 173
Egües, Blas, 18
Egües, Richard, 16
Ellington, Duke, 43, 44, 49, 56
Escuela Nacional de Arte (ENA), 45, 88
Espinel, Vicente, 185
Estivil, O., 17
Evans, Bill, 43, 47, 104

F

Faílde, Miguel, 9, 185
Fajardo, José, 16, 186
Farlow, Tal, 62, 95
Fellové, Julián, 42
Fernández, Joseíto, 11
Filiú, Román, 61
Fischer, Clare, 95, 96, 174
Fitzgerald, Ella, 11
Flores, Pedro, 15
Flynn, Frank Emilio, 17, 58, 184
Formell, Juan, 18, 21, 29, 33, 188

G

Garay, Sindo, 10
García, Andy, 16
García, Bernardo, 42, 56
Getz, Stan, 53, 57
Gillespie, Dizzy, 2, 44, 53, 57, 58, 167
Giral, Alberto "El Men," 41, 87
Gismonti, Egberto, 50
Goines, Victor, 46
González, Sara, 58
Goodman, Benny, 13
Gramatges, Harold, 38
Grand Theater of Havana, 49
Granz, Norman, 17, 39, 40
Great American Music Hall, 96, 97
Grenet, Eliseo, 4, 53
Grever, María, 15
Grupo AfroCuba, 48, 61
Grupo Afrocuba de Matanzas, 8, 79
"Guapachá," Amado Borcelá, 41
Guerra, Marcelino, 27
Gutiérrez, Julio, 17, 184
Güines, Tata, 17, 58

H

Habanero, Sexteto, 187
Hancock, Herbie, 43, 46, 53, 57, 165, 170
Hargrove, Roy, 61, 208
Hart, Billy, 57
Havana National Symphony Orchestra, 41
Hernández, Braulio, 42
Hernández, Kiki, 41, 87
Hernández, Mario "El Indio", 61
Hernández, Rafael, 15, 50
Hernández, René, 15
Hierrezuelo, Lorenzo, 10

I

Instituto Superior de Arte (ISA), 45
Izquierdo, Pedro, 17, 81, 185

J

Jara, Victor, 55
Jarrett, Keith, 61, 90
Jazz at Lincoln Center Orchestra (JALCO), 46, 49
Jazz Jamboree, 44
Jobim, Antonio Carlos, 1
Joel, Billy, 58
Johnson, James P., 37
Jorrín, Enrique, 10, 16, 181
Joya, Gastón, 63
Justiz, Pedro "Peruchín," 17, 38, 47, 170, 186

K

Karl Marx Theater, 49, 58
Kelly, Wynton, 43
Kenton, Stan, 13
Kessel, Barney, 62, 95
Kristofferson, Kris, 58

L

Lang, Lang, 50, 167
Lara, Adalberto, 60
Lara, Agustín, 15
Lecuona, Ernesto, 4, 13, 15, 37, 39, 41, 47, 50, 103, 171, 173
Lee, Peggy, 47
Linares, María Teresa, 65, 78
Lins, Ivan, 49, 207
Lloyd, Charles, 89, 90
López, Orlando "Cachaíto," 54
López, César, 60, 61

INDEX

López, Israel "Cachao," vii, 10, 15, 16, 17, 171
López, Orestes "Macho," 10, 179
López, Oriente, 48
López Nussa, Ernán, 45
Los Muñequitos de Matanzas, 8, 50, 79, 168
Loussier, Jacques, 166
Lundvall, Bruce, 44, 57, 58, 59,

M
Machado, Manuel, 60, 63
Machín, Antonio, 13
Manga, Mario, 49
Manolito y Su Trabuco, 19
Márquez, Basilio, 61
Márquez, Tito, 48
Mariza, 49
Marsalis, Wynton, 49, 177
Martí, José, 1, 11, 178
Martínez Griñán, Luis "Lilí," 14, 22
Martínez, Pedrito, 49
Mason, John, 6
Masucci, Jerry, 58
Matamoros, Miguel, 15
McClure, Rob, 57
McLaughlin, John, 58
McRae, Carmen, 47
Melián Álvarez, Reynaldo, 63
Méndez, José Antonio, 11, 38, 178, 186
Milanés, Pablo, 11, 48, 58
Miranda, Andrés "Negrón," 61
Miyares Hernández, Carlos, 63
Monk, Thelonious, 47
Montaner, Rita, 13, 39,
Monterey Jazz Festival, 89
Montgomery, Wes, 95
Montreux Jazz Festival, 58, 88, 93
Morales, Carlos Emilio, 41, 42, 47, 53, 54, 55, 56, 60, 61, 62, 87, 88, 95, 102, 104
Moran, Jason, 167
Moré, Benny, 15, 170, 173
Mozart, W. A., 45, 168
Mulligan, Gerry, 54
Munguía, Juan, 59, 60, 104,

N
National School(s) of Art, 45, 88
Newport Jazz Festival, 57, 58, 93
N.G. La Banda, 19, 59
Nueva Canción, 11
Nueva Trova, 48

O
Olatunji, Babatunde, 65
Oquendo, Manny, 17, 187
Orquesta América, 16
Orquesta Aragón, 16, 58
Orquesta Cubana de Música Moderna (OCMM), 41, 42, 53, 88, 177
Orquesta del Teatro Musical de la Habana (OTM), 40, 41, 43, 49, 87
Orquesta Ritmo Oriental, 180
Orquesta Sinfónica Nacional, 170, 172, 206
Ortega, Rafael, 39
Ortiz, Fernando, 3, 22, 23, 68, 73, 173, 180
Oréfiche, Armando, 13
O'Farrill, Chico, 13

P
Padrón, Julio, 61
Palmieri, Eddie, 17, 187
Pastorius, Jaco, 58
Pérez Prado, Dámaso, 15, 187
Peruchín, Pedro Justiz, 17, 38, 47, 170, 186
Piñeiro, Ignacio, 12, 189
Plá, Enrique, 42, 53, 54, 55, 56, 60, 61, 62, 89, 100, 101, 102,
Portillo de la Luz, César, 11, 15, 38, 186
Portuondo, Omara, 11, 48
Powell, Bud, 43, 206
Prats, Jaime, 13
Puente, Ernest Anthony "Tito," 15, 16, 96, 186
Pérez, Danilo, 50

Q
Quesada, Emilio, 94

R
Ramos, Miguel, 66
Repilado, Francisco "Compay Segundo," 10
Reyes, Jorge, 61
Rivera, El Niño, 186
Rivero Alarcón, Lázaro "El Fino," 62
Rodríguez, Arsenio, 14, 22, 26, 62, 168, 183, 187
Rodríguez, Silvio, 11, 48, 180
Rodríguez, Tito, 15
Rojas, Ñico, 38
Romeu, Antonio María, 43, 50, 168
Romeu, Armando, 13, 53
Romeu, Camerata, 43
Romeu, Zenaida, 43, 168
Ronnie Scott's Nightclub, 59, 85, 90, 94, 95

INDEX

Ros, Lázaro, 63
Rubalcaba, Gonzalo, 50, 102
Ruiz, Rosendo, 10, 16

S

Salvador, Emiliano, 44
Sánchez, José Pepe, 10, 180, 189
Sandoval, Arturo, 41, 45, 46, 53, 55, 56, 57, 59, 87, 88, 94, 95, 171, 173
Santamaría, Mongo, 102
Santana, Carlos, 16, 17, 96, 97, 102,
Saquito, Ñico, 10
Sarduy, Carlos, 63
Saumell, Manuel, 9, 37, 166, 203
Seeger, Pete, 11
Sexteto Habanero, 187
Septeto Nacional de Ignacio Piñeiro, 12, 187
SFJAZZ Center, ii, vii, 50, 166
Shearing, George, 43
Sillins, Susan, vi, 46, 102
Silver, Horace, 43, 88
Simone, Nina, 47
Simons, Moisés, 13
Sinatra, Frank, 11
Smith, Arnold Jay, 53
Smith, Frederic, 43,
Somavilla, Rafael, 53
Stills, Stephen, 58
Sublette, Ned, 78
Summers, Donna, 53
Swingle Singers, 166

T

Taborn, Craig, 165
Taylor, Billy, 43
Taylor, Cecil, 165
Taño, Tony, 42, 43,
Teatro Amadeo Roldán, 170
Thompson, Alfredo, 61
Torres, Juan Pablo, 42, 53
Tropicana Nightclub, 14, 37, 39, 40, 89, 92
Tropicana Orchestra, 39
Trueba, Fernando, 48, 103
Turina Pérez, Joaquín, 37, 38
Tyner, McCoy, 47, 101, 171

U

UNESCO, 8, 46, 78, 176, 187
Urfé, José, 183

V

Valdés, Bebo, vi vii, 17, 37, 38, 39, 40, 43, 46, 47, 48, 61, 89, 96, 103, 168, 171, 184
Valdés, Gilberto, 89
Valdés, Mayra Caridad, 61
Valdés, Merceditas, vii, 56
Valdés, Oscar, 41, 42, 43, 54, 55, 56, 58, 60, 61, 62, 88, 90, 93, 97, 101
Valdés, Oscarito, 60, 61
Valdés Chicoy, Jorge Luís, 61
Valle, Orlando "Maraca," 60, 61,
Vargas, Chavela, 48
Varona, Jorge, 42, 53, 56, 59, 60
Vaughan, Sarah, 11
Velasco, Germán, 59, 60, 96, 104
Vento, Julio, 41, 87,
Vera, María Teresa, 10
Village Vanguard, 62, 101, 102, 171, 204, 206
Villalón, Alberto, 10
Vitier, Sergio, 42, 56
Voice of America Jazz Hour, 47

W

Wallace, Wayne, 45
Wang, Yuja, 165
Washington, Grover Jr., 100
Williams, Tony, 58, 62
Winston, Yochanan Sebastian, 87
Withers, Bill, 100

Y

Young, Victor, 104
Yulo, El, 92

Z

Zalba, Javier, 60
Zawinul, Joe, 90, 206

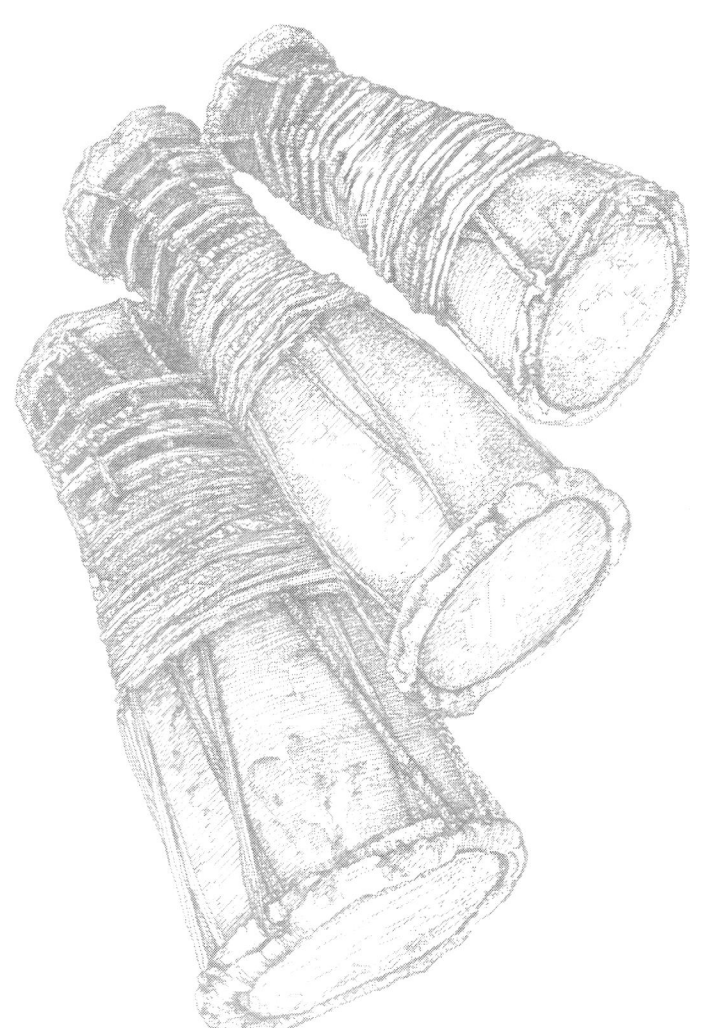